ACTIVE GAMES FOR CHILDREN WITH MOVEMENT PROBLEMS

ALAN BROWN
University of Newcastle upon Tyne

P·C·P
Paul Chapman
Publishing Ltd

First published 1987
by Harper and Row Ltd

Reprinted in this edition by
Paul Chapman Publishing Ltd
144 Liverpool Road
London N1 1LA

British Library Cataloguing in Publication Data
Brown, Alan
   Active games for children with movement problems.
   1. Sports for physically handicapped children
   I. Title
   796'.01'96   GV709.3

ISBN 1 85396 148 5

Typeset by Katerprint Typesetting Services, Oxford
Printed and bound by Athenaeum Press Ltd, Newcastle upon Tyne.

B C D E F G   5 4 3 2 1 0

for
Jenny Brown

CONTENTS

Foreword ix
Acknowledgements x
Introduction xi

1 THE ACQUISITION OF GAMES SKILLS 1
The perceptual-motor process 3
A classification of motor tasks 8
Stages of learning 10

2 THE EFFECTS OF HANDICAP ON
PERCEPTUAL-MOTOR PERFORMANCE 16
Cerebral palsy 18
Spina bifida 23
Muscular dystrophy 25
Asthma 26
Cardiac disorders 27
Epilepsy 28
Summary 29
Learning difficulties 30

3 SELECTION AND ADAPTATION OF ACTIVITIES 36
Selection of activities 36
Evaluation 37
Task analysis 41
Performer analysis 43
Adaptation of games 46

4 TEACHING THE BASIC SKILLS 50
Structuring the teaching programme 51
General body management 54
Techniques of projecting objects 59
Techniques of receiving and acquiring possession 74

   Striking skills 82
   Lesson plan: Level 1 90
   Lesson plan: Level 2 93
   Lesson plan: Level 3 94

5 INDIVIDUAL AND PARTNER ACTIVITIES 95
   Beanbag aiming games 96
   Games for severe arm involvement 108
   Wall games 112
   Miscellaneous games 118

6 GROUP GAMES 124
   Chasing games 125
   Aiming games 126
   Simple ball games 138
   Miscellaneous games 144
   Relays 147

7 TEAM GAMES 161
   Invasion games 162
   Net games 185
   Striking games 194

8 MAJOR TEAM GAMES 204
   Volleyball 205
   Cricket 209
   Hockey 213
   Basketball 220
   Badminton 225

9 GAMES TEACHING IN THE MAINSTREAM SCHOOL 230
   Attitude 232
   Individual records 233
   Individualized teaching 233
   Support personnel 234
   Peer teaching 235
   Selection of activities 236
   Education for leisure 237

   Index 239

FOREWORD

Alan Brown is, I believe, the only author of a book dealing with physical education for children with disabling conditions who is himself a parent of such a child. He is also an academic with sound research background, is a practical teacher of physical education, was a professional sportsman and remains an enthusiastic and active amateur. All these facets of Alan's life help to illuminate what is a most important addition to the literature of physical education.

Alan Brown was impelled into the world of disability by the birth of his daughter who was diagnosed as suffering from cerebral palsy. She is now happily a University undergraduate but at birth the prognosis was not good.

Twenty years ago he began learning and teaching; weekly he taught (and still teaches) in a special school; he established the Northern 'Spastic' games and developed coaching methods for disabled athletes. This book is the accumulation of years of teaching, testing theories, reading, debating with colleagues, at home and abroad and, most important of all, checking out his ideas with those most concerned — the young people themselves.

While games play a major role in mainstream schools, in special schools there is often more emphasis on individual activities. Children with a wide range of physical and mental disabilities have become skilled in dance and swimming. Games, on the other hand, have often been taught badly in both special and mainstream schools. Whereas dance and swimming have been so structured as to eliminate chance of failure, many children have turned away from all aspects of physical education and recreation because of failure in games. Even adults sometimes have difficulty in coping with failure. Alan Brown shows how a careful analytical and systematic approach to games skills and competitive situations can eliminate failure and make every child a winner.

Many who teach in special schools lack an understanding of the principles of skill acquisition. P.E. specialists have this background but lack an understanding of medical conditions and the competence to break down skills into easily assimilated steps. Both groups will find this book a veritable goldmine.

Recently I chaired a lecture by Alan Brown at a D.E.S. National Course. The response of delegates to his presentation demonstrated most clearly that practising teachers are looking for the clear systematic approach this book offers. But it is NOT simply a 'cook book'; all the practical material is based on sound academic research and the way is pointed for those who wish to read more deeply.

Lilian Groves
University of Durham
former president P.E.A. of Great
Britain and Northern Ireland

ACKNOWLEDGEMENTS

I am indebted to David Johnstone, headmaster of the Percy Hedley Spastics Centre in Newcastle upon Tyne, for his friendship and patience in making me understand even a few of the problems of cerebral palsied children. His constant encouragement and belief in the value of physical education led me in the development of a full programme at the school.

Dr D. Savage, formerly senior lecturer in clinical psychology at Newcastle and currently Professor of Psychology at Murdoch University, Western Australia, led me through the cognitive maze of experimental psychology. My wife Eileen, acted as my sounding board and read every single word of the manuscript with infinite patience and critical appraisal. As an experienced teacher her advice was invaluable. Mrs Anne McPhee typed the manuscript with an accuracy and speed that removed many of the worries of authorship. I am greatly indebted to Phil Robinson, departmental technician, for the fine quality of his photographs and the drawing of the diagrams.

Finally, I am grateful to the hundreds of cerebral palsied children from the Percy Hedley Spastics Centre who have given me so much pleasure by their efforts in learning movement skills over the last twenty years.

A.B.
October 1985

INTRODUCTION

The inspiration for this book came from a series of visits I made some years ago to special schools within the United Kingdom. The purpose of the visits was to examine at first hand the physical education curriculum presented to handicapped children. I found great variations in the training, qualifications and experience of the staff responsible for the teaching of physical education across a broad spectrum of special schools. I also saw evidence of good practice, particularly in the areas of educational gymnastics, swimming and dance. Perhaps it is significant that these activities are largely individually based. Many games lessons were observed, but only in rare cases were there any signs of genuine quality teaching. Children were seen to be playing games, but the fundamental skills and techniques of the games had not been previously established. In discussions with teachers it emerged that they were unsure of what to teach, how to teach, and how to cope with the varied handicapping conditions within a group games situation. This book is based on twenty years' experience of teaching games to children suffering from cerebral palsy, spina bifida, specific learning difficulties and other associated movement problems. It is intended as a source of material for teachers in special schools. The implications of the 1981 Education Act suggest that many more disabled children will be integrated within the normal school setting. I hope that this material will prove of service to specialist physical education teachers, offering them some ideas as they confront the problems of handling handicapped children within a regular games class.

Games are played for fun. This must always be the prime objective for teachers in presenting a games programme to handicapped youngsters who have missed out on many of the pleasurable experiences in life as a result of their condition. Great enjoyment can be gained from successfully taking part in a social games situation, whether winning or losing. Satisfaction, however, can only come from successful performance and in taking a full part within the game. This means more than fringe participation: it means total involvement, and this can only happen if the child has developed adequate skills to take his or her place within the game on merit. Games are much more than fun: they are an important medium for the achievement of educational goals in physical, psychological, social and emotional areas.

Oliver (1972) stated: 'Play is often synonymous with games and it is worth noting that there is still a large body of opinion which claims that games and sports comprise the most effective medium for the socialisation of the individual.' Games and sports are a most important part of our present culture and exert a great influence on the developing child. Keogh *et al.* (1979) and Gordon and McKinley (1980) have identified the difficulties of social interaction and the unhappiness in play situations that result from the poor motor skills of children with movement problems. Whiting *et al.* (1969) noted the way in which clumsy children avoided participation in social play and game situations because of their lack of motor skills. A vicious circle thus develops where the child participates less in social situations because of poor skills, thereby creating fewer opportunities for essential practice of skill, and so the cycle goes on. The end result may be total withdrawal from social play situations for fear of failure and rejection.

The underlying philosophy of this book is that *success breeds success.* Through careful selection of games material and the use of appropriate teaching methods the individual child is faced with learning situations where goals are achieved and successful social integration is allowed to occur. The vast majority of social contacts for children occur in play, and success in play settings is highly valued, leading, it is hoped, to social acceptance within the peer group. Cratty (1970) stressed this when he stated: 'For the educator to ignore the marked influence that game success has on the social acceptance of children and adolescents is to ignore an important dimension of the value system with which youngsters are surrounded.'

Success in play activities which are highly valued within the peer group is likely to have a marked positive effect on the development of a child's self-concept. Conversely, failure and rejection will have an adverse effect and create problems in the development of personality traits. A programme of games teaching which is based on the fulfilment of individual needs, the steady achievement of personal goals and skills, and the application of these skills in a carefully arranged social setting is a sound basis for the development of a more confident self-concept. The way handicapped children transfer this confidence to new learning experiences is very evident. It is well described by Oliver (1972).

The major aims of any physical education curriculum are the acquisition of skill and the development of physical fitness. This is equally true of programmes geared to the needs of handicapped children. As skill develops and children are able to play an increasing part in games requiring the expenditure of great energy, the important attribute of cardiovascular endurance will develop as the amount of gross motor activity increases. Brown (1975) reviewed the literature on the effects of exercise on the working capacity of handicapped children and showed the beneficial effects of exercise programmes.

I make no apology for my belief that the more physically handicapped the child, the more important are the personal and social effects of games.

It must be stressed that games are only one part of the whole physical education curriculum. A prescriptive teaching model is described in the chapters that follow. This has been found highly effective in making handicapped children more skilful. The more severely disabled the child, the greater is the need for individualized instruction; thus the desirability of a prescriptive approach becomes apparent. This method is not the only approach in the teaching of physical education; teaching strategies will vary with the quality of the teacher, the area of study in physical education, and the severity of the child's disability. In educational gymnastics and dance the acquisition of motor skills provides avenues for creative, expressive and aesthetic experiences, and teaching methods will guide the child through discovery of movement in problem-solving situations.

Mosston (1966) produced a stimulating treatise on teaching styles related to the full range of physical education. Mauldon and Redfern (1981) discuss problem-solving methods related to the teaching of games within the primary school. Many different styles of teaching can be effective in varying situations. The material in this book is very easily adapted to any teaching style appropriate to the special abilities or special needs of children. However, the prescriptive model is presented because severely handicapped children are unable to explore their environment and experiment with play apparatus in the same way as normal children. It is a method based on the progressive achievement of success and the avoidance of constant failure. There is no single right way or wrong way, no immediate panacea, only a teaching method that is appropriate to the subject area and the needs of the children in producing effective learning. Neither are there easier or more difficult teaching styles. The choice of teaching styles ought not to be influenced by difficulty, only by efficiency and effectiveness in producing valuable educational experiences.

The first three chapters present a simple theoretical background as a basis for the principles by which the later chapters on the development of practice are organized. In Chapter 1 I highlight some selected aspects of learning and perceptual-motor performance as an aid to understanding the nature of skill. In Chapter 2 the effects of handicap on perceptual-motor performance of children are reviewed as guidelines for the teacher who is unfamiliar with the major problems of teaching handicapped children. The principles of selecting and adapting material for games are outlined in Chapter 3, which also presents a prescriptive model of teaching. Because successful teaching of handicapped children is so dependent upon task analysis and performer analysis, the principles underlying these processes are established.

The games programme in the long term will have three dimensions:

1. *Developmental.* A developmental programme in the primary school is designed to promote the necessary perceptual-motor attributes and skills

to allow for participation in games. We are seeking to teach the basic 'tools of the trade'.

2. *Adapted*. When children are so severely handicapped that they cannot develop the necessary competence in perceptual-motor skills, the environmental demands must be adapted and modified to simplify participation within the limitations of their disability.

3. *Sport and physical recreation*. Following a successful developmental and adapted programme, children should be in a position to choose those games activities which allow for social integration and from which they gain satisfaction and pleasure for lifelong leisure. These may be competitive, cooperative or purely recreational.

From Chapter 4 onwards this book is organized in sequence to fulfil these three-dimensional objectives. Chapter 4 is devoted to the teaching of basic techniques as the foundation on which the whole games programme is built. The sections on individual, group and team games follow in the normal hierarchical development of games training and indicate the adapted nature of the activities listed. It is hoped that they will provide a source of material for the teacher, the PHAB club, the youth club leader, and for organizers of community sports clubs for the disabled. The list is by no means exhaustive, but it is my sincere hope that the material will prove of value to the educators of handicapped children.

A.B.

REFERENCES

Brown, A. (1975) Review: physical fitness and cerebral palsy, *Child: Care, Health and Development*, Vol. 1, pp. 143–152

Cratty, B.J. (1970) *Perceptual and Motor Development in Infants and Children*, Macmillan, London

Gordon, N. and McKinley, I. (Eds) (1980) *Helping Clumsy Children*, Churchill Livingstone, Edinburgh

Keogh, J.F., Sugden, D.A., Reynard, C.L. and Calkins, J.A. (1979) The identification of clumsy children: comparisons and comments, *Journal of Human Movement Studies*, Vol. 5, pp. 32–41

Mauldon, E. and Redfern, H.B. (1981) *Games Teaching* (2nd edn), McDonald & Evans, Plymouth

Mosston, M. (1966) *Teaching Physical Education: from Command to Discovery*, Charles E. Merrill, Ohio

Oliver, J.N. (1972) *Physical activity and the psychological development of the handicapped*. In J.E. Kane (Ed.), Psychological Aspects of Physical Education and Sport, Routledge & Kegan Paul, London

Whiting, H.T.A., Clarke, T.A. and Morris, P.R. (1969) A clinical validation of the Stott test of motor impairment, *British Journal of Social and Clinical Psychology*, Vol. 8, pp. 240–279

Chapter 1
THE ACQUISITION OF GAMES SKILLS

A knowledge of how children learn motor skills is fundamental for the teacher in building up a programme of games teaching and choosing a method of instruction appropriate to different games situations. A complete review of the problems related to skill acquisition is beyond the scope of this book, but certain important principles relevant to the teaching of games skills to handicapped children are presented below. The non-specialist teacher of games wishing to develop a more knowledgeable approach is recommended to read Knapp (1963), Whiting (1969), Schmidt (1975), Kerr (1982), Singer (1982) and Marteniuk (1976). Specialist physical education teachers will be interested in the work of Keogh and Sugden (1985).

All who study this subject area must appreciate the complexity of motor function and understand the sequence of events occurring in the development of control over motor function. The basic unit of motor function is a motor action, that is, any overt muscular act from blinking an eye to raising a hand. A series of consecutive motor actions produces motor behaviour, which, when purposefully directed towards a particular goal, is known as motor performance. The repetition of a particular motor performance and its modification and refinement by learning to give a smooth and efficient result produces a motor skill. Each succeeding stage of motor function requires greater cerebral activity and competence than the preceding stage. Skill, therefore, develops in a hierarchical manner with each stage dependent upon the development of competence in a previous stage in the sequence. A hierarchy must be seen as a graded sequence of ordered events.

Knapp (1963) defined skill as 'the learned ability to bring about predetermined results with maximum certainty, often with minimum outlay of time or energy, or both'. This statement requires elaboration. The skilled performer is able to reduce the discrepancy between an intended performance and the subsequent response with consistency and accuracy. Skill shows up in a performance that is smooth, efficient in terms of physiological energy consumption, and accurate; the hallmark of a good performer is that he or she appears to have time when the less skilled are hurried. It must be stressed that motor skill is acquired through a learning process. This is also true of cognitive skills, social skills and games skills. The term 'skill' may also be used to describe a task, such as the skill of a forehand drive in tennis.

There is often some confusion over the difference between the concepts of learning and performance. Kerr (1982) defines learning as 'the relatively permanent change in performance resulting from practice or past experience'. We cannot see learning and it is only possible to know that learning has taken place by observing performance. The observation of changes in performance must take place over a period of time sufficiently lengthy to confirm that the improvement is permanent and not due to chance. Learning is, therefore, measured by changes in performance of a given task, when consistent accuracy is achieved. Performance, on the other hand, is only a temporary occurrence in the time it takes to complete a task; it is a function of motivation and experience, and therefore variable. Learning would not be considered to have occurred where changes in performance are due solely to the effects of growth, or increases in strength through maturation, or, on the other hand, to deterioration of the neuromuscular system as a result of trauma, hospitalization or accident. For example, when a child rises from a quadriped crawling position to the vertical and begins to take a few walking steps the movement pattern could not be described as skilful. The child can only take this important step in development when he is ready as a result of the growth and maturation process. When better performance is seen as the result of practice or of exposure to experience, where improvement occurs through a complex cognitive, perceptual and neuromuscular refinement, then learning has taken place.

In teaching young children the emphasis is on the refinement of fundamental movement patterns, and the development of more specific skills is dependent upon this base. The development of skill can, therefore, be viewed in two phases:

1. The development in early life of those movement skills where maturation is a predominant factor in improvement. These skills are common to the species and are known as phylogenetic skills. The timing and acquisition of these skills are critically due to opportunity for movement and the normal maturation process. Normal children develop these skills as they grow but handicapped children, deprived of movement experience, exhibit grave deficiencies. The acquisition of established movement patterns in sitting, crawling, walking, balancing, running, reaching and grasping provides the potential for further skills to develop. This process will be discussed later.

2. Recreational skills necessary for participation in games activities. These skills are peculiar to the individual. They do not develop as a result of maturation and they are specific to any given task. Improvement of efficient performance can only occur as the direct result of practice.

Thus the acquisition of skill can be seen as a progressive and sequential process on a hierarchical continuum.

THE PERCEPTUAL-MOTOR PROCESS

It is now generally accepted in physical education that discussions on the control of movement and the acquisition of skill are related to a simple model of perceptual-motor performance (see Figure 1.1). Arnheim and Pestolesi (1978) define the perceptual-motor process as 'the managing of information coming to the individual through the senses, the processing of the information, and then the reacting to the information in terms of some behaviour'.

This information-processing sequence can be very simply described as operating in four related stages:

1. *Input.* Sensory information is received through the sense organs and transmitted to the brain for processing.
2. *Decision making.* Incoming sensory information arrives from all of the sensory modalities and appears to be organized through the process of perception into a pattern which is recognized and compared with past experience. On the basis of pattern recognition an appropriate decision to take action is made.
3. *Output.* As a result of the decision to act, the appropriate body action is executed as a motor response.
4. *Feedback.* The consequences of the motor act can be seen or felt as correct or incorrect responses and then evaluated. Some form of feedback information is relayed back to the sensory and decision-making channels as an error-sensing mechanism.

The whole pattern of performance is, therefore, an integrated process of sensation, perception, decision making and motor action. Provided that the sense organs function normally, through seeing and feeling in particular, sensory information passed as nerve impulses to the brain tends to be fairly accurate, although sensory capacity in individual children will vary considerably. The perception of the incoming sensory stimuli is of prime importance to the learner in the performance of games activities. Perception is the interpretation of those stimuli which makes them recognizable and meaningful. According to the nature and extent of past experience we recognize patterns of stimuli, compare them, then react accordingly. Our choice of movement response is dictated by the ability to recognize a previously remembered pattern and make instant sense of the information. Because perception is based on the interpretation of sensory stimuli according to past experience, it follows that this is a function that can be learned. The development of perceptual abilities in young children is of basic concern to the physical education teacher because they are the base on which simple perceptual-motor skills are learned. Ball games form a large part of the games curriculum. For children to cope effectively with a ball that is travelling

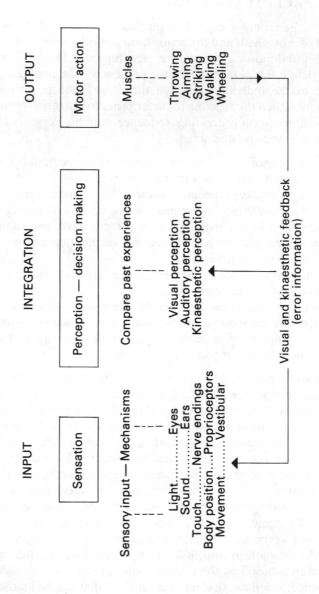

Figure 1.1   The perceptual-motor process model

towards them they must be able to perceive the distance, direction, speed and flight arc of the movement of the ball. This is a learned ability and without it the children could not play successfully. For example, in catching a ball children must be aware that a ball is about to be thrown and that they must pay attention to the thrower. From the initial postural movements, combined with the throwing action of the thrower, they will gain a preliminary warning of when and where the point of release is likely to occur. As soon as the ball is released they monitor the flight of the ball, predict how far and how fast it has been thrown and estimate the time it will take to reach them. The ball is visually tracked against a background of walls, ceiling, other players and light fittings, and they must be able to differentiate the ball from the background. Based on a prediction of the ball's flight path, they decide early to initiate certain gross movement patterns by moving the whole body into the line of flight to intercept. Fractionally later they begin to prepare for the catch by deciding when to place the hands in position and precisely where they will need to be. In the early stages of learning, the placement of hands may be controlled by either visual checking or kinaesthetic awareness, or both. At the correct moment they must then close the grasp to coincide with the arrival of the ball and allow the hands to cushion the impact. Different kinds of information concerning the success or failure of their action is now immediately available to them, as feedback. This may be visual in seeing the ball drop, or they may feel the ball strike the wrong part of the hand or they may hear a helpful comment from the teacher. The results of such actions are remembered and stored for future reference and comparison in similar tasks. Through the use of feedback the learner evaluates the performance and also the adequacy of his original objective. If either of these is inadequate, then modifications to further attempts at the movement are made. As this sequence is followed so the objectives and the performance become more efficient and appropriate.

The problem for the teacher and the children is in analyzing where the breakdown in performance occurred, for an error at any point in the chain of events could be responsible. They may have made faulty judgements, based on inaccurate visual perceptions about where the ball would arrive, the hands may not have been in the correct position through faulty kinaesthetic awareness, or their decision to move may have been too slow to allow time for the correct movements to take place.

The learning process in this sequence is well described by Holt (1984):

At the very beginning the child may not appreciate that the action of the thrower is connected to the arrival of the ball. When he does realise the connection he tends to watch the thrower all the time and only very belatedly realises that he must move his arms and hands, and so when he does raise them the ball has gone by. He then learns to break his visual fixation on the thrower and learns to watch the ball coming towards him.

He gets the timing right and gets his hands in position at the correct time. As spatial positioning of the arms and hands improves, the whole action takes on a better appearance. A great deal has gone into learning to make a two-handed frontal catch, and much more still has to be acquired. However, having reached this stage as a basis, the child can go on to make side catches, one-handed catches, and the many more difficult catches he will encounter on the playing fields.

This process is the same for normal and handicapped children, but handicapped children need to learn the task of catching a ball initially at a lower operational level in order to achieve any success.

KINAESTHESIS

While vision and hearing are critical sensory modalities through which we receive information in games which involve seeing a ball and hearing it struck, other perceptual abilities are equally important to learning and performance. We also receive cues which come from within the body as we move. The perception of movement or muscle sense is known as kinaesthesis. Muscle sense makes us aware of the positions of our limbs in space, the directions in which they are moving — in general, it is an awareness of body movement. Sensations arise from sense receptors located in those muscles and joints of the body which are sensitive to changes in muscle tension and joint position and are known as proprioceptors. These, together with sensations from the balance mechanisms within the inner ear and the vestibular system, provide a continuous self-regulating feedback system to the cerebrum and cerebellum, thereby effecting the internal control of movement. Proprioceptive feedback is critical in helping us to remember the feel of a movement or a change in body position. Sound kinaesthetic perception is critical to the development of balance, body awareness, and the important perceptual abilities of laterality and directionality which control our awareness of space. Muscle sense develops in relation to specific movement experiences. It is important, therefore, that children have the opportunity for a wide experience of many varied movement situations so that they may acquire a full repertoire of kinaesthetic perceptual abilities which form the foundations for future learning of movement skills.

PERCEPTUAL-MOTOR ABILITIES

The basic perceptual abilities underlying our capacity to learn motor skills can be mainly seen as visual perception, auditory perception and kinaesthetic perception. The integration of these with a variety of motor responses over a long period will lead to the development of visuo-motor coordination, eye–hand accuracy and eye–foot coordination. These are learned abilities and fundamental to the acquisition of skill in games. They can be seen as the base of the pyramid on which we build our hierarchy of learning games. The material in Chapter 4 is sequenced as much for the development of perceptual-motor ability as it is for the learning of games skills. Physical education in the kindergarten and first school is geared to laying down the foundations of general body management and to perceptual-motor training. Excellent programmes for the development of basic body management through perceptual-motor training can be found in Arnheim and Pestolesi (1978), Holle (1976) and Frostig and Maslow (1970). Arnheim and Pestolesi state,

> The basic body management programme attempts, through a sequential task-learning process, to assist children in becoming more successful in managing their bodies in a wide variety of movement situations. At the same time it attempts to provide the child with movement experiences that are multisensory in nature. In essence, this programme strives to provide children with tasks that are appropriate for their particular maturation and readiness levels while at the same time stimulating integration of the nervous system in order that increasingly more complicated motor activities may be accomplished.

Within the games context we are seeking to establish a base in the development of ball sense and muscle sense.

The concept of skilfulness in games can cause some confusion in the mind of the teacher because of the widely different situations that occur in varying types of games. In basketball, a team game, skill is shown by the ability of a player to be in the right place at the right time, select the appropriate technique, and make the correct decision according to the demands of the situation. The game is made up of a series of techniques or subroutines involving passing, catching, dribbling and shooting, together with tactical awareness. It is possible to be technically proficient without necessarily demonstrating true skill in that a choice of techniques inappropriate to the immediate situation produces a failure. In group games and team games the ability to read the game is paramount in becoming a skilful player. On the other hand, certain games are predominantly games where technical excellence is essential for successful performance. It is impossible to take part in partner activities such as tennis, badminton or ten-pin bowling unless the ball, shuttle or bowl can be manipulated and directed accurately. We must often, therefore, distinguish between skill and technique. Technique is the basis of an action, the movement pattern necessary to bring about the desired effects of the action. Skill is the ability to produce the correct technique on demand, at the right moment, successfully and consistently. It is the total power to control the action. Normal children acquire the essential games techniques relatively easily through play and show widely differing performance according to their individual abilities. Without demonstrating tactical awareness they can nevertheless play group and team games of a low order and develop understanding of tactical game principles during their play. Handicapped children do not show this same technical proficiency; therefore it is essential that they are taught the basic principles before they are introduced to games where decision making and adaptability to a changing environment are critical factors in performance.

The hierarchy of learning games skills can therefore be presented as a simple model (Figure 1.2).

Figure 1.2   Hierarchy of learning games skills

Team games
Group games
Individual and partner games
Basic techniques
General body management
Perceptual-motor abilities

A CLASSIFICATION OF MOTOR TASKS

There have been many attempts to develop classification systems for motor skills. These are valuable where they increase understanding of the relative degree of difficulty of tasks as an aid to selection of material appropriate to the movement problems of children with special needs. Tasks in physical education vary from the simple to the highly complex, and we need to know the component factors inherent within any task which affect the degree of difficulty presented. Where groups of tasks exhibit common characteristics it may be possible to choose teaching methods that are more appropriate to the various task clusters.

Sugden (1984) has described a classification system, adapted from the work of Gentile *et al.* (1975) and Speth-Arnold (1981), that is simple to use and valuable in placing the problems in some sort of order. Although the classification system was never intended to describe the degree of task difficulty, the implications for use with handicapped children are obvious, and the experienced teacher will be able to formulate a progression in difficulty within each of the identified categories. Sugden examines the demand placed upon the individual when performing different types of movement:

1.   The body is stable.
2.   The body is moving, and some tasks may require limb manipulation.
3.   The environment is stable and, therefore, predictable.
4.   The environment is variable.

In aiming a beanbag at a skittle, or shooting a netball at a low basket, the task is totally predictable as the body is stable and the environmental conditions are constant. The task is, therefore, relatively simple according to the physical demands and the height, distance and force judgements that will vary with the chosen task. When two stationary players pass a ball between them they are stable, but the flight of the ball is a variable factor. This task demonstrates an increase in difficulty dependent upon the type of ball used, the distance between the players, and the spatial demands of the ball flight related to the type of pass. When both players attempt to pass and catch while on the move, the bodily and environmental demands become unpredictable and a great increase in task difficulty may be observed.

This particular task classification can provide a rough assessment tool for the identification of movement problems in children as they attempt to learn games skills. Through careful observation of children's movements as they perform different types of tasks we can identify the particular areas of performance that require remedial help. For example, if children demonstrate problems in performing any movement task where the body is stable and the environment is constant, then the problem may be identified as being motor in origin. On the other hand, if they perform well in that situation but find difficulty when either the body or the environment are variable and unpredictable, then the problem is likely to be perceptual, shown by their inability to adapt to the changing conditions.

A simple model illustrates the relationship between the categories of motor tasks (see Table 1.1). This straightforward classification is valuable for the practising teacher and is based upon a sequence of skill taxonomies that are of interest in the way they identify task characteristics in a different manner. These skill taxonomies are briefly summarized below.

Poulton (1957) proposed a continuum of 'closed' and 'open' skills. In closed skills the performer concentrates on internal feedback through the kinaesthe-

Table 1.1   Relationship between categories of motor task

	Body stable	Body moving
Environment stable	Standing, kneeling, sitting Limb manipulation: 　reaching for a stationary object; 　playing bowling games; 　aiming at a skittle; 　setting a shot in basketball	Walking, crawling, running, wheeling Limb manipulation: 　reaching for a stationary object; 　laying up a shot in basketball
Environment changing	Standing, kneeling, sitting Many group games: 　aiming in dodgeball games; 　catching a moving ball; 　hitting a rounders ball	Running, wheeling, crawling Team games: 　passing to a partner; 　catching a moving ball; 　clearing a shot in badminton

tic sense, and in open skills adaptability of response to a changing environment is all important, with varying environmental demands graded between the two ends of the scale. Extrapolating from the work of Poulton, Knapp (1963) discussed a continuum of skills ranging from those which are mainly habitual through to those which are mainly perceptual. Fitts (1965) placed movement skills into three categories: discrete tasks of short duration with a clear beginning and end; serial tasks with a beginning and end but where a sequence of events follow one another in rapid succession; and continuous tasks that involve a series of movements where the performer has to make frequent and sometimes unpredictable adjustments to his actions in response to changing environmental conditions. Singer (1982) reviewed the many task classification systems and clarified the common task characteristics. He listed the analysis of task characteristics under the following headings:

1. *Degree of bodily involvement* — a continuum of gross motor skills involving large muscle groups to fine motor skills requiring precision of movement and eye–hand coordination.
2. *Length and control of movement* — classified in terms of discrete, serial and continuous.
3. *Environmental control* — classified under the situational demands on the performer as open and closed skills.
4. *Cognitive involvement* — classified according to the need for the performer to understand strategy that might help in handling information related to identification of cues, anticipation and decision making.
5. *Feedback availability* — ranging from slow activities where feedback is ongoing and appropriate responses can be made to activities where feedback is terminal, that is, available on the completion of the movement task when the outcome can be seen or felt.

Singer (1982) lays stress on the importance of these factors for the teacher in performing a task analysis to simplify the demands of the task for a learner with movement problems.

STAGES OF LEARNING

Games skills must be learned. They can be improved as a result of trial and error methods, but learning will be made easier by sound guidance from the teacher. The continual feedback to the learner of information related to his most recent performance is vital to the learning process.

The role of the teacher is vital in providing appropriate guidance throughout the practice of a motor skill. Beginners notoriously attend to too many cues in a skill-learning situation. Teachers, on the other hand, often provide so much information to beginners at once that they confuse the issue in the minds of children. The three main forms of guidance used by teachers are verbal, visual and manual.

VERBAL GUIDANCE

Verbal directions are too often beyond the comprehension of young children. The more complex the skill, the less valuable verbal instruction is prior to practice. Words are best used to draw the attention of the learner to the task in hand and to cue the action. In particular, they may be used to direct attention to certain aspects of a demonstration felt to be of most importance at that moment. Verbal instruction should therefore be brief and in simple language. The author remembers drawing the attention of a severely disabled boy to the essential mechanics of aiming a beanbag at a skittle standing on a table: 'Line up your eyes, the beanbag and the target before throwing.' The reply 'Please sir, what's a target?' was a chastening experience.

VISUAL GUIDANCE

Use of demonstration is fundamental at all levels of learning motor skills in presenting an all-action visual picture of the movement task. It must be remembered that children will attempt to imitate what they have seen, so the demonstration must be a sound facsimile of the task and directly related to the ability of the children. Where the children have a motor disability affecting the execution of a desired movement pattern, then the demonstration should replicate the disability. Demonstrations to children in wheelchairs should be performed from a wheelchair to provide the children with an exact movement to copy.

MANUAL GUIDANCE

When dealing with disabled children this means putting the performer's body through the required movements to help feel the pattern of movement. It may also be of great help in movements requiring force to *resist* the action, thereby helping them to feel the power of the movement or to time the release of an object, particularly in antigravity actions such as throwing.

It is important that teachers should understand some of the changes that take place during the learning process and appreciate the relevance of the correct type of guidance at the right time. In the previous section a classification of motor tasks was described. It is apparent that different techniques of instruction may be necessary for tasks requiring *adaptability to a changing environment* where visual perception is a major factor, and tasks where *technically correct movements* are needed. Children have limited capacities for processing information, so the teacher must help to highlight the essential stimuli of a task and focus the children's attention selectively on the most important cues appropriate to both the type of task and the stage of learning reached. In the early stages of learning a perceptual-motor task, it is well known that what the child sees is the most important factor affecting the rate of learning as a beginner sorts out the important visual cues from the environment. As the visual cues are accommodated, kinaesthetic feedback becomes more important in controlling the rate of learning. For example, consider the case of a golfer first learning to drive a ball off the tee. He looks at the flag, places his feet in position, visually checks his position in relation to the ball, visually re-checks that his feet are lined up on the flag, and places the club head behind the ball. In trying a preliminary swing he may visually check the club position at the top of the swing. Throughout the movements he is constantly working out the sequence of events in his mind at a conscious level. After considerable practice the sequence of movements becomes refined and any further improvements are in the feel of the movement. At the conscious level his thoughts change from 'What am I doing?' to 'How am I doing it?'. As the quality of the golf swing becomes constant and he no longer thinks about it he is able to concentrate his whole attention on the ball and his estimate of distance and direction from the hole. Eventually the act of driving becomes automatic, a subconscious function. Any improvements occurring at this stage will be related to the feeling of the movement pattern. This process of working through the learning of a motor task from the conscious to the unconscious level is common to all motor tasks. Fitts and Posner (1967) have identified three stages of learning in the acquisition of motor skill, thus clarifying the type of information that the teacher must present at the appropriate phase of the learning process. Clearly the stages are not discrete but part of a continuous process, although they are valuable in describing the early beginnings, the practice stage and the final phases of skill learning.

THE COGNITIVE PHASE

When a beginner approaches the learning of a new motor skill the main function of the teacher is in helping him to understand the nature of the task. The learner must appreciate the objectives and develop an overall picture of the problem as he formulates a preparatory plan of action. The major role of the teacher is in directing the attention of the learner to the important stimuli of the situation and, where necessary, to simplify the initial practice situation by removing irrelevant elements which might cause distractions. Marteniuk (1976) suggests that

> included in the idea of the skill at this phase of learning are the relevant environmental cues that control or regulate the movement. In other words, the learner must not only have an idea of the movement involved but must also be able to recognise and process those cues in the environment to which the movement must be matched. For closed skills this may represent a relatively simple approach for this initial stage of learning.

The situation for open skills is obviously more complex because of the changing nature of the environment and the need to adapt to the change. In certain cases cues appear in sequence, enabling the performer to anticipate and predict likely events. Considerable cognitive activity takes place as the learner plans out the strategy for performing the sequence of movements. Verbal input and description needs to be translated into movement action and the learner will often 'talk' his way through the initial responses. A demonstration of the whole task is essential and key words will be used to make the performer attend to the most important aspects of the demonstration. For example, in an aiming task, such as shooting at a basket, the learner will be asked to look at the basket, line up the ball with it, and keep the ball on line throughout the shot. These are visual cues and critical in the initial stages of learning as the performer tries to understand the intentions of the movement pattern. The learner may make a great many mistakes at this stage, but improvement is rapid as incorrect movement responses are discarded in favour of more successful ones. By careful task analysis and knowledge of the performer's ability, the teacher ought to be able to lead the child through this stage fairly quickly.

THE ASSOCIATIVE PHASE

Once the learner appreciates the nature of the task and how to tackle the problem, he moves into the next phase of learning. This is the associative phase where practice of the skill is critical in refining the movement pattern. Here, the learner comes to terms with the feel of the movement and the correct timing of the sequence of actions. In shooting at a basket the emphasis will be placed on the accuracy of the arm action, the use of the wrist in developing power, and getting the feel of how much force is required appropriate to the distance from the basket. In the first phase the beginner learns to sort out directional cues in terms of left, right and upwards and hits the basket consistently without necessarily putting the ball through the ring. Once these cues are established and cognitive activity diminishes, the learner will, as a result of practice, refine the motor action in terms of muscular power and begin to drop several shots through the ring. Changes in technique tend to be small and errors minimal as performance improves. As learning develops the learner becomes much more aware of errors as they occur and is able to adapt accordingly. Handicapped children show deficiencies in proprioceptive feedback at this stage, so manual guidance techniques are often necessary to reinforce the feeling of the actions. This second phase of learning is far more prolonged than the first and is where, through constant repetition of the learning experience, the learner begins to reduce the number of errors in his performance. Attention must be directed towards understanding the continuing performance and the effects of changed actions upon the quality of that performance. A great deal of patience and persistence is required by both teacher and learner at this stage. The teacher must keep motivation high by matching the difficulty of the task to the ability of the performer through sound task analysis. The child must practise being successful.

THE AUTONOMOUS PHASE

The final phase of learning is shown when the skill is performed with a lower level of conscious attention so that the movement pattern becomes automatic. At this stage the performer automatically utilizes kinaesthetic feedback in controlling the action and is therefore free to concentrate his attention on other important elements within the environmental situation. This is characterized by a fluency of action, even under the stress of playing a game in which opponents attempt to interfere with the performance; the performer is able to scan the immediate area, look for other players and decide which tactical actions are needed. The focus of attention for the teacher at this last stage in skill acquisition is in helping the child to make the correct decisions by increasing his tactical knowledge and awareness and by making a much more detailed analysis of technical errors.

It can thus be seen that the key role of the teacher is to review performance constantly and help the learner retain information from previous stages. This is done to compare intention with actual performance and to analyze why there were differences. Teachers can help by matching the key aspects of performance and intention, and guiding the performer to concentrate on those important aspects throughout the three stages of learning.

REFERENCES

Arnheim, D.D. and Pestolesi, R.A. (1978) *Elementary Physical Education*, C.V. Mosby, Saint Louis, Minnesota
Fitts, P.M. (1965) *Factors in complex skill training*. In R. Glaser (Ed.), Training Research and Education, John Wiley, New York
Fitts, P.M. and Posner, M.I. (1967) *Human Performance*, Brooks–Cole
Frostig, M. and Maslow, P. (1970) *Movement Education: Theory and Practice*, Follett, Chicago
Gentile, A.M., Higgins, J.R., Miller, E.A. and Rosen, B.M. (1975) The structure of motor tasks, *Movement*, Vol. 7, pp. 11–28
Holle, B. (1976) *Motor Development in Children*, Blackwell Scientific Publications, Oxford
Holt, K. (1984) *Movement studies*. In A. Brown *et al.* (Eds), Adapted Physical Activities. Proceedings of IVth IFAPA Symposium, London, pp. 2–11, International Federation of Adapted Physical Activity
Keogh, J. and Sugden, D.A. (1985) *Movement Skill Development*, Macmillan, New York
Kerr, R. (1982) *Psychomotor Learning*, Saunders College, New York
Knapp, B. (1963) *Skill in Sport*, Routledge & Kegan Paul, London
Marteniuk, R.G. (1976) *Information Processing in Motor Skills*, Holt, Rinehart & Winston, New York
Poulton, E.C. (1957) On prediction in skilled movements, *Psychological Bulletin*, Vol. 54, pp. 467–478

Schmidt, R.A. (1975) *Motor Skills*, Harper & Row, New York
Singer, R.N. (1982) *The Learning of Motor Skills*, Macmillan, New York
Speth-Arnold, R.K. (1981) *Developing sport skills*. In Motor Skills: Theory into Practice, Monograph 2
Sugden, D.A. (1984) Issues in teaching children with movement problems, *British Journal of Physical Education*, Vol. 15, No. 3, pp. 68–70
Whiting, H.T.A. (1969) *Acquiring Ball Skill*, G. Bell, London

Chapter 2
THE EFFECTS OF HANDICAP ON PERCEPTUAL-MOTOR PERFORMANCE

The selection and adaptation of material included within the games curriculum must be seen in relation to the special needs and the movement problems of children. The problem for physical education specialist teachers in the normal school setting is that although they are expert in their subject area they are unfamiliar with the movement problems of children with special needs. These children are too often excluded from games lessons; furthermore, where they are integrated inappropriate lesson material and inappropriate teaching methods are used. In this chapter some of the movement problems shown by handicapped children are identified and clarified and some methods of minimizing or overcoming their difficulties in learning games skills are suggested.

It is not only beyond the scope of this book but unnecessary in this context to present the aetiology and medical history of every form of handicap; where necessary, further references are provided. The more common conditions are described, together with those handicaps that entail particular difficulties. It is important that the movement characteristics should be understood in relation to their effect on perceptual-motor performance and skill learning; the implications for teaching in physical education are described merely as guidelines. The main focus is the effect on function and on the capacity for motor learning.

Before considering specific types of handicap, we need to examine the major problems that interfere with or prevent correct performance in gross perceptual-motor skills.

1. Lack of previous experience. Handicapped children often perform poorly because they have been overprotected and sheltered and have thus missed vital years of movement experience. As a result, they often approach new tasks with fear and trepidation and lack the developed abilities to make judgements based on experiential learning.
2. Hand and arm impairment. Most games skills involve the use of the hands; a handicap of hand function in terms of strength or control is a

Figure 2.1 Perceptual-motor process model (catching a ball)

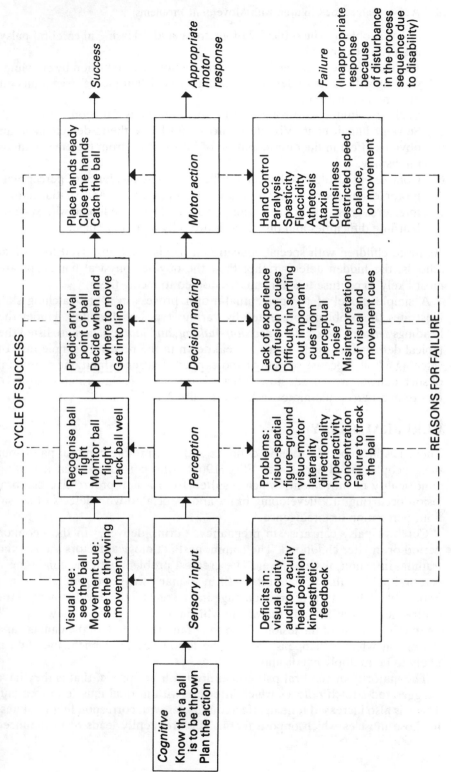

major problem. The difficulty of grasping and releasing in cerebral palsy is a prime example.

3.   Ability to move with freedom. The restriction of locomotion by crawling, walking with assistive devices, or using a wheelchair places strict limits on movement potential.
4.   Lack of voluntary control as a result of cerebral dysfunction.
5.   Sensory impairment. Visual, auditory and kinaesthetic defects have an obvious effect in the discrimination of information from the environmental display.
6.   Complex psychological learning difficulties. The incidence of perceptual-motor disorders of a visual-motor, visuo-perceptual and spatial nature interferes grossly with the learning process. These are linked with specific learning difficulties and discussed more fully at a later stage.

As more children with special educational needs are transferred to normal schools, the hidden defects rather than the obvious physical handicaps are most likely to confuse teachers unaccustomed to facing them.

A simple model of the perceptual-motor process in a ball-catching skill illustrates the problems presented by various types of disability. Under the headings *sensory*, *perception*, *decision making*, and *motor action* are listed the typical defects that might cause a breakdown in the relatively simple task of catching a ball. Because so many handicapped children exhibit one or several of such deficits, we can see how difficult it is to analyze the primary causes of failure in a perceptual-motor task (see Figure 2.1).

CEREBRAL PALSY

There is still some variation in defining and interpreting cerebral palsy, but most people would agree with Ellis (1967), who considered that it was an abnormality of movement, which resulted from a non-progressive cerebral lesion occurring in a developing brain and associated with defects of sensation, perception or intelligence.

Cerebral palsy can arise in pregnancy, during delivery, in the neonatal period or in later childhood. The commonest aetiological factors are anoxia, trauma, infection, fits and fever. The greatest problem with the condition of cerebral palsy is that it manifests itself in so many ways and generalization is impossible. The effects of brain damage interfere with the development of the central nervous system and the way in which the characteristics show depends on the specific site of the lesion within the brain, the extent of the damage and the age at which it happens. Where the lesion occurs at birth, the child is likely to be multiply handicapped.

The majority of cerebral palsied children will be spastic, that is they have exaggerated stretch reflexes which interfere with normal muscle movement. There is also increased tone in affected muscles with corresponding weakness in those muscles which oppose them. This frequently leads to pronounced deformities of major joints such as hips, shoulders and wrists. Spasticity tends to affect the main muscles involving flexion, with the extensor muscles being weak, producing a flexion deformity. Postural control is therefore difficult and voluntary control of movement in the affected limbs is very limited. In severe cases all four limbs are involved and we have a spastic quadriplegia. If the lower limbs only are affected, this is a paraplegia; where an arm and a leg on the same side of the body are involved this is known as a hemiplegia. In spastic paraplegia only the legs are affected and many will eventually walk with or without aids, although gait patterns are awkward with internal rotation of the hips and ankle joints. Those affected are permanently on their toes through excessive contraction of the achilles tendon. Head and arm control tend to be good and many become quite skilled in games involving the hands, although as a group they exhibit problems of visuo-motor control. The vast majority of spastics are below normal intelligence levels compared with other types of cerebral palsy.

The second most common type of cerebral palsy is athetosis caused by damage to the basal ganglia located in the cerebrum. Athetoids demonstrate an excess of involuntary movements and, in particular, will experience these when attempting volitional acts such as reaching for a pencil or a ball. They show a total lack of control and exhibit movements that are without purpose, unpredictable and lacking in any form of coordination. Lack of head control is a major problem in physical education as the head jerks about and to one side as gross body movement is attempted; this obviously affects visual focusing in ball games. Athetoids are less likely to be of low intelligence. Unfortunately they may be regarded as mentally retarded by the layman because of their appearance, often characterized by dribbling from the mouth, and their great difficulty in control of speech.

The third commonest group are those suffering from ataxia resulting from a lesion in the cerebellum. As the cerebellum is the main centre for organization of feedback information related to muscular coordination and kinaesthesis, this produces problems of balance. Ataxics are lacking in balance and although many are able to walk their gait is like that of a person who is drunk: they stumble and wave their arms and legs about in an effort to maintain balance. They have great difficulty in placing their feet to avoid obstacles and have problems in reaching for objects because they stretch too far.

There are other types of cerebral palsy less frequently met, but the majority of these fall into the spastic, athetoid and ataxic categories and obviously present very different problems. The needs of those affected vary greatly. A more detailed account of the movement characteristics of cerebral palsy can be found in Holt (1965) and Price (1980).

The most obvious characteristic of the cerebral palsied child is therefore a pronounced motor dysfunction, but this is only one aspect. Johnstone (1975) suggests that perhaps this is not the most important problem in the total development of the child. On closer acquaintance we find the child may be further handicapped by a wide variety of other associated disorders resulting from the initial brain damage. Almost 50 per cent of such children are mentally subnormal with IQs below 70. Added to this, cerebral palsied children are more likely to have defects of vision and hearing than their normal peers. Further, many of them have articulatory problems; in some cases these are so severe that communication by speech becomes impossible. In cerebral palsy we also find the familiar learning difficulties of distractibility, perseveration, poor attention span, faulty body image, deficits in visuo-motor and visual–perceptual skills, auditory imperception and inadequate receptive language. These psychological problems are well documented in Holt and Reynell (1967).

The complex problem in teaching is the vast range of severity within any group and the vast range of multiple handicap within any individual. Disability will range from the very slight to the extremely severe, indicating that with these children, more than any others, we need to organize a programme based on individualizing the teaching.

IMPLICATIONS FOR TEACHING

Because of the widely varying types and severities of handicap within the overall condition of cerebral palsy it is imperative to have an individual profile of each child indicating the specific motor handicap, specific movement patterns to avoid because of stretch reflexes, perceptual-motor problems, and specific learning difficulties. Performer analysis and task analysis techniques will be necessary in almost all cases in order to simplify and adapt most activities. Because the children are easily distracted, it is necessary to produce an environment free as far as possible of external stimulation; yet the immediate teaching apparatus must be highly stimulating in order to focus attention on the task in hand. This may mean quiet pastel shades on walls, diffused lighting, the avoidance of glare from windows, and, in certain instances, screened-off areas for individual practice. On the other hand, multicoloured play balls, targets and beanbags will serve to focus attention on the task and help figure–ground discrimination. The severely disabled, particularly young children, will require one-to-one support while learning basic skills. In the primary school, children should, where possible, be removed from their wheelchairs for physical education and placed in their most comfortable functional position on gymnasium mats. There will be exceptions to this rule, of course, in the case of those suffering from excessive hyperactive involuntary motion and after surgery of the lower limbs. One important task that the child must be taught, in cooperation with the physiotherapist, is independent movement to and from a wheelchair.

Before any cerebral palsied child can take part in games activities it is critical that a stable position is established from which he can operate with the head and hands under some degree of control. According to individual postural development, this will vary from standing, sitting, straddle legged, kneeling, lying over a foam cushion wedge, to being confined in a wheelchair. Athetoid and ataxic children often perform best after they have been stabilized in a kneeling position from which they can take part in a vast range of activities. In general, games should be selected that tend to reduce the excitement factor as this only increases involuntary movement in athetoids and elicits the stretch reflex spasm in spastics. It has been found that high ball flight often causes similar problems as the children cannot predict the flight and lose the ball, show fear of the ball, and constantly over reach. The use of large beanbags allows maximum participation in group and team games for all types of cerebral palsy. Apart from groups of spastic paraplegics and hemiplegics, it is generally necessary to modify ball flight in all activities. Where possible the game situations need to be slowed down both as regards the speed of the ball and the movement of the players.

Despite these problems, cerebral palsied children have been found to develop considerable skill in adapted games, and the social benefits of group and team games should not be underestimated. It is impossible to generalize, and it must be stressed that the *type* of cerebral palsy is not as important as the *severity of the handicap* in dictating selection and adaptation of games activities. Most hemiplegic children can develop skill with their good hand and foot and can take part in even major games in a relatively unrestricted environment. Spastic paraplegics often show compensatory development in arms and shoulders and after a period of training exhibit great skill in games involving the use of hands and arms. Ambulant paraplegics have balance problems and, therefore, should not be required to cover large areas of space too quickly. Wheelchair paraplegics on the other hand show great skill in manipulating their transport and can play a great range of team games once they have successfully learnt how to collect a ball from floor level. Wheelchair quadriplegics show a wide range of ability; they too, dependent upon their arm use, can take part in team games where the rules have been adapted. They can take part with success in individual and partner activities based on discrete performance of single response-type activities involving aiming and throwing, throwing and catching, and simple striking skills.

The most difficult groups of children to teach are the athetoid and ataxic. Because of their difficulties in ball-tracking, fast ball games are never successful and produce the most bizarre movement patterns. They need to be quietened down and kept calm during games playing. When ball flight has been modified and the fear element removed by using soft balls, they can develop skill in catching or hitting rolled or bounced balls. Fine manipulative skill is impossible and all movement should be adapted to a gross pattern where possible. They play quite well in group games of a quiet nature where speed of activity is minimal, and they can show evidence of a high level of skill in aiming games. The normal practice in aiming games, however, is to prepare for the action by taking several preliminary swings along the line of aim prior to throwing. In their case this only serves to wind them up and exaggerate and distort the involuntary movement pattern; hence the object may fly off at a tangent. They tend to aim better and release more accurately if they are taught to relax first, breathe deeply, go floppy, then release the object in one sudden movement.

Another problem that causes difficulty for cerebral palsied children as they learn new skills is their poor body image, linked as it is with deficient awareness of movement through impaired kinaesthesis. A progressive programme aimed at the identification of body parts and awareness of changes in body position during movement needs to be developed before any success can be gained in the acquisition of games skills. Thus, a multisensory approach to learning is often necessary, particularly in the recognition of cues during motor action. Dunn (1984) suggests a sequence of cues found to be effective with the severely disabled which seem particularly useful in dealing with cerebral palsy. These cues are ordered according to their complexity:

1. Verbal cue is given — the child is told what to do. If the child fails to respond or responds incorrectly, move to step 2.
2. A demonstration of the skill (visual cue) is combined with the verbal cue. If the child does not respond or responds incorrectly, move to step 3.
3. A demonstration of the skill (visual cue) is combined with the verbal cue, and the child is given physical assistance in the form of manual kinaesthesis.

The object of the hierarchy is to help children perform physical tasks at the highest cue level possible. Many cerebral palsied children with grasp-release problems can be helped to time the moment of release by a sequence of (1) a sharp shout of 'Now!', (2) touching the arm at the correct time, (3) manhandling the arm through the movement pattern and reinforcing the timing with a shout. Eventually the child should respond to the task without the need for any form of manual assistance.

A further point for consideration is the unique nature of the movement problems for each cerebral palsied child, and we must always stress function rather than style. The idea of normal movement development is totally foreign to the problems of cerebral palsied children. As a result of exposure to experience and through practice, each child will develop some understanding of his abilities and work out his own method of performing. The use of trick movements that work well is a feature in dealing with the cerebral palsied. Each child may come up with a different solution to any given movement task and we must accept this, if it works consistently.

In an attempt to produce relative homogeneity within a physical education class, Price (1980) proposes a simple classification based on motor function rather than the type of cerebral palsy. He suggests three distinct groups:

1. Ambulant children — those who can walk, with or without assistive devices. Those with minimal impairment can be introduced to the full range of games activities. Others with more serious movement problems can perform games activities of a more sedate nature.
2. Independent wheelchair users — poor leg control but with strong arms and reasonable control. He suggests that these children could be grouped with the paraplegics so long as similar standards are not expected as some trunk and arm involvement is almost always present.
3. Dependent wheelchair users — use of electric chairs is indicated because neuromuscular control is so poor. One-to-one assistance is almost always necessary and games where no speed of reaction is required should be chosen. Aiming games present the obvious outlet.

At first glance there is no obvious weakness in this general system of grouping for physical education, but the practicalities may present problems within a small special school population in obtaining class numbers of a viable size and of a comparable age range. In the end, teaching will still be based on mixed ability methods. The implications of such a system within the recreation context are, however, very interesting. Such a grouping within community sports clubs for the adult disabled would solve many organizational problems and allow large groups of people with relatively similar abilities and interests to take part in recreational games for lifelong leisure. Some large comprehensive schools may be identified under the 1981 Education Act as centres for the integration of children with special needs and Price's proposed grouping system may have important implications for the organization of special classes and for the organization of after school activities in intra-mural and extra-mural sport.

A fairly lengthy description of cerebral palsy has been drawn in the belief that if the teacher can overcome the problems presented, no other handicapping condition demonstrates quite the same degree of difficulty.

SPINA BIFIDA

Spina bifida is a general term, referring to a developmental defect of the spinal column in which the arches of one or more of the spinal vertebrae have failed to fuse together so that the spine exhibits a gap in the vertebral wall. Anderson and Spain (1977) give a full account of the medical, educational and psychological problems of children with spina bifida. After cerebral palsy, this is now the second most common physically handicapping condition in childhood. The extent of neuromuscular involvement will depend upon the site of the lesion and the degree of damage to the spinal cord. Where lesions occur in the sacral region, muscular problems may only show as a flaccidity or weakness in the lower legs and the feet and the child may learn to walk quite well. Damage occurring in the lumbar and lower thoracic areas almost always results in complete paraplegia together with loss of sensation and anaesthesia. Fait and Dunn (1984) indicate that innervation of the muscles concerned with urinating comes from the sacral level of the spine, therefore, bladder paralysis is almost universal. Incontinence of the bowel and bladder is a feature of low lesion spina bifida. Lesions which occur at a higher spinal level in the cervical region generally show no paralysis although there may be some involvement of the muscles in the arms.

In the majority of cases of spina bifida the most serious associated problem is the incidence of hydrocephalus. This is caused by a blockage of the ventricle within the cranial cavity causing the build up of excessive quantities of cerebrospinal fluid. In the untreated state this produces gross enlargement of the head, brain damage, possible educational subnormality and ultimately an early death. Modern technological advances have produced a shunt valve, the Spitz–Holter, inserted into the ventricle, which drains the fluid into the blood stream. A low-pressure valve, located behind the right ear, controls the flow of fluid as pressure builds up. This valve can be felt under the skin, but the whole area tends to be highly sensitive to the touch. No special care need be taken during activity sessions, except that the teacher must be aware that damage to the valve could occur as a result of direct contact from a body or a hard ball in flight. Any damage may result in a blockage of the valve. Such damage produces blinding headaches, some drowsiness and projectile vomiting. In such circumstances the child must be immediately taken to the nearest hospital for emergency treatment.

The main features of spina bifida, therefore, exhibit as impairment of mobility, incontinence, some intellectual impairment, learning problems of distractibility in cases of hydrocephalus, and problems of social and emotional development as a result. In most cases, however, the musculature above the site of the spinal lesion functions very well and many children demonstrate pronounced compensatory development of arms, shoulders and upper torso.

IMPLICATIONS FOR TEACHING

Price (1980) has produced an excellent summary of considerations for a teacher in the selection of appropriate activities for spina bifida children. He suggests that physical education programmes should be centred upon:

1. activities which can be pursued in wheelchairs;
2. activities in which the children can participate sitting or lying down on the floor.

Price does, however, add a note of caution and lists other factors that must be borne in mind when considering the appropriateness of particular activities.

1. Non-weight-bearing bones with no tonic muscle covering become very brittle and are easily fractured. Paralysed limbs are anaesthetic and,

therefore, the child feels no pain when an injury occurs. Thus children at risk are advised to wear calipers during very active pursuits. Floor activities can also produce problems as paralysed legs are dragged around. Children ought to use gymnasium mats for protection as they may be more sensitive to friction burns than others. They must also be taught to manoeuvre from wheelchair to floor or onto apparatus.

2. Incontinent children normally wear a bag for the collection of urine, attached either to the thigh or the abdomen. Hard physical exercise promotes the flow of urine and the plastic bags can easily come adrift. Care needs to be taken to avoid positions where spillage can occur.

3. Spitz–Holter shunt valves do not prevent children from taking part in physical education, but some care is necessary to avoid a direct impact in the ear area.

4. Paraplegics often have stronger arms than normal but show evidence of a lower-order performance in manual dexterity, hand–eye coordination and fine motor control. This may be due to the prolonged effects of movement deprivation but can often be overcome by the patient provision of a movement programme over a long period.

Although special teaching methods are not necessary for most spina bifida children, some adaptation will be required in the learning of ball skills to help cope with their visuo-motor problems. Following a structured individual programme, most children show evidence of great ability in games activities that do not require too much mobility.

MUSCULAR DYSTROPHY

Muscular dystrophy is one of a group of diseases where progressive muscle weakness is the main feature. The most common form of the disease likely to be found in schools is Duchennes muscular dystrophy. Typical of the disease is a progressive pattern of muscular weakness becoming apparent in the early years of life with a gradual deterioration of posture and muscle function until early death occurs at around 20 years of age. No cure exists and education and therapy programmes are geared to delay the onset of deterioration by keeping the child active as long as possible within the limits of progressive fatigue.

IMPLICATIONS FOR TEACHING

In the early stages of the condition muscular dystrophy children are not helpless and should be encouraged to do as much as possible while taking care not to overstrain the cardiovascular system. They are not suffering from the neuromuscular control problems of brain or spinal damage and can, therefore, be presented with a wide programme of basic games tasks where skill, rather than strength, is emphasized. During the period when they are confined to a manual wheelchair they may still take part in group and team games of a social nature, provided that allowance is made for their muscular weakness and early fatigue. Lightweight bats and long-handled sticks simplify participation in striking games. It is critical that they are made to feel part of their peer group, and games should be selected that emphasize the socialization and recreational values of the activity. Simple adaptations to the rules of team games and to the mobility factor in performance can be made to include them within the group.

Once children have progressed to the use of an electric wheelchair the main problems of participation arise, but this time the movement potential may be negligible. Price (1980) suggests that at this stage they are in much the same position as quadriplegics and can be treated in a similar manner. Provided that they can operate an electric wheelchair successfully they can be positioned as a goalkeeper in certain team games. Their cognitive abilities remain intact, so they can take a part as a team coach or officiate as a referee. Depending upon the extent of the disability, many children will still be able to take part in the simplest aiming games and even static passing activities. The use of assistive devices, such as chutes attached to the front of the wheelchair, enable them to play bowling games of many varieties. In most cases they will require assistance on a one-to-one basis, but some independence can be retained by attaching thin cords to the objects thrown for easy retrieval.

As deterioration increases the whole process is heartrending for both teacher and child, and the attitude of the teacher is critical in establishing an atmosphere of fun within every games lesson. Although they are outside the normal active scope of physical education, many games have been adapted for play on a table and they provide a great deal of fun for the child with muscular dystrophy. These include table football, table shuffleboard, table ten-pin bowls and table cricket.

ASTHMA

Asthma is a disease of the bronchial tubes or the lungs, or both. An asthmatic attack is characterized by breathlessness, coughing and wheezing, tightness in the chest and excess formation of mucus. These attacks may be induced by the inhalation of smoke, dust, cold dry air, pollen and other irritating substances. The anomaly in asthma is that 'although over 80 per cent of asthmatics are susceptible to exercise as a trigger for bronchoconstriction, exercise is now accepted as a form of therapy in the control of the severity and duration of attack' (Jones, 1984). Jones also shows that with increased cardiovascular fitness and efficiency, there is an improvement in the vast majority of asthmatics by a decrease in frequency, severity and/or duration of asthma attacks.

IMPLICATIONS FOR TEACHING

The problem for the teacher is to introduce asthmatic children to physical activity which will promote physical well-being without triggering off an attack through a bout of too vigorous exercise. Mallinson (1985) suggests that these children need a longer period of warming up than normal children and advises the use of interval training principles where activity is interspersed with short periods of rest so that breathing returns to normal. In general, short bouts of exercise lasting 5 minutes cause little distress, provided that the activity is not too intense, whereas activities of longer duration cause distress. A games programme where the children work for approximately 5 minutes then rest for a similar period is, therefore, indicated. More important perhaps is that children should know when they reach their limit and stop to rest. Whenever any signs of distress appear rest is critical. Jones (1984) also suggests that humidified air may be a factor in the decrease in exercise-induced bronchorestriction and therefore the environmental conditions within a gymnasium need to be controlled. Many children suffering from asthma carry Ventalin or Intal inhalers to relieve bronchial constriction, and recent research suggests that they should take their preventative treatment at least 15 minutes before an exercise session is due to start.

Many asthmatic children in normal schools are often excused from physical education when, in fact, there is much they could do indoors. Outdoor games are less encouraged as the children are so sensitive to climatic conditions. The gymnasium or sports hall should be kept as clean as possible to avoid dust in the atmosphere. Games of badminton doubles and volleyball are suitable where short rest periods can be taken periodically.

Provided that the rate and duration of exercise in indoor games lessons is controlled and treatment taken prior to activity, asthmatic children can take part in a relatively unrestricted programme of games. They exhibit no other physical handicap and the sporting world is full of heroes who suffer from forms of asthma which they control.

Teachers of asthmatic children should learn how to cope with an asthma attack and how to help a child to take medication correctly. A useful guide is prescribed by Heggarty (1985).

CARDIAC DISORDERS

Although cardiac disorders can not be compared with many other handicapping conditions in that voluntary control of movement is unaffected and there are few other secondary disorders, nevertheless they are of critical importance to the physical education teacher because of the inherent danger to the child. Because of the widely varying degrees of severity in association with a particular cardiac problem, the diagnosis and prescription of games activities must be made on the recommendation of the child's doctor or specialist. Cardiac disorders may be congenital malformations or may be acquired, often as the result of childhood rheumatic fever. The important information needed by the teacher hinges upon the safety aspects of exercise prescription. The teacher must request information regarding the exercise tolerance level and be given a clear indication of a child's capacity to handle various work loads.

Games vary greatly in their exercise demands from very static basic skill practices to quiet, relaxed games of lawn bowls or putting to highly active team activities. Provided that sound medical advice is given to the teacher, and the child is made aware of his limitations, the child can take a part in activities based on skill rather than gross activity. It is easy to categorize games by exercise and effort requirement at mild, moderate and vigorous levels so that an appropriate selection of activities may be made. It is important to the social development of a child with a cardiac disorder that he can relate to the play activity of peers and develop skills of a more gentle nature for life-long leisure.

A caution is necessary concerning the use of competition in games where winning becomes too important: in the excitement of a game the child may go beyond the normal restraints. Many group and team games can be adapted for play on a cooperative basis, and these activities offer great scope for the inclusion of children with cardiac disorders.

EPILEPSY

Because of effective controlling drug regimens, epilepsy is no longer the problem it was. Now most epileptic children are educated in the normal school environment. Epilepsy is, however, prevalent among children with neurological problems, particularly cerebral palsy, and therefore it is of concern to teachers in a special school. So long as epileptic children are clearly identified, little restriction is necessary in the selection of suitable games activities. Where the child suffers from multiple handicap it is the perceptual-motor handicap that must be taken into account for teaching, not the epilepsy. The teacher needs to be aware of some of the conditions that might increase the chances of a seizure so that they may be considered in planning the play environment.

1. Hyperventilation or holding the breath, particularly during activities requiring endurance.
2. Conditions of stress. These may include psychological stress, emotional stress and excessive excitement. The author has experience of a child having a seizure brought on by the excitement and adrenalin flow of a National Athletics championship.
3. Direct traumatic damage to the head.
4. Excessive alcohol consumption. But it is to be hoped this does not apply to children.

Usually, however, most children have their seizures well under control and are able to take a full part in the normal games programme.

In the unlikely event of an attack, the teacher needs to be aware of very basic first aid procedures and this will only apply to the grand mal attacks.

1. Keep calm and do not panic the rest of the class.

2. Lay the child on his side with the face slanted down to allow the tongue to remain clear and any vomit or saliva to drain.
3. Once the attack has subsided, allow the child to have a rest or even to sleep.
4. If the jerky movements have not stopped after approximately 5 minutes, or if they recur, then a doctor should be called.

In certain aspects of the physical education programme safety must be a prime consideration in planning, which mainly consists of very close supervision during swimming sessions and the avoidance of heights in a gymnasium. This is less of a problem in games and the teacher's main concern is to control the level of excitement developed within games situations.

SUMMARY

I have discussed some of the problems associated with the more common handicapping conditions found in schools and have highlighted certain implications for the teacher of physical education in terms of selection, adaptation and safety. There are many more forms of handicap to be found, but it is beyond the scope of this book to present a full description of all of them. Interested teachers wishing to further their knowledge are recommended to read Fait and Dunn (1984), Price (1980), Crowe et al. (1981) and Sherrill (1982). In particular there is a vast range of orthopaedic handicaps to be found in both special schools and in the mainstream setting. These have not been dealt with because where loss of ambulation or limb function occurs the intelligent teacher will find little difficulty in adapting games activities to match the motor handicap.

A further group of children hover on the fringe of being identified as handicapped. These are the children that Sugden (1984) described as 'children with movement problems'. Elsewhere they have commonly been called 'clumsy children' or 'physically awkward'. These children exhibit many behavioural problems which stem from inadequate motor performance, but their main difficulty is a lack of proficiency in motor skills. Most of these children are to be found within the normal school environment where their problems are inadequately understood. The very limited skills level of these children precludes their participation in a normal school games curriculum and they try to withdraw from all situations which expose their inadequacies. Further reference may be made to Keogh et al. (1979), Gubbay (1975), Walton (1961), Sugden (1975) and Wall and Taylor (1984). The principles of assessment, prescription, task analysis, individualized instruction and programme structuring, on which the teaching methodology of this book are based, are singularly appropriate to the needs of these children.

The handicapping conditions discussed may be summarized as follows:

1. Neuromuscular disorder, characterized by difficulty in the control of movement with impairment of coordination and linked with many asso-

ciated psychological disorders. Teaching must be individualized and careful task analysis and environmental structuring is necessary.

2. Cardio-respiratory problems, characterized by the early onset of fatigue. Care needs to be taken in assessing exercise tolerance. Safety considerations are important in selecting activities which do not overtax the child.
3. Disorders resulting in progressive muscular weakness. In these conditions the games programme is gradually reduced in activity as the condition progresses.
4. Disorders resulting in loss of function or paralysis. A careful selection of games activities is needed to match the residual function and ability of the child.

Price (1980) produced interesting and useful guidelines for the teacher in assessing the effects of handicap on the selection of appropriate physical activity. He has suggested that the following questions should be answered before the child is allowed to participate in vigorous physical activity:

1. What sort of disorder are we dealing with? Is it neuromuscular, muscular, orthopaedic, respiratory or cardiac? What secondary characteristics must be considered, such as brittle bones, vertigo, muscle spasms, epilepsy or the side effects of medication?
2. Is the condition progressive or non-progressive?
3. Which body segments are affected and to what extent? Are the affected parts to be used or is movement of them to be restricted?
4. Will participation in any particular form of physical exercise aggravate the child's condition?

If we have satisfactory answers to these questions, then we are in a better position to relate the principles of selection and adaptation of activities specifically to the needs of the individual child.

LEARNING DIFFICULTIES

The learning difficulties under discussion are the hidden handicaps that interfere with performance as children try to solve movement problems. These handicaps are a feature of cerebral palsy in particular, but they are certainly not confined to children with overt physical disabilities. Many children in the normal school, with no obvious handicap, demonstrate movement problems as they attempt to learn new skills and these hidden handicaps are often hardest for teachers to understand. The causes of these problems are difficult to pinpoint but minimal cerebral dysfunction and certain environmental factors involving emotional stresses can be identified. Morris and Whiting (1971) list these problems as behavioural characteristics associated with disturbances in perceptual-motor functions. A basic understanding of some of these specific learning difficulties is necessary because of their implications for teaching strategies in planning a lesson.

DISTRACTIBILITY

This is the inability to focus attention on any task, object or person within the immediate environment. These children respond to all extraneous visual or auditory stimuli around them and their attention is, therefore, distracted. They tend to overreact to everything and find it impossible to discriminate between the relevant aspects of a task and irrelevant stimuli such as bright colours, the sound of a passing bus, a fly on the wall, or the work of the nearest child. As a result they have a very short span of attention.

In dealing with the problem the teacher must structure the immediate teaching environment so that external distracting stimuli are reduced. In the first instance this may involve a plain gymnasium decor in quiet pastel shades and the removal of superfluous apparatus during games lessons. During work on a one-to-one basis the child should be placed in his own personal space away from the distractions of other children. Attention needs to be focused on one task at a time until the child is successful; then a slight increase in difficulty should be tried before moving on to the next task. Tasks that are discrete, with a single response, may be learned better than continuous tasks requiring too great an attention span. Although the background should be as free of stimulation as possible, it is important that the immediate play apparatus should be excessively stimulating and bright coloured beanbags and multicoloured playballs are useful. Activities should be selected that provide the child with a high expectation of success; therefore some evaluation of the initial starting point for teaching is needed, followed by a step-by-step progressive approach. From a recreational standpoint the distractible child will achieve greater success in individual and partner activities than in team games.

HYPERACTIVITY

Hyperactive children are constantly on the move and have difficulty in sitting down or standing quietly. They show an excessive level of energy, are often quite aggressive and have difficulty in focusing their attention on one thing at a time.

The implications for teaching are similar to those when dealing with distractibility in many ways. Modifying the environment to eliminate distracting influences and focusing on one simple task at a time have been found to work successfully. Many tasks can be modified to slow down the rate of response and to enable continuous tasks to be performed at a slow steady rhythm. Slow music may be used in an effort to make the child move to the rhythm, even in bouncing and catching tasks. Rules of group games need to be very simple with attention focused on one particular skill, and games should be selected in sequence to alternate the quieter activities with the more vigorous. In any one game, quiet periods need to be organized to slow down these children — perhaps a time out to discuss rules or game tactics.

PERSEVERATION

Perseveration is the difficulty that children have in shifting their attention with ease from one activity to another. Their attention seems to be locked into one particular response behaviour. Faced with a different task, the child may continue with the same response as before. This leads to constant repetitive behaviour at tasks where some success has been achieved, and an inability to move on.

This problem is partly solved by having distinct task stations spread around a gymnasium. The site for each task is clearly separated from the others; in each case the chosen task should be distinctly different from the preceding tasks. Tasks should be regularly changed and made as dissimilar as possible. This may follow the pattern often used in primary schools where practice stations are set up for the individual practice of various basic skills instead of teaching them on a group basis.

DISSOCIATION

Dissociation implies a deficit in perceiving objects as a whole. These children see parts of things but are unable to see the relationship of the parts to the whole task. They often react only to small aspects of the total task which makes their behaviour appear rather weird.

The choice of teaching method is important in dealing with dissociation and emphasis ought to be placed upon whole–part–whole techniques. The child observes or tries the total performance of the task, the task is then analyzed into achievable parts, and finally the whole task is attempted. The subtasks should be as large as possible and the child should be encouraged to perceive the relevance of these to the main task. Constant referral to the main task must be undertaken to help the child see the relationship between task and practice subroutines.

Children who experience specific learning difficulties will often demonstrate deficiencies in perceptual-motor performance related to laterality and directionality; very poor body awareness; visual, auditory and kinaesthetic perception; and figure–ground discrimination. Laterality is an awareness of left and right within the body and the ability to control the two sides of the body separately or simultaneously. Many children have difficulty in establishing their preferred dominant handedness. Directionality is an awareness of left, right, front and back and up and down in space. This external awareness of direction develops from laterality and the two are inextricably linked. Problems of laterality and directionality will obviously lead to a deficit in general spatial awareness.

The effects of these disorders may be considerably minimized through a planned intervention programme of compensatory education. A full description of systems of perceptual-motor training is beyond the scope of this book, but these were well reviewed by Morris and Whiting (1971) and more recently by Fait and Dunn (1984).

When dealing with children who suffer no obvious physical handicap but show evidence of specific learning difficulties, it is critical that teachers have access to a full psychological report which clearly identifies the problem areas. With this knowledge, the teacher is better able to plan a programme geared to the specific needs of each child. Most remedial programmes currently in use are based on a system of behaviour modification.

BEHAVIOUR MODIFICATION

The major principle in behaviour modification is the structuring of events within the environment to promote learning patterns and thus enhance the learning process. In this approach, goals are set by the teacher and the intervention programme is geared to elicit those goals. Immediately after the child performs a task reinforcement is provided. Positive reinforcement may be praise from the teacher, peer attention or a particular treat which is dependent upon acceptable performance. The teacher must experiment to discover what type of reinforcement works for each individual child. Negative responses may also be used to indicate displeasure at the way in which the task was performed. The underlying principle is that positive reinforcement of a task well done increases the probability of a repeat performance, whereas a negative response from the teacher decreases that probability. Many tasks in physical education are self-reinforcing and the consequences of a skilled action can be seen to be either accurate or inaccurate by the performer. It is important that the teacher sets short-term objectives which are within the range of the ability of the child so that goals are achieved and reinforcement occurs regularly through success.

TEACHING STRATEGIES

It may be useful to summarize some of the basic principles involved in the teaching process for children with specific learning difficulties.

1. Structure the teaching programme and the whole routine of the school setting. This merely means planning for success and getting the child accustomed to the environment. Lesson plans are repeated and very carefully followed so that the child knows *precisely* where to go, what to do, and how to do it.
2. The teacher sets the short-term objectives for each individual and carefully monitors progress. Instruction is individualized.
3. Tasks are presented in a progressive sequence.
4. A multisensory approach will be necessary in the presentation of tasks using visual, verbal and physical guidance, particularly in the demonstration phase of teaching.

5. Immediate reinforcement must be provided after performance. In the early stages of learning, reinforcement may be provided for the accomplishment of very simple tasks. At a later stage of learning more complex accomplishments should be rewarded. Unsatisfactory behaviour should become redundant after a period of no reinforcement.
6. Provide a teaching environment that is free from irrelevant stimuli and utilize learning materials that are highly stimulating in themselves. Where necessary reduce and isolate the space in which an individual works.
7. Introduce the child to social games on an individual and partner basis and be prepared to allow for constant repetition of successful activities. Where children can be integrated into a group or team situation, reduce the overall excitement factor by decreasing the competitive element.

In this chapter the major problems of performance by children with disabilities have been analyzed and basic principles have been established relating to methods of presenting appropriate material. Later discussion will centre on the fundamental principles of selection and adaptation of games within a structured programme of teaching. The remaining chapters include the material for a games curriculum in a progressive sequential order of presentation. Teachers will be able to select material appropriate to the age, abilities and movement problems of their children.

REFERENCES

Anderson, E.M. and Spain, B. (1977) *The Child with Spina Bifida*, Methuen, London

Crowe, W.C., Auxter, D. and Pyfer, J. (1981) *Adapted Physical Education and Recreation* (4th edn), C.V. Mosby, Saint Louis, Minnesota

Dunn, J. (1984) *Data-based psychomotor instructional systems for the severely handicapped*. In A. Brown *et al.* (Ed.), Adapted Physical Activities, Proceedings of IVth IFAPA Symposium, International Federation of Adapted Physical Activity, London

Ellis, E. (1967) *The Physical Management of Developmental Disorders*, Heinemann, London

Fait, H.F. and Dunn, J.M. (1984) *Special Physical Education* (5th edn), Saunders College, New York

Gubbay, S.S. (1975) *The Clumsy Child*, W.B. Saunders, London

Heggarty, H. (1985) Childhood asthma and sport, *British Journal of Physical Education*, Vol. 16, No. 4, p. 124

Holt, K.S. (1965) *Assessment of Cerebral Palsy*, Pt I, Lloyd–Luke, London

Holt, K.S. and Reynell, J.K. (1967) *Assessment of Cerebral Palsy*, Pt II, Lloyd–Luke, London

Johnstone, D.D. (1975) *Assessing the needs of children with cerebral palsy*. In Proceedings of National Council for Special Education Conference, Bradford

Jones, D. (1984) *Exercise prescription for persons with asthma*. In A. Brown *et al.* (Ed.), Adapted Physical Activities, Proceedings of IVth IFAPA Symposium, International Federation of Adapted Physical Activity, London

Keogh, J.F., Sugden, D.A., Reynard, C.L. and Calkins, J.A. (1979) The identification of clumsy children: comparison and comments. *Journal of Human Movement Studies*, Vol. 5, pp. 32–41

Mallinson, B. (1985) Exercise programme for asthmatic children, *British Journal of Physical Education*, Vol. 16, No. 4, p. 121

Morris, P.R. and Whiting, H.T.A. (1971) *Motor Impairment and Compensatory Education*, G. Bell, London

Price, R.J. (1980) *Physical Education and the Physically Handicapped Child*, Lepus Books, London

Sherrill, C. (1982) *Adapted Physical Education and Recreation* (2nd edn), William C. Brown, Dubuque, Iowa

Sugden, D.A. (1975) Clumsy children, *British Journal of Physical Education*, Vol. 6, p. xiv

Sugden, D.A. (1984) Issues in teaching children with movement problems, *British Journal of Physical Education*, Vol. 15, No. 3, pp. 68–70

Wall, A.E. and Taylor, J. (1984) *Physical awkwardness: a motor developmental approach to remedial intervention*. In A. Brown *et al.* (Ed.), Adapted Physical Activities, Proceedings of IVth IFAPA Symposium, International Federation of Adapted Physical Activity, London

Walton, J.N. (1961) Clumsy children, *Spastics Quarterly*, Vol. 10, No. 1, pp. 9–21

Chapter 3
SELECTION AND ADAPTATION OF ACTIVITIES

SELECTION OF ACTIVITIES

If we are to succeed in designing a sound programme of skills learning for disabled children, it is essential to adopt a systematic approach. The important choice of suitable material for inclusion in a games programme cannot be based on haphazard ideas or random sampling. Before we even begin to plan, the critical decision that must be taken is what to teach. What factors ought to be considered before we choose games tasks and activities for the physically disabled child? Obviously this depends upon the needs of each child in terms of current skill level, age and stage of social development.

The first criterion is that the children should be successful and gain fun and enjoyment from the activity. This means that we should carefully choose activities at which they can achieve success within their current limited skill level. From this start we can then structure all skills learning from the simple to the complex, in a hierarchical manner.

We know from observation of the weaknesses inherent in children's performance, but we try to ignore these problems where possible and build upon existing strengths. When we build upon strength and success is achieved, motivation will be enhanced.

It is necessary to consider reasons why we include any activity within the programme. Will it be of educational value to the child? Will successful achievement of a particular task be of particular benefit in allowing interaction with peer groups? Will it lead to further development or is it merely an end in itself? Activities need to be chosen as means to achieve educational ends; they are not objectives in themselves. The activities listed later have been arranged in a structured way to simplify the process of selecting individual programmes for each child. They are a sequenced approach to the problem of individualizing a programme of learning games skills.

EVALUATION

Before we begin to select a programme of activities it is essential to have a very clear idea of the capabilities of each child, and this implies some form of simple assessment. The practising teacher, recognizing the widely varied nature of severely handicapped children within any group, is likely to prefer the use of criterion-referenced tasks as a method of evaluating the performance levels of children. These will help to identify the strengths and weaknesses of each child in a games environment and establish the base line for beginning a remedial programme. The use of criterion-referenced tasks is an integral part of assessment based upon the content of the games curriculum itself and is geared to a simultaneous evaluation of both the learner and the teacher. The teacher makes out a checklist of performance objectives based on a hierarchical continuum of sequentially ordered activities. This assumes that simple tasks of a low order are necessary for the acquisition of more complex higher-order tasks. Progress through the checklist is an indicator of the advancement that a child has made. Criterion-referenced checklists in games skills may, therefore, be used in three ways:

1. *Diagnosis* — assessing the present level of performance of each child.
2. *Prescription* — deciding the short-term objectives to be set in the games programme. This involves the careful selection of teaching material for the forthcoming block of lessons.
3. *Evaluation* — determining how much learning and improvement of performance has taken place throughout a given period of teaching. Where little or no progress has been made, then a further, more in-depth, assessment must be made to evaluate the teaching process and the specific problems facing the learner.

Using the information derived from checklists, the teacher can produce a profile on each child, demonstrating current performance and progress made in any given period. This monitors the rate of learning and simplifies the prescription of future objectives within the games curriculum. Although checklists may be in continuous use during lessons, it is important that they are used at least at the beginning and end of each half-term.

Experienced teachers will wish to make up their own checklists based on their expert knowledge, but examples are given here to simplify the procedure. The basic skills of aiming and throwing, catching and striking are quoted. The techniques are listed in an approximate sequential order of progressions, but the particular order of achievement may change according to the type of handicap suffered by each child and the aspect of behaviour affected. Each child can be checked for performance in a simple games setting and a tick recorded on the checklist. A failure is recorded with a cross in the 'No' column. The checklist will then clearly indicate the strengths of the child as a starting point for the selection of suitable activities; it will also identify the weaknesses as future objectives for learning. Once achievable skills have been identified these can be related to appropriate social games by referring to Chapters 5, 6, 7 and 8 for lesson material.

EVALUATION CHECKLIST: AIMING AND THROWING

	Yes	Almost	No
Throw beanbag overhand into a circle from 1 m distance	☐	☐	☐
Throw beanbag overhand into a circle from 2 m distance	☐	☐	☐
Throw beanbag overhand into a circle from 3 m distance	☐	☐	☐
Throw beanbag overhand into a box from 1 m distance	☐	☐	☐
Throw beanbag overhand into a box from 2 m distance	☐	☐	☐
Throw beanbag overhand into a box from 3 m distance	☐	☐	☐
Slide beanbag underhand into a 1 m circle from 2 m distance	☐	☐	☐
Roll large ball to partner from 2 m distance	☐	☐	☐
Roll large ball to partner from 6 m distance	☐	☐	☐
Throw beanbag overhand at wall target sized 2 × 1 m from 2 m distance	☐	☐	☐
Roll large ball between two skittles 1 m apart from 2 m distance	☐	☐	☐
Roll large ball between two skittles 1 m apart from 6 m distance	☐	☐	☐
Throw small foam ball underhand at wall target from 2 m distance	☐	☐	☐
Throw small foam ball overhand at wall target from 2 m distance	☐	☐	☐
Throw quoits onto a stickboard from 2 m distance	☐	☐	☐
Throw beanbags or small foam balls through a swinging hoop	☐	☐	☐
Roll a large ball at a skittle from 3 m distance	☐	☐	☐
Roll a large ball at a skittle from 5 m distance	☐	☐	☐
Throw a beanbag for distance, any style — 3 m	☐	☐	☐
Throw a beanbag for distance, any style — 5 m	☐	☐	☐
Bounce a medium-sized ball to a partner — 2 m apart	☐	☐	☐
Bounce a medium-sized ball to a partner — 3 m apart	☐	☐	☐
Throw a beanbag through a netball ring 1.5 m high	☐	☐	☐
Throw a foam ball through a netball ring 1.5 m high	☐	☐	☐
Throw a medium-sized ball through a netball ring 1.5 m high	☐	☐	☐
Pass a large ball to a partner — two-hand underhand, 2 m apart	☐	☐	☐
Pass a large ball to a partner — two-hand chest pass, 2 m apart	☐	☐	☐

Yes Almost No

Pass a large ball to a partner — one-hand overhand, 2 m
   apart ☐ ☐ ☐
Play simple target games with a partner ☐ ☐ ☐
Play simple target games in a group of three plus ☐ ☐ ☐
Play simple dodgeball game in a group ☐ ☐ ☐

EVALUATION CHECKLIST:
CATCHING AND GAINING POSSESSION

Trap with both hands a large ball rolled from 2 m ☐ ☐ ☐
Trap with both hands a large ball rolled from 4 m ☐ ☐ ☐
Trap with both hands a large ball rolled from 6 m ☐ ☐ ☐
Catch a large beanbag tossed from 2 m distance ☐ ☐ ☐
Catch a large beanbag tossed from 4 m distance ☐ ☐ ☐
Drop a large ball from head height and cradle catch after
   the bounce ☐ ☐ ☐
Cradle catch (two arms) a large ball bounced from 2 m ☐ ☐ ☐
Cradle catch (two arms) a large ball bounced from 4 m ☐ ☐ ☐
Catch a large ball (hug to body) tossed from 2 m ☐ ☐ ☐
Catch a large ball (hug to body) tossed from 4 m ☐ ☐ ☐
Touch an object swinging side to side ☐ ☐ ☐
Catch a large suspended ball swinging back and forward ☐ ☐ ☐
Catch in both hands a large ball bounced from 2 m ☐ ☐ ☐
Catch in both hands a large ball bounced from 4 m ☐ ☐ ☐
Catch in both hands a large ball tossed from 2 m ☐ ☐ ☐
Catch in both hands a large ball tossed from 4 m ☐ ☐ ☐
Catch at chest height (hands facing forward) a ball tossed
   from 2 m ☐ ☐ ☐
Catch at chest height (hands facing forward) a ball tossed
   from 4 m ☐ ☐ ☐
Play roll and catch with a partner; count score ☐ ☐ ☐
Play bounce and catch with a partner ☐ ☐ ☐
Play throw and catch with a partner; hug ball to body in
   cradle ☐ ☐ ☐
Play throw and catch with a partner; use hands only ☐ ☐ ☐
Play throw and catch in a group of three plus on the move ☐ ☐ ☐
Play simple passing games in a group ☐ ☐ ☐

EVALUATION CHECKLIST: STRIKING GAMES

Hit a stationary foam ball forward with hand or fist ☐ ☐ ☐
Kneeling, hit forward a large foam ball rolled from 2 m ☐ ☐ ☐
Kneeling, hit forward a large foam ball rolled from 4 m ☐ ☐ ☐

	Yes	Almost	No
Keep up a large balloon by hand tapping — 5 times	☐	☐	☐
Keep up a large balloon by hand tapping — 10 times	☐	☐	☐
Drop a large foam ball and hit at a wall after the bounce	☐	☐	☐
Hit a large foam ball at a wall, after a bounced underhand feed	☐	☐	☐
Rebound a foam ball against a wall with hand or fist	☐	☐	☐
Hit a foam ball forward with the hand, tossing gently from 1 m	☐	☐	☐
Hit a foam ball forward with the hand, tossing gently from 2 m	☐	☐	☐
Hit a foam ball forward with the hand, tossing gently from 3 m	☐	☐	☐
Hit a large stationary ball forward using a narrow bat	☐	☐	☐
Hit a large ball forward off a tee (cone) using a narrow bat	☐	☐	☐
Hit forward with a narrow bat a large ball rolled from 2 m	☐	☐	☐
Hit forward with a narrow bat a large ball rolled from 4 m	☐	☐	☐
Hit forward with a narrow bat a large ball bounced from 2 m	☐	☐	☐
Hit forward with a narrow bat a large ball bounced from 4 m	☐	☐	☐
Hit forward with a narrow bat a large ball tossed from 2 m	☐	☐	☐
Hit forward with a narrow bat a large ball tossed from 4 m	☐	☐	☐
Hit a stationary ball two-handed with a hockey stick	☐	☐	☐
Play continuous pat bounce with padder bat and foam ball	☐	☐	☐
Rebound a foam ball against a wall with a wide bat	☐	☐	☐
Pat bounce a large ball with the hand while stationary	☐	☐	☐
Pat bounce a large ball with the hand while on the move	☐	☐	☐
With foam ball and hand, play continuous pat bounce with a partner	☐	☐	☐
With bat and ball, play continuous pat bounce with a partner	☐	☐	☐
Serve a volleyball underhand against a wall	☐	☐	☐
Bounce a large ball around obstacles	☐	☐	☐
Dribble a ball around obstacles with a hockey stick	☐	☐	☐
Hit two-handed with a narrow bat a large ball bounced from 4 m	☐	☐	☐
Hit a large ball tossed from 4 m	☐	☐	☐

One of the major problems for the teacher to solve in preparing a games programme geared to the needs of individual children is the need to reduce the teacher–pupil ratio considerably. The teaching of a severely disabled child often requires a one-to-one relationship and this can be difficult to achieve. In the small-class teaching situation of the special school it is easier to obtain help from other staff, such as physiotherapists, occupational therapists, speech therapists, class teachers and students, who are all interested in studying another aspect of educational development. In addition, within the partial residential situation, there are housemothers, child-care assistants, community service volunteers and other aides who can lend assistance in handling individual children. The situation is very different when the class teacher in a normal primary school is faced with one or two disabled children within any class. One solution which has been found to work well is the use of peer teaching within the class where able-bodied children take turns to play on a one-to-one basis with a handicapped child in the basic skill part of the lesson. In the secondary school this system will also work but can be supplemented by the use of older, mature teenagers coming in to help with younger groups. The author has considerable experience of handling a wide range of disability within any secondary group. A senior secondary school class within a special school included a 14-year-old severe athetoid (see Chapter 2) confined to a wheelchair. He had no control whatsoever over arm or trunk movement, but it was discovered that he could exert considerable control over his lower leg and left foot. Eventually he was given an electric wheelchair with the control mechanism situated on the left footrest. For physical education lessons he was moved into a manual wheelchair with the footrests removed to allow some manipulative control with his left foot. Regardless of what the remainder of the class were doing in the early skill-learning phase of a games lesson, he would work to a prescribed programme of skill development with the assistance of an able class mate to feed him accurate balls to his left foot. The remainder of the class took turns to work with him and they were challenged to see how accurately they could produce a variety of ball feeds to him. Over a long period of time he learned to trap a rolled or bounced ball, to manipulate the ball into a favourable position to kick, and to aim at a wide variety of targets. Each stage of his learning was carefully planned and great development of skill with his left foot occurred. During the group and team games phase of every lesson he was totally integrated as a result of careful adaptation of the rules of the game. All passes were rolled to him, without interception, and opponents could not move to within 2 m of his wheelchair. The remainder of that class took great pleasure from his achievements and accepted the challenge to see that he was successful in his efforts. Help can, therefore, be obtained in one way or another to solve the problems of individualized teaching. Adult assistance, however, is required with the assessment procedure to help run through criterion-referenced measurement.

TASK ANALYSIS

Once a selection of appropriate activities has been made, it is likely that children of mild and moderate handicap will proceed to learn the chosen tasks, even if some adaptation of the learning environment is required. This will not occur with the severely disabled because they find even the most basic skills difficult to perform. We should remind ourselves that we are teaching children, not activities, and the focus of all attention must be the child. The tasks we choose are distinct means to the end of making the child successful by working always from the most simple to the more complex. Where the severely disabled child cannot perform a basic movement task in a play situation, then he is excluded from the social benefits of that situation. We must begin somewhere and the child must find success. This leads to the principle of task analysis where a skilled task is broken down into its component parts so that we can identify each part, place it in order of difficulty, and produce a sequence of subroutines which make up the whole task. The child then achieves gradual success in the performance of each phase, proceeding through the progressive continuum of subroutines until finally success is achieved with an approximate model of the whole skill. This compares with the traditional system of progressive practice used by physical education teachers, but at a more finite level. To begin a task analysis we must be able to identify clearly the cognitive and perceptual-motor components of each task, then place them in order from the most simple to the most complex. In the same way we can analyze the components that make up a game before we introduce it to the severely disabled. For example, there are many quite difficult components involved in the apparently simple game of beanbag bowls. To play the game involves the following factors:

1. to understand the objectives of the game — cognitive;
2. to be able to maintain a stable kneeling or sitting position — motor ability;
3. to attend clearly to the white beanbag and the coloured beanbags and discriminate them from the surrounding floor — visual and figure–ground discrimination;
4. to focus on the white beanbag and the coloured beanbag to be thrown;
5. to judge the direction and distance from the white beanbag — perception;
6. to possess a certain degree of eye–hand accuracy and eye–hand coordination;
7. to discriminate colour and recognize your own beanbags;
8. to judge the force required to throw the beanbag accurately — kinaesthetic perception;
9. to be able to grasp the beanbag, produce a throwing pattern of movement and release the beanbag at the appropriate moment.

We have here a progressive chain of events through which we can proceed until we can identify the point at which the performance breaks down. At the breakdown stage we must then decide whether the step between phases is too great for the child to master and assess whether we can further simplify the particular phase at which breakdown occurs so that progress may continue.

There is a danger that the progressive sequence may become too fragmented and divorced from the end goal. At each stage of successful performance it is essential that the child sees the relationship between his isolated practice and the attainment of the ultimate skill. This is important for the continuous development of insight, understanding and acceptance of the need for practice and is a key role for the teacher in motivating the child. The child must always see the relevance of what he practices within the context of the game.

PERFORMER ANALYSIS

After using criterion-referenced checklists and the application of detailed task analysis, we know what the child can and cannot do. We have collected a great deal of information relating to the end product — the performance of a task. Unfortunately this does not tell us why the child cannot perform certain simple tasks. This vital 'process' information must be obtained differently, in particular by careful clinical observation of the manner in which a child attempts a task. We must focus on an analysis of the performer and find out the underlying reasons why his performance fails. For example, the problem for the teacher in a simple ball-catching situation is to discover exactly when the breakdown in perceptual-motor performance occurs. Are the problems due to faulty visual scanning or to faulty perception of bounce, ball flight, speed, distance or direction? Are they due to inability to make quick decisions, lack of previous experience in the situation or, in the end the result, a total inability to produce the correct motor response because of severe motor dysfunction? This observation must be carried out in an orderly manner and take place over a number of task repetitions to check for consistency by the performer and allow the teacher time to follow another checklist sequence. Top-class sports coaches are often advised to check a performer from head to toe, and this can be sound advice to follow. A cricket coach, for example, will assess the form of a batsman, over a series of repetitions of a stroke, by observing in sequence:

1. the preparatory stance of readiness;
2. the head position before and during the stroke;
3. the position of the shoulders throughout;
4. the grip on the bat handle;
5. the early backlift;
6. the position of the feet and movements during the stroke, from start to finish;
7. the overall body shape throughout the movement.

Careful observation of head and feet movements, in terms of speed and direction, helps establish whether a player is able to judge the length, speed and direction of the ball after delivery. This is a useful analogy to use in assessing the performance of handicapped children in skills involving eye–

hand coordination and eye–hand accuracy. The answers to a number of simple questions relating to the observation of movement in a games context can reveal valuable information:

> Can he maintain a stable starting position?
> Can he concentrate, focus upon and follow a moving object with his eyes?
> Does he begin to move into the path of an incoming object?
> Can he keep the body balanced as he moves?
> Do the arms and hands move early to prepare for the final execution of the task?
> At the final point of contact with a ball, are the hands or feet there too early or too late?
> Is the final movement of hands accurate or wildly misplaced?

The answers to these questions, when related to our existing knowledge of sensory impairment, motor impairment and specific learning difficulties, will help in planning a teaching strategy to overcome or avoid the problems. Many schools now have video cameras with a playback facility which offers a valuable opportunity for more careful observation of movement problems. This makes possible a retrospective group appraisal of learning problems by the whole teaching team from various disciplines, thus increasing the accuracy and efficiency of observation.

The current level of performance of the child has, therefore, been assessed by use of a criterion-referenced task checklist, the tasks themselves have been analyzed in fine detail ready for simplified learning stages, and the major individual performance weaknesses have been identified through accurate clinical observation. These stages in the planning process are not self-contained units but part of an overlapping and continuous instructional procedure based on a sequential achievement of short-term objectives. By matching the various processes we can now prescribe specific remedial programmes that are enjoyable, challenging and successful.

For example, let us apply this process to learning games which involve aiming. We know from observation of child development that as children grow older they develop the skills of aiming and throwing in the following sequence:

> in a downward direction;
> in a forward direction;
> in an upward direction;
> at moving targets.

The selection of aiming tasks must, therefore, follow this developmental sequence.

The throwing patterns involved in aiming develop from simple overhand actions, first to an underarm action and then to sidearm and other individual styles. This sequence must also logically be followed unless prevented by movement problems. For simplification, these throwing patterns need to be subjected to task analysis (see Chapter 4).

The specific perceptual-motor problems of each child must be identified:

1. Head position — eye focus.
2. Throwing pattern — motor impairment.
3. Stable body position.
4. Grasp-release difficulties. What cues (verbal, manual, etc.) are required to help the child time the point of release.
5. Spatial or other perceptual difficulties.
6. Learning difficulties — distractibility, perseveration.

At this stage we may begin to prescribe a developmental programme based on the following careful systematic procedure:

1. Modify starting positions and throwing actions.
2. Simplify the perceptual and motor aspects of the aiming task.
3. Start with beanbags aimed at floor targets. Increase the distance gradually.
4. Increase the distance further, introducing guiding lines on floor.
5. Aim at low wall targets. Increase height and distance.
6. Aim at swinging targets.
7. Aim at moving balls, hoops, etc.
8. Introduce individual, partner and small group games at the appropriate stage — for instance, beanbag bowls, shuffleboard, boule, boccia.

This is a form of prescriptive teaching which works well with handicapped children as they achieve success step by step. Throughout the learning process we monitor what the child has achieved while constantly identifying the areas where he may need specific help. The whole cycle of the teaching process, therefore, evolves into a clear systematic pattern:

1. Identify clear short-term objectives within the games curriculum.
2. Assess the abilities and weaknesses of each child using criterion-referenced tasks and observation.
3. Select and prescribe appropriate learning tasks.
4. Adapt and simplify the learning and performance variables by task analysis.
5. Use the learned skills in social games situations as appropriate.
6. Evaluate the progress of each child by criterion-referenced measurement, identifying areas of weakness through observation.
7. Set new goals and short-term objectives as a result of the re-evaluation.

A long-term programme based on systematic teaching should achieve the aims of a developmental curriculum by promoting the necessary perceptual-motor attributes and basic games skills as foundations for participation in games for education and leisure.

When dealing with severely disabled children it is essential to be realistic. We must appreciate that because of the extremely severe nature of their handicapping condition many children will never progress beyond a very limited level of performance. Even when children have not developed the basic perceptual-motor abilities it is still possible to include them in social games of a group and team nature by providing an adapted games programme.

ADAPTATION OF GAMES

The principle of adaptation of a games programme is to simplify the performance levels necessary for children to gain maximum participation regardless of their degree of handicap. In the previous sections we have discussed the careful selection of activities suited to the ability of individual children based on task analysis and performer analysis, leading to modifications of initial learning situations. Now we must look at ways of integrating a heterogeneous group of disabled children so that they can play together. This is based on adaptation of the games material to match the disability of the children.

In Chapters 4–8 specific adaptations of most of the activities are described, but these are by no means the only ones. Teachers will wish to adapt other common activities or games of their own invention and, therefore, they must be able to understand certain basic principles of adaptation in relation to the range of handicapping conditions with which they are dealing. This is best seen in relation to the perceptual-motor process model whereby we think of performance in terms of cognition — visual input; perception, integration of information systems, decision making; and finally the motor action at the output stage. The whole skill task may be analyzed and simplified at any of these stages to enable children to participate at a lower order of performance.

The degree of adaptation needed will obviously depend on the severity of handicap of the participants. The less they are disabled in perceptual-motor function the less the activity will need to be modified. It must be borne in mind that the main objectives in adaptation are to allow the children to achieve success while taking part, and to gain enjoyment. A general rule to consider might be that the rules, techniques, equipment and playing environment for a game should be changed as little as necessary so that the game is safe but also retains as many elements of the normal game as is possible. Where possible, the nature of the game should be clearly recognizable by the children so that they may identify with the game as it is played by their non-disabled peers.

SIMPLIFICATION OF MOTOR PROBLEMS

1. Substitute walking or wheeling for running parts of a game.
2. Substitute lighter apparatus to improve control over implements. Light plastic bats are much easier to handle and can be managed in one hand.

3. Allow able-bodied runners to run for or to push disabled wheelchair players.
4. Larger balls can be introduced to simplify catching and striking techniques.
5. The size of the playing area can be made smaller, thereby reducing the amount of gross motor activity proportionately.
6. Increase the number of players in a team to reduce the amount of space for which each player is responsible.
7. Modify starting positions to achieve a stable, more balanced position from which certain skilled actions can be performed. Athetoid and ataxic children, for example, perform much better in batting and catching games from a kneeling position where the head is relatively still and jerky movements are reduced.
8. Decrease the length of a pitch or distance from targets in aiming or throwing activities.
9. Restrict certain players to a specific position on court according to their freedom of movement — for example, shooter in netball, front court in volleyball.
10. In net games the height of the net considerably affects the speed of play. A higher net produces a slower game by forcing a higher and slower ball flight. The players must, of course, have good enough arm control to clear the net. Use of a lower net speeds up the game but makes throwing and batting easier.
11. The substitution of beanbags and foam balls decreases the distance the implement travels and reduces the play area accordingly.
12. Large bladders or overinflated beach balls simplify batting procedure in net games.
13. Substitution of large beanbags instead of balls simplifies grasp and release problems.
14. Use a chute for the severely disabled in bowling activities.

SIMPLIFICATION OF PERCEPTUAL PROBLEMS

1. Use of multicoloured playballs helps to reduce the visuo-motor problems of perceptually impaired children.
2. Ball flight must be modified to suit children with spatial problems and the tempo of a game must be reduced to match the slower perceptual-motor responses of the children. The ball service in a game may be reduced in difficulty and progressively graded as skill improves:
   (a) rolled;
   (b) bounced;
   (c) thrown underhand.
   The size of the ball affects visual tracking ability; larger balls are easier to follow in flight.

3.   The degree of bounce may be reduced by using many foam and low-bounce balls now freely available on the market.

4.   Overinflated bladders and beach balls tend to float in the air and thus slow down the responses needed from players. Balloons may be substituted in net games, but care must be taken when hyperacoustic children are present in case of a loud burst.

5.   Simplify and reduce the number of decisions a child has to make within a game.

6.   Adapt the starting position of the child and the flight of the ball to ensure that both the hands and the ball are always within the visual field. This lessens the degree of proprioceptive control required.

SIMPLIFICATION OF THE PLAYING ENVIRONMENT

1.   Rule changes may be made to simplify performance in any game so long as the game remains recognizable, particularly to older players. The rules controlling performance by certain individual players within a game may be slightly different to compensate for varying degrees of handicap:

(a) Different types of service in striking games according to ability — rolled, bounced, thrown, etc.

(b) 'Safe ball' rule — in passing games defending players may not infringe within 2 m of a severely disabled player or overguard. Only a team mate may take the ball from him.

(c) Shorten the duration of a game by reducing the period of time or the total of points necessary for a win.

(d) In volleyball and other net games some players may catch the ball while the more able must bat or strike.

(e) Prevent the more able players from dominating play totally by restricting their role. The 'no-return-pass' rule in invasion games creates greater opportunities for the less able to take an active part (see 'Invasion games', p. 162).

2.   During group or team games, select children for playing positions according to their movement potential. The role of the goalkeeper is obvious but, in general terms, in invasion games the more handicapped players should play either in defence or as attackers in front of goal, with the more mobile players acting as midfield fetchers and carriers. With a fairly homogeneous group, positional responsibilities, on the other hand, ought to be shared.

3.   Reduce the fatigue factor in certain cases where necessary by:

(a) shortening the game period;

(b) allowing freedom of player substitution on a regular basis;

(c) switching the role of tired players to that of referee or linesman for a rest period;

(d) substituting cooperative practice for the competitive game situation;

(e) reducing the tempo of the activity in several of the ways listed above;
(f) reducing body contact situations by introducing 'no-running' and 'no-tackling' rules in team passing games.

FURTHER READING

Fait, H.F. and Dunn, J.M. (1984) *Special Physical Education* (5th edn), Saunders College, New York
Vodola, T.M. (1981) *Project Active. Developmental Physical Education — Low Motor Ability*, C.F. Wood, Bloomfield, Connecticut
Wessel, J.A. (1976) *Project I CAN*, Michigan State University, East Lansing, Michigan

Chapter 4
TEACHING THE BASIC SKILLS

LAYING THE FOUNDATION

When a normal child reaches school age he has already acquired a fair degree of perceptual-motor competence in gross body movements, in manual dexterity in handling small objects and in coordination of eye and hand over large muscle movement. These will vary from control of running, jumping and climbing to scribbling, drawing and manipulating educational toys. General body management is already well developed and postural orientation involving balancing, dodging and skipping is quite good.

It is probably true to say that although ball skill has not developed the child has had experience of playing with balls of various sizes and textures and has begun to perceive some of the properties of ball flight, such as bounce, speed, direction and weight. Limited development of eye–hand coordination and eye–hand accuracy in manipulation of objects will have occurred in throwing, catching and hitting. General body management and manipulation of objects tend to develop one after the other, although in alternating phases, and they form the basis of the games skills programme in a school.

Unfortunately this is not true of most handicapped children, who come to school with a much lower level of developmental motor functioning. So, it is vital that learning general body management and manipulative skills related to games playing should begin as early as possible to lay the foundation for future recreational competence. In long-term planning it is important to consider the level of physical, mental and social maturity in choosing which skills to teach and when to introduce them. Oliver and Keogh (1967) showed that, with clumsy children, when a skill has been missed at an early stage it is not then available to assist in the learning of more complex skills at a later stage.

Planning a normal progressive programme in games skills is usually based on a knowledge of child development in perceptual-motor abilities and social maturation, which are age related and based on normative behaviour. The criteria for planning a programme to cover sequential periods of development for handicapped children should be related to the norm, but allowance should be made for their delayed and retarded physical and social development. In brief, it appears that normal children progress through the following social play stages: playing as individuals on their own; playing on their own but alongside other children; sharing and taking turns with play equipment; cooperating with other individuals in self-testing activities; competing against other individuals; cooperating and competing as part of a small group; and finally cooperating and competing as part of a team unit. Handicapped children follow the same pattern of social development but at a slower and much more variable rate of progress. This is a major consideration in planning.

STRUCTURING THE TEACHING PROGRAMME

Taking account of varied social maturation problems, together with the very great range of perceptual-motor impairment present in handicapped children, we can see how difficult programme planning appears. A programme based solely on identification of individual movement problems does not always take account of the social needs of the child. It is necessary to structure an individualized programme suitable for the physical needs of each child, but this must also be seen in the more general context of social development.

To simplify the process more generalized stages of skill development are suggested, related to degree of perceptual-motor handicap. These developmental stages are related to performance rather than age and take account of skill levels necessary for varying social interactions. The three proposed levels of skill progression are based on a perceptual-motor analysis of performance difficulty without reference to age or to any handicapping condition. The age factor must never be an important element in structuring programmes for severely disabled children, as they learn much more slowly. There is no way of knowing how quickly a severely disabled child will make progress, and the amount of time spent at each performance level must be based on individual evaluation. Certainly the more time that is spent on learning and consolidation in the early stages the more are the chances of the child being motivated later by successful achievement. The three proposed divisions of skill progression are termed levels rather than stages. The word 'stage' suggests that after a period of practice the child will automatically proceed to the next stage of development. This may not be true for a severely disabled individual whose handicaps preclude more advanced performance. Nevertheless, assessing the child's level of performance and improvement may provide a clear indicator for selection of appropriate activities later.

LEVEL 1

Level 1 skills consist of the most basic techniques involving limited judgements of space, direction and timing, with simple motor actions. Teaching may be organized on a one-to-one basis using whatever help is available. Formal structured learning situations of the prescriptive type dominate. At this level the teacher may have to help with the maintenance of a stable posture; manual guidance and verbal cues are almost always needed. The manipulation of objects in flight are too complex at this stage and most skills are performed at floor level. If insufficient adult help is available, children may be asked to operate at a more advanced social level by working with a partner before they are ready. Because of the degree of physical handicap a child may not be able to work on his own and retain possession of an object that rolls away out of control. Help is required to feed and receive objects and to provide important motivation and feedback on performance. For example, a child needs someone to whom he can roll a ball or from whom the ball can be stopped; also he needs help in returning objects after he has aimed them at a target. Successful achievement of the basic techniques of aiming, throwing, bouncing, rolling, hitting and stopping are the foundation upon which simple individual and partner games are based. Some non-ambulant children may never progress beyond this basic competence level, but they should be encouraged to progress as far as possible. Lack of competence at a higher skill level is not a total barrier to participation in larger group activities but may only be a guide for appropriate adaptation of environmental conditions. While technical performance may remain at Level 1, the children can still be included in more advanced activities that have been suitably simplified.

Some examples of the activities that children ought to be able to perform at the end of a programme aimed at this level are listed below as a simple guide.

Assume a stable position with the head still and the hands free.
Push or roll a large ball to a partner.
Stop a large ball rolled from a partner.
Push and stop a pendulum ball.
Hit a stationary ball.
Throw and catch a large beanbag.
Aim a beanbag at various targets.
Participate in simple aiming games with a partner.
Participate in simple group games cooperatively.
Manipulate a large ball at floor level with a bat.
Participate in simple relays based on basic skills.
Demonstrate an understanding of the principles of throwing, catching, hitting, passing and aiming in simple situations.

LEVEL 2

Level 2 skills are represented by more advanced techniques involving more complex perceptual judgements and showing a greater degree of control over motor actions. These skills underlie performance in partner activities and socially orientated group games. Children should demonstrate a greater awareness of the effects of their actions on others and, as a result, demonstrate at least an elementary understanding of game principles and objectives. Children should learn to cope with bouncing balls and limited situations where the ball is in full flight. The most important element at this level is the interaction of children while they practise as a gradual lead up to social cooperation and competition in groups. Some children may still require some manual guidance as they learn throwing and catching skills, and verbal cues may still be necessary to focus attention on the proposed action for children with moderate learning difficulties.

At the end of a teaching programme most of the children should be able to:

Demonstrate some control over throwing, catching and bouncing balls both stationary and on the move.

Catch a large ball with both arms.

Play throw and catch with a partner.

Play hit and catch with a partner.

Demonstrate the ability to play rebound off a wall individually and with a partner.

Play catch and throw over a net with a large beanbag or one bounce with a ball.

Demonstrate an understanding of the rules of simple group games.

Show an elementary understanding of some principles of play in group games.

Show an ability to cooperate with others in group games and compete as a member of a small team.

LEVEL 3

Level 3 skills encompass the full range of techniques where manipulation of a ball in flight and the ability to cooperate with other players dictate participation. Several aspects of skilled performance may be practised in sequence rather than in isolation. For example, the child may learn to receive a ball, dribble for several paces, and then pass to another player or shoot. This is an advanced sequence of events for a child with movement problems and may be the key to full participation with his peers in a range of games. Understanding of basic game tactics will be closely related to the practice situation in group and team games.

At the end of a programme the less severely disabled children should be able to:

Perform some of the techniques involved in cooperation and competition in the more complex group and team games.

Show an understanding of the basic principles of play and tactics in invasion games, net games and striking games.

Take an active role in group and team games suitably adapted for them.
Demonstrate their own preference for particular activities at a recreational
level.

No clear division can possibly exist between the three levels of performance:
individual children will demonstrate markedly varying levels of ability across
the full spectrum of games skills. Nevertheless, the three suggested levels of
performance may help in evaluating the current skill status of any child and
therefore serve as rough diagnostic indicators for prescribing activities appropriate to the needs and ability of each particular child. They may also serve in
organizing relatively homogeneous groupings of children for out-of-school
recreational clubs.

The material in Chapters 5 and 6 on individual and partner activities and
group games, respectively, could not be arranged strictly according to the
suggested levels of performance because of the difficulty in accurate classification, but it has been organized in a progressive sequence from the simple to
the more complex. This will simplify the selection of follow-up activities at all
levels of performance.

Throughout this chapter the basic techniques, which are the foundation
skills for playing games, have been analyzed and arranged into a series of
progressive learning experiences. Great care has been taken to create a
logical hierarchy in the sequence of skill acquisition so that the child, with
practice, will always succeed.

GENERAL BODY MANAGEMENT

The activities of general body management allied to certain manipulative
skills form the foundations of a programme in games training. The ability to
move around with relative freedom, to stop under control, to change direction quickly and to relate personal movement with or in opposition to
someone else is the basis of general body management in games. Although
physically handicapped children will show major deficiencies in all or some
areas of movement control, they can nevertheless demonstrate remarkable
improvement as a result of meaningful practice. The gross motor actions
important in games training are running, crawling, wheeling, sitting, kneeling, stopping, changing position from lying to kneeling to sitting, dodging,
swerving, pivotting and turning, and stopping and starting. In addition, these
actions may be performed forwards, backwards and sideways in different
directions, as well as at varying levels from low floor level, medium kneeling
or bending level, to a high standing position. The ongoing body coordination
requirements in a game are highly variable and it is necessary for children to
show some degree of control in a wide variety of situations as they stoop for a
ball, crawl for a ball or dodge away from an opponent. Despite their degree of
handicap, children need to develop their gross movement skills at the same

time as they learn the manipulative skills of throwing, catching and striking. Quite apart from movement within their own personal space, games playing requires an awareness of general space in a games area. Except in the very early stages of learning individual skills, children are never alone as they move in space. Other children will be using space alongside them, and the logical development of their skill leads to sharing space and working with or against a partner until they can perform in a large space with a group of other children without interference in a cooperative manner. For many children with spatial difficulties a large playroom is a fearsome place and they need careful training to overcome this fear.

These aspects of general body management where the children develop body awareness, particularly of the body in action, have been well taught in movement education lessons within the United Kingdom, but they have not always been specifically related to the teaching of games skills. It is suggested that, apart from the normal movement education lessons that feature within a primary school programme, the first 5–10 minutes of an indoor games lesson could profitably be spent on aspects of general body management, particularly with young children. It is beyond the scope of this text to present a full programme of such activities. There are many excellent books on movement education for normal children on the market, but a limited range of activities are suggested here as a guideline to the selection of warm-up actions at the start of a lesson with young children. They are not related to age, and selection will depend on the performance levels of the children.

LEVEL 1

1. Establish a sitting position with feet on the floor using foam mattress or benches.
   (a) Identify body parts. The class teacher demonstrates a movement and verbalizes the task using a multisensory approach to reinforce basic body awareness.
   'This is my nose; touch your nose.'
   'These are my ears; touch your ears.'
   The children repeat the words as they perform the motor action.
   'Touch right hand to left toe.'
   'Touch left hand to right elbow.'
   'Place your hands upon your head.'
   (Children repeat: 'I place my hands upon my head.')
   (b) Change the shape of the body.
   'Stretch tall.'
   'Curl small.'
   'Stretch wide.'
   'Touch the floor; stretch high.'
   'Look to left, centre, right, up at the ceiling, down to the floor.'

Use a suitable piece of music and perform the movements to a steady rhythm.

2. Establish a back-lying position on a mat.
    'Raise the right leg; now raise the left leg.'
    'Hands by the sides, lift the right arm, now the left.'
    'Raise both arms; touch hands above your face.'
    'Curl small, stretch tall, stretch wide.'
    'Cover as much space as you can on the floor.'
3. (a) 'Roll to the side and kneel on all fours.'
    'Raise the right arm; raise the left arm.'
    'Look up, down, to the right, to the centre, to the left.'
    'Roll on to your right side, curl small, stretch tall.'
    'Roll to your left side, curl small, stretch tall.'
    (b) 'Crawl forwards, backwards, sideways.'
    'Crawl as fast as possible; stop on command.'
    'Crawl as slowly as you can.'
    'Crawl to the beat of a drum; count the steps.'

Figure 4.1   Mats 2 m × 1 m arranged in a rectangle

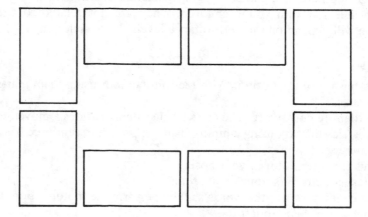

'Crawl forward around the mats' (see Figures 4.1 and 4.2).
'Crawl backwards around the mats.'
Crawl and follow the mats. Verbalize direction 'I turn to the right', etc.
Crawl along a line.
Crawl and change direction on the teacher's command.
'Turn right', 'Stop!', 'Turn left', 'Move backwards', 'Stop!', 'Crawl sideways left'.
(c) Ambulant children may perform all of the body actions from a standing position.

Figure 4.2   Staggered arrangement of 2 m × 1 m mats

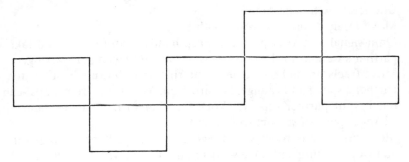

4. Move freely around the gymnasium, avoiding other children. Look for free space. Change speed and direction. Stop on command. How quickly can you move off into a new space from a stationary position?

LEVEL 2

1. (a) Move freely around the room dribbling a large ball with hands or feet. Move on command — 'Right', 'Left', 'Stop!', 'Move backwards', 'Sideways right', 'Stop!', etc. Avoid other children and find empty space. (Locomotor action appropriate to degree of handicap.)
    (b) Move around and change direction on a signal. Avoid other children. Can you change direction and move in a curved path? Can you stop dead and turn sharply when you move off?
    (c) Move and change speed and direction with the rhythm of a drum beat.
2. Movement with a partner.
    (a) Kneel on a mat facing each other.
    Try to mirror your partner's movements on command.
    Arms raise sideways; count one, two, three, four.
    Arms raise as high as possible; count one, two, three, four.
    Arms raise forwards to touch hands.
    Circle both arms forwards; count one, two, three, four.
    Circle both arms backwards; count one, two, three, four.
    (b) Body alphabet exercise.
    Work together on the floor and, using both of your bodies together, make the letters M, O, T, H, V, Y, etc.
    Start at floor level and work as high as possible.
    (c) Move around the room at the same speed as your partner, crawling, wheeling or walking.
    Change speed and direction on a signal and stay close. On the command 'Stop!' try to be in touching range of your partner.
    Avoid other pairs and use free space.
    (d) Play follow-my-leader in pairs trying to match your partner's movements.

LEVEL 3

1. Cooperate with a partner.
   Move freely around the room with a partner.
   On a signal face your partner, grasp hands, lean forward and take your partner's weight. Push gently against him. (Crawling or walking.)
2. Move freely around the room to the rhythm of a drum beat. Match your partner's speed and changes of direction. When the drum stops, can you touch your partner's hand? Work together to keep at the same speed. Change speed of rhythm to fast and slow.
3. Move around the room staying close to your partner. Change direction and stop to command. One works at floor level with the other at a higher level, e.g. low crawling, high kneeling, bear walking, full walking. Change places.
4. Play simple dodging and chasing games on a competitive basis.

DODGE AND MARK

Children work in pairs 1 m apart. One is the dodger and the other the chaser. On a signal the dodgers all move away and try to get free, closely followed by the chasers. On a signal all stop still. Can you touch your partner? Change positions. Teach for changes in pace, direction and use of other players to block the route of the chaser.

FREE AND CAUGHT

Two or three players are the chasers trying to catch the remainder. They touch as many players as possible. Any player touched must stay still but may be freed by a touch from a free player. The objective is for the chasers to have as many stationary players as possible in a given time.

Obviously these simple games relate closely to the gross body actions involved in marking players in group and team games and make excellent warm-up activities for a games lesson. They form a logical lead-up to many dodgeball games.

The activities listed here under the broad title of 'General body management' are not meant in any way as a comprehensive programme but merely as examples for the selection of a progressive sequence of learning activities. There are available many programmes of gross body coordination, perceptual-motor training or educational gymnastics (Cratty, 1969; Means and Applequist, 1974; Schurr, 1975; Arnheim and Pestolesi, 1978; Vodola, 1981). With young children the multisensory approach of utilizing verbal, auditory, visual and movement cues simultaneously in a rhythmical pattern follows the teaching of Professor Andras Peto, founder of Conductive Education for Brain-injured Children (Cotton, 1970).

TECHNIQUES OF PROJECTING OBJECTS

AIMING AND THROWING

In general the development of throwing skills precedes the acquisition of catching ability and in planning a programme it must be understood that to play 'throw-and-catch' requires accurate throwing of the object before the complex problem of catching may really be tackled successfully.

In normal children three basic patterns of one-handed throwing develop: the overhead, the underhand and the sidearm. When throwing for accuracy many young children will use the underhand throwing method because this is often the easiest to control. The overhead throw is most used when power is needed, but many physically handicapped children cannot develop the whip-like action of this style as they throw with the arm only, cannot produce the body action, balance badly, and allow the elbow to drop close to the side of the body causing a pushing action to occur. For those children who are able to reproduce a more normal style it is important that the teacher can analyze the task into its sequential movement parts and provide feedback on teaching points to help the performer.

THE OVERHEAD THROW

1. Establish a stable position sideways to the direction of throw — whether standing, sitting or kneeling. Provide support where necessary.
2. Hold the object in the base of the fingers, not in the palm of the hand.
3. Raise and extend the throwing elbow upwards and backwards to approximately shoulder height with the forearm extended and pointing upwards. Manual guidance may be necessary to establish the feel of the movement.
4. Initiate the throwing action by transferring the weight forward on to the front foot or lean the front shoulder forward into the action for seated or kneeling performers.
5. Start the arm throw by leading with the elbow, followed by the wrist and fingers. The sequence of extension of the arm in a forward direction is critical in developing a smooth action — elbow, wrist, then finger flick. Give verbal cues or manual guidance where necessary to cue the release point.
6. The whole body then follows through with a full arm extension in the direction of the target.

Because of the power generated by the overhead throw it is the main style used in fielding games where distance is required, but it is also accurate where a fairly standard movement pattern has developed.

THE UNDERHAND THROW

The underhand throw is often used where accuracy is needed in aiming or bowling activities, but it is difficult to achieve distance in throwing since body rotation is limited and the arm action is straight. The greatest problems facing handicapped children in developing underhand throwing are the establishment of a good stable throwing position and difficulty in grasp/release. Children in wheelchairs must have the arm rests removed to allow freedom of arm and shoulder action, and in many cases a high-kneeling position on the floor affords a well-balanced position which is high enough to gain a full free straight arm swing.

The main teaching points for accuracy are as follows:

- Establish a balanced position high enough to allow a free arm swing.
- Use a smooth straight arm swing forward and back in line with the target.
- Keep the arm action in line with the target and close to the body.
- The eyes must be above the arm swing and in line with the target.
- Keep in line the eyes, the hand and the target.
- Release the object at the end of the forward swing and before the arm swings up. (The higher the target, the later is the ball or other object released.)

Some further points for ambulant throwers operating from a standing position are:

- Line up eyes, hand and target.
- Swing back the arm straight and on line with the target.
- Step on to the front foot towards the target.
- Make a smooth, straight arm swing forward, close to the body and on line.
- Release the object just past the line of the front knee.
- Watch the object all the way to the target during the follow through.

The development of an accurate underhand throw opens up the opportunity for immediate participation in many simple aiming or bowling games.

THE SIDEARM THROW

The sidearm throwing pattern allows for the use of body rotation and for a longer backswing; therefore it is more efficient than the underhand technique in throwing for distance. Where accuracy is required, the sidearm throw creates greater problems as the arm is travelling in an arc during the long swing and the point of release of the object is critical. Only at the midpoint of the swing, level with the shoulder, is the hand travelling in a forward direction. Gauging the point of release, and in fact being physically capable of effecting a satisfactory form of release, can be a great problem. Modifying the starting position by turning a wheelchair side-facing or turning a kneeling player into a sideways position helps to fix the arc of the throwing arm in a general forward direction and may give a point of reference for release over the shoulder of the non-throwing arm. In certain circumstances when dealing with individuals of impaired proprioceptive and kinaesthetic awareness it may be found that they need more concrete cues to fix the point of release. For example, if the straight arm swing is guided in an upward direction, with the body positioned sideways to the direction of throw, at the top of the swing, the upper arm comes in contact with the side of the head and this is the tactile cue for grip release. This method is valuable in training quadriplegic children, with associated spatial disorientation, who have no concept of angles of release. It provides reinforcing information to produce forward throwing at a reasonable upward angle of release. Adaptations of the sidearm throwing techniques have been found to be very effective in teaching several types of cerebral palsied children, but attention must be paid to the problem of grasp/release in affecting left–right directional accuracy. As a technique used in throwing for distance by physically handicapped children it is efficient, regardless of whether the performer stands with an aid, sits or kneels.

Teaching points

- Establish a stable position sideways to the direction of throw.
- Rotate the upper body backwards as the arm swings back straight.
- Bend the non-throwing arm (where possible) across the chest and in line with the throwing arm through the line of the shoulders.
- Begin the throw by flinging the non-throwing arm forwards and upwards, immediately followed by the smooth, straight swing of the throwing arm. The shoulders rotate forwards during the action.
- Release the object from shoulder high or above (depending upon whether distance or accuracy is required). For long throws the ideal angle is 45°.
- When throwing for distance, the arm swing must be from a low position at the rear of the swing to a high position at the appropriate point of release.

Apart from these standard methods of throwing one-handed, other techniques may evolve from individual needs and abilities. Two such typical styles useful for the severely disabled child with very limited range of movement at the shoulder joint are the modified sidearm throw and the rear-facing technique.

MODIFIED SIDEARM THROW

The major problems to overcome in developing this technique are to produce a reasonable arm swing within the limits of the disability and to focus attention on the difficulty of grasp/release in deciding when to let go of the object. Most severely disabled children using this technique have a problem of being unable to relax, and it has been found that the more usual preliminary swings prior to the final throw only serve to 'wind up' the state of muscular tension and distort the pattern. This may be solved in many instances by creating a posture of total stillness before throwing, with no preliminary movement leading up to the sudden throw. Arm rests must be removed from wheelchairs on the side of the throwing arm.

Teaching points
- Position the thrower in a sitting position sideways to the direction of throw with the shoulder of the throwing arm pointing sideways at the target.
- Hold the object in the fingers, not in the palm of the hand, and rest the object in the lap. For a right-handed thrower resting the right hand at the side of the left hip increases the length of arm swing, provided that the position can be maintained in a totally relaxed fashion.
- Line up the head, the hand holding the object and the target.
- Relax.
- Start the arm throw sideways by leading with the elbow, followed by the wrist and finger extension. The final release is by a sharp extensor flick of wrist and fingers in a backhand manner. The length of arm swing, control of the timing of the backhand flick, the height of the final flick and the point of release dictate the control of either distance or accuracy.

This technique can be successfully used in many aiming games with small objects and in certain athletics field events using a beanbag.

REAR-FACING THROW

This technique was first developed in throwing events in athletics for the severely disabled, but it can be used in many games and is most suitable for severe cases of cerebral palsy. Because of the lack of flexibility and the poor range of joint movement in cerebral palsy, it is often not possible to apply force against an object through a wide range; the rear-facing technique begins to solve this problem. Throwing distances may be steadily increased, but accuracy remains a problem as the performer often cannot visually monitor the results of a throw. Compensation must be achieved by a great deal of verbal feedback on direction from the teacher.

Teaching points
- Position the wheelchair with the child facing to the rear and the back of the wheelchair pointing down the direction of throw.
- Hold the object in the fingers and rest the hand in the lap.
- Relax and flop in the chair if necessary.
- Initiate the throw by firing the elbow upwards and backwards. The forearm fires upwards as near to the vertical as possible as the arm is extended, and the final release of the object is by an extensor wrist flick from as high a position as possible overhead.
- The object is released above the shoulder of the throwing arm.

In many ways the action resembles trying to swot a fly off the ceiling with a backhand action. Accuracy can be gained by those children who are able to turn their head sufficiently, prior to the throw, to follow the flight of the object; they can then modify the action in terms of direction.

Five basic methods of throwing an object have been discussed, but in the end there may be as many effective methods as there are individual children.

TEACHING METHODS

In a variety of games where aiming is the basic skill, the target may be stationary as in bowls or quoits or moving as is the case in passing to other players. It is, therefore, critical that before junior school children are introduced to games involving the projection of objects they should be exposed to a great deal of experience at simple aiming activities. With physically handicapped children, particularly those suffering from brain damage, the more usual stereotyped patterns of throwing cannot be performed because of motor impairment problems. The teacher must set up problem-solving situations which allow the children to experiment and discover individual patterns of movement which are efficient in producing reasonable accuracy. This approach should lead to the children learning to apply techniques in a variety of situations and should also lead to their understanding fundamental principles about the mechanics of aiming. They therefore engage in practical exploration of throwing situations which are, in fact, structured by the teacher. The teacher sets an overall task within a certain theme and the children explore various methods of performance within the general theme. However, there may be many passive children deprived of previous play experience who need to be stimulated by a much more directed approach where movement patterns are prescribed then copied by the child. This is when the general principles of performer analysis and evaluation together with task analysis need to be applied.

The direction and flight of a thrown or bowled object depend upon the arc described by the throwing hand prior to release and the timing of the point of release. Timing the point of release refers to whether the object is released early or late during the arm action. Children can only learn such principles by experiencing the effects of a variety of movement patterns on the flight of objects in relation to targets. Normal children can often acquire an understanding and a feeling for the necessary movements fairly quickly. When dealing with severely disabled children it is necessary to decide how much supplementary information must be provided to help them in the learning situation. If they cannot achieve success early in the practice, how much special assistance is required and through which sensory modalities is the assistance best presented? For example, to help such children develop kinaesthetic awareness of a throwing pattern it may be valuable if manual guidance is given by holding the wrist of the throwing arm, waiting until the arm is relaxed and then moving the hand quickly through the action. Repetition of this pattern of movement is most helpful if the child is able to concentrate solely on what the action 'feels' like. A sharp verbal cue can be given by the teacher to stimulate and prompt the correct timing of the release point. Similarly, by placing manual resistance on the leading surface of the throwing hand the child is required to move the hand and arm through the desired action and in the correct direction. This is the same as the proprioceptive facilitation techniques used in physiotherapy for brain-injured children.

Visual guidance can be provided in aiming where the child is required to roll, throw or bowl an object along a line or a channel drawn on the floor. The importance of having both eyes over the line looking at the target and moving the hand along the line before release become quickly apparent. As the distance between partners is increased, so the child should begin to appreciate the significance of the factors which influence speed, distance and direction to reach the partner.

Quite apart from the motor actions required, aiming at targets involves considerable judgement of horizontal distance, perception of space, ball flight and appreciation of force patterns. Participation in these games situations should lead to improved perceptual development in eye–hand accuracy.

PLANNING THE PROGRAMME

The many factors for consideration in planning a developmental scheme of work that is progressive and sequential include (a) a careful analysis of throwing tasks by degree of motor difficulty and (b) a similar analysis which takes account of the perceptual factors involved in performance. The motor action will be affected by the size, weight and shape of the object as the child will find smaller objects much easier to handle initially. Beanbags and foam tennis balls are obviously easier to hold as they are light and they shape to the hand or can be held in the fingers. Targets are vital in setting up throwing tasks in order that the spatial factors of direction, distance and level are developed together with the throwing pattern. Progressively grading the degree of difficulty involved in the perceptual-motor process of aiming and throwing will also include siting targets in relation to the position of the thrower. The usual sequence of development follows a clear pattern:

1. Aiming and throwing from a seated or standing position in a *downward direction*. Large targets should be at floor level and non-bounce objects simplify the problems. All techniques of throwing can be used.
2. Throwing at targets *which are level* with the performer in a *forward direction* — for example, skittles on a bench or chair, wickets, etc. Again, all throwing techniques can be used, including rolling or sliding objects along the floor with an underhand throw (bowling action).
3. Throwing at targets in an *upward direction* such as wall targets, basketball rings, etc.
4. Throwing at *moving targets*.

Planning a progressive scheme of learning will take these stages into account.

In addition to considering these factors specifically related to the task development, the teacher will need to evaluate the abilities of individual children in order to assess how much assistance is required initially and how much adaptation may be necessary.

ASSESSMENT OF THROWING POTENTIAL

Although any attempt to assess the most appropriate starting level for the individual child will take account of chronological age, this is rarely a major factor. Much more important elements are the stage of perceptual-motor development that the child has reached and the severity of the disability that interferes with performance. The following will need to be assessed.

Position of stability

The most efficient starting position which is stable, as upright as possible, and allows for freedom of arm and shoulder movement, must be established. This will vary from standing unaided, standing with aids, sitting in a wheelchair without arm rests, kneeling upright, to lying prone on the floor. The decision of whether or not to move the child out of the wheelchair will depend upon how much freedom of controlled posture he can achieve on his own. There are many seating devices now on the market which can solve this problem. Plastic-covered foam chair shapes, soft play cushions and bags, and wedge-shaped foam cushions are now freely available. The use of such apparatus means that even the severely disabled can be placed in sitting positions at floor level. Wedge cushions can be placed under the chest of prone lying children so that the arms and shoulders are raised high enough off the floor to allow for a range of controlled movement sufficient to play with a ball.

Grasp/release

Assess the ability to grasp objects and release them at will in a number of directions. Does the child require verbal or tactile cues to prompt when to let go?

Locomotor ability and balance

How well can the child move about and change position under his own steam? The child may be ambulant in some form or another, mobile in a manual wheelchair, mobile in an electric wheelchair, or may be able to crawl on all fours; the form of controlled movement will dictate the suitability of more advanced throwing activities.

Visual perception

Eye-focusing is important in following the track of an object, and it is necessary to assess if a child can, in fact, focus attention on the target. This is obviously simplified if the child is positioned so that the head remains still throughout the action. The implications for athetoid and ataxic children are obvious in attempting to gain stability. Does the child require assistance in trying to focus attention on the target? How might this best be achieved?

Understanding instructions

Degree of mental subnormality will affect the child's ability to understand instructions, and we must evaluate how the child reacts to different teaching cues and types of reinforcement. In general, activities are best introduced by demonstration and imitation rather than through verbal cues to performance.

Control of arm action

Within the limited range of arm movement in severely disabled children we must discover which specific arm actions they can control. In which plane do they have the widest range of movement? Can they raise one or both arms overhead? In which direction and over what range do they have the most control?

A DEVELOPMENTAL PROGRAMME OF AIMING AND THROWING ACTIVITIES

Level 1: beanbags

1. From a sitting or kneeling position pick up beanbags and drop them into a box. Hold the beanbag as high as possible then release from above the box.
2. As above, but sort two colours of beanbags into separate boxes. Make the child reach further by moving the boxes.
3. From a sitting position aim to throw beanbags into a large hoop placed on the floor in front of the child. (For overhead throw, check elbow extension in throw.)
4. Throw beanbags down into a range of receptacles placed at floor level at varying distances in front of the thrower. Beat your score.
5. Throw beanbags forward for distance from an overhead throw. Beat your best marker.
6. Throwing for distance, experiment with various styles of throwing. Beat your best marker.
7. Throw the beanbag down onto the ground to make the loudest possible noise.
8. Throw beanbags into shapes or pictures drawn on the floor (faces, circles, squares, etc.). Name the target before throwing. Beat your best score.
9. Throw beanbags to knock down two skittles. The skittles may initially be set up on wood blocks to raise them nearer to the thrower. Move the skittles further away as success is achieved and reduce to one skittle. Mark lines on the floor to measure distance from the target. How far away can you move and still hit the skittle?
10. Throw beanbags at a large beach ball on the floor and try to move it. Start close to the ball and gradually increase the distance.
11. Aim beanbags to hit targets drawn or stuck on a wall. The targets may be numbered concentric circles or a series of shapes set at different heights. Lines may be drawn on the floor to indicate distance from the wall and the distance thrown should be progressively increased. In these activities the children must judge horizontal direction, the force of the throw and the vertical height of the target.

Basket shooting, note the large beanbag

12. Throw beanbags into a bucket. After three successful throws, move the bucket a little further away.
13. Throw beanbags through a large hoop suspended from a beam. The hoop should initially be at chest level for the thrower. As success is achieved the hoop can be raised and the throwing distance from the hoop increased.
14. To achieve a moving target, a hoop can be set swinging from left to right. The child aims to throw through the hoop.
15. To form a swingball target, a large ball is suspended from a beam or netball ring and set swinging from left to right across the thrower's vision. The flight path of the ball is predictable and the child must assess its speed, distance and arc before deciding *when* to initiate the throwing action. This can be performed as an individual or group activity. Scores are for direct hits.
16. Throw beanbags through a netball ring set at the appropriate height. Raise the ring and increase the distance.

The above activities may provide a basis for a developmental programme of aiming skills for handicapped children. As the skills are acquired and social development occurs, there are many aiming games which can be played on either a cooperative or competitive basis. The aiming activities have been listed in an approximate sequential order of development, but within their performance other basic factors of progression need to be considered:

1. Progress from a starting position of kneeling or sitting to standing, where possible.
2. Progress from aiming and releasing downwards to a forward direction, then to upward targets, then at moving targets. Grasp/release to throwing.
3. Start with large targets and reduce the size as skill develops.
4. Begin aiming from close range and increase the distance from the target.

In learning to aim and throw at targets, beanbags have been suggested as the best starting point because they simplify the perceptual-motor performance. Beanbags slide along the floor after landing, so the thrower does not have to judge bounce or flight problems; furthermore, as they do not roll away they can be easily retrieved for repetitive practice to continue without too much delay. As movement patterns become established, other objects may be introduced in a similar manner. All of the above activities can also be used with 6–8 cm diameter foam balls. The list of activities is in no way exhaustive, and the experienced teacher will select and adapt activities most appropriate to the abilities of each child.

UNDERHAND THROWING

Underhand throwing techniques may be developed through similar progressive practices using beanbags, foam balls or rubber quoits. These objects reduce the grasp–release problems for children with hand and arm impairment and, of course, they do not bounce.

1. From a kneeling or sitting position toss quoits onto a floor target.
2. Toss quoits into a hoop on the floor.
3. Toss quoits into a box or bucket.
4. Toss quoits along a line drawn on the floor. One point is scored if the quoit ends up on the line.

Figure 4.3   Numbered boxes into which quoits are thrown

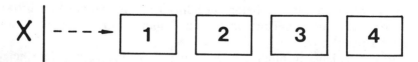

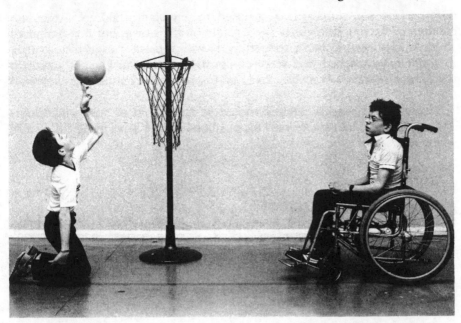

Shooting at a low basket

5. Toss quoits into boxes drawn on the floor (see Figure 4.3). Number the boxes progressively to raise the score as the distance increases from the thrower, as in shuffleboard. Beat your score.
6. Ring-the-stick — toss quoits to land over a pegboard, skittle or cone on the floor.
7. Wall targets — toss quoits at a variety of targets marked on a wall.
8. Toss quoits through a suspended hoop.
9. Swinging hoop — as with beanbags.
10. Swingball target.

   The basic aims are to develop an underhand pattern with a spinning action of the wrist, to time the moment of release and to reduce unsuitable movements.

PROJECTING BALLS

Normal children acquire the technique of throwing, rolling and bouncing balls as a result of extended practice and individual experimentation in a variety of situations. They project the object, chase after it and retrieve it in many ways. Catching or stopping is closely associated with throwing. Moving to retrieve the object is difficult for handicapped children and this must be considered in planning the programme. The organization of practice may need to be very different for non-ambulant as opposed to ambulant children. Ambulant children of varying disabilities can operate on their own, but non-ambulant children may need to work cooperatively with a partner even though they may not have reached that stage of normal social behaviour. If sufficient teaching assistance is available, then one-to-one teaching situations can be set up.

Severely handicapped children should be moved out of their wheelchairs and manipulated into stable working positions at floor level using sitting aids where necessary.

LEVEL 1

Rolling and stopping a ball

1. Astride sitting, legs apart, facing a partner or helper 1.5–2 m away. Place both hands on top of the ball and push it away to the partner. Increase the distance between pairs. Stop the ball by placing both hands on it. Use large balls.
2. Astride sitting, roll the large ball one-handed, aiming between the

Basketball shooting pratice

Rolling at skittles, note the use of wedge cushions

partner's legs. Place one hand behind the top of the ball and push. Stop with two hands.
3. As above but stop with one hand. Use either hand alternately.
4. Astride sitting, with legs closer together, hold the ball at the side of the legs and roll with one hand aiming to the side of partner (see Figure 4.4).

Figure 4.4   Rolling a ball aimed to the side of partner

5. Kneeling as high as possible, roll the ball with both hands straight to a partner. Increase the distance.
6. High kneeling, roll the large ball to the side of a kneeling partner so that he has to reach for it.
7. High kneeling, roll the ball one-handed and try to stop the ball one-handed.

8. Roll the ball to a partner down a channel 50 cm wide marked on the floor.
9. Roll the ball along a line to a partner.
10. Roll the ball to a partner so that it passes between two skittles 1 m apart.
11. Roll the ball to knock down a skittle placed in front of a partner. If the distance is kept short and the skittle is placed within reach, the partners can stop the ball, replace the skittle themselves and keep the activity going.
12. Develop practices by rolling the ball at a variety of targets, gradually increasing the distances and reducing the size of the target.

The experienced teacher will decide how much assistance is needed by children at different levels of ability. As far as possible, children should be allowed to experiment for themselves, but it will often be necessary to use direct teaching methods to establish important teaching points. At the lowest levels of ability and with the most severely disabled children some manual support may be needed to maintain a stable position, but sitting aids are preferable because they give independence. For children with severe hand and arm impairment, lengths of plastic guttering can be used as chutes down which to roll the ball from a wheelchair position.

All of the developmental practices listed above, which are used for large balls, may be used in the sequence for teaching and handling of small balls with one hand. Airflow balls of different sizes have very low bounce properties and can be easily handled. Although badly disabled children can often roll or throw small balls at targets quite successfully, they cannot genuinely become involved in many small-ball activities because of the difficulties inherent in catching and retrieving them. The use of small-ball activities within the programme for young children is therefore unrealistic when the disability is severe.

LEVEL 2

Bouncing a ball (medium to large size — 15 cm plus)

Bouncing a ball is usually performed in one of two ways. In the first, the ball is thrown or released to the floor, then caught after the bounce; in the second, it is struck by the hand to the floor, then repeatedly patted to the floor. On the other hand, the ball may be bounced towards another player; this is an important technique allowing two handicapped players to combine together in throw-and-catch play. Patting the ball repeatedly is not really a throwing technique but the beginnings of striking skill. It will be discussed later.

1. From a high kneeling position, hold a large ball in two hands and release it to the floor. Catch the rebound by hugging the ball to the stomach. The ball should initially be held with one hand on either side and dropped by moving the hands out to the side.

Bounce passing

2. From a high-kneeling position, hold the ball with one hand above and one hand below, then bounce the ball firmly with pressure from the top hand. Catch the ball after two bounces.

3. From a high-kneeling position, bounce the ball against a wall and collect the return. The ball should be bounced on the floor first before making contact with the wall; thus it bounces quite high but does not rebound far from the wall.

4. From a high-kneeling position, bounce the ball once to a helper so that it reaches him at above knee height. Stop a rolled return.

5. From a high-kneeling or standing position, bounce the ball for a partner to catch.

6. Bounce the ball to a partner so that on its way it hits a large floor target such as a hoop.

7. Bounce the ball along a line to a partner.

8. How many bounce passes can you make to your partner without dropping the ball?

Bouncing a ball to a partner will usually be performed with a two-handed push from the chest or a two-handed forward throw from head height.

Teaching points
- Hold the ball with fingers and thumbs behind the ball.
- Spread the elbows out to the sides.
- Push the ball away, extending the arms and wrists very quickly.

LEVEL 3

Throwing a ball at this skill level involves cooperation in passing to other players, both stationary and on the move. It is a major lead up to the development of group games. As this is closely related to catching, a brief list of practices appears at the end of the following section.

TECHNIQUES OF RECEIVING AND ACQUIRING POSSESSION

The ability to acquire possession of a ball that has been played is a major landmark for any child in learning to play many games. Once a child can catch a ball successfully, he is in a position to participate in cooperative and competitive games situations with peers. The skills of throwing and catching are fundamental to a vast range of games opportunities.

The problem of catching a thrown ball involves a complex combination of perceptual interpretation of visual stimuli in tracking the flight path of the ball, predicting when it will arrive, anticipating where to move, and finally the motor action of being in position and placing the hands to trap it. When a ball is thrown towards a catcher, several variables are present within the flight path: direction in terms of left and right; speed; and height in terms of a trajectory which must be judged. The visuo-motor problems of many handicapped children will often prevent the successful accomplishment of such a seemingly simple task for visual monitoring of ball flight in three-dimensional space is not a simple matter. A high degree of eye–hand coordination, good control over both hands and fairly sophisticated perceptual abilities are required.

A realistic appraisal of the abilities of severely handicapped children will suggest that such a skill will always be beyond their capacity. The problem is, therefore, how to simplify performance so that they succeed, for they must succeed somehow. Simplification may involve reducing the confusion of stimuli from the visual display, thereby simplifying the decision-making process; it may also involve the use of alternative materials to simplify the motor actions. Large balls are easier to handle than small ones and they are easier to see. Catching a small ball requires very accurate visual tracking ability, and fine manipulation and placement of the hands is necessary with only a small margin of error between success and failure. Provided that a large ball is accurately thrown with a low flight arc, the catching act becomes more of a gross perceptual-motor task as the ball can be cradled into the body with both

Passing and receiving

arms, even if the hand placement is not accurate. When a ball is rolled along the ground, the pathway of the ball becomes two-dimensional in both speed and direction; therefore it is easier to monitor and stop, particularly when the bright multicoloured texture of the ball highlights it against a plain floor surface. Athetoids, ataxics and children with spatial–perceptual problems find it much easier to catch a ball which is bounced rather than thrown. This does not involve a change of visual focus of attention from high to low, as the eyes can remain steadily fixed on the ball throughout the performance. Kneeling or sitting for stability also improves catching ability for the same children because this tends to reduce unwanted extraneous body movements and fixes the head and eye position rather better than standing.

The experienced teacher will use evaluative techniques in deciding whether a disabled child is likely to develop the specific perceptual-motor abilities needed in catching tasks or at what stage constant adaptation is necessary to enable participation to occur successfully.

SUMMARY OF FACTORS AFFECTING PERFORMANCE

Before planning a developmental sequence of progressive learning situations in the techniques of catching a ball, it may be useful to summarize the factors which control the degree of difficulty in the performance of young children. Such a summary is given in Figure 4.5. By simple permutation of the factors, the teacher can manipulate the learning environment and adapt the level of difficulty of the task to the ability of each child.

Figure 4.5   Summary of factors controlling performance in young children

---

Ball size
Large ball (simple) → small ball (difficult)

Ball colour
Provide a clear contrast between the ball and the background.
Darker colours are easier to see against a neutral mat surrounding.

Ball speed
Slow (simple) → fast (difficult)

Ball flight

Simple	rolled
	bounced to the midpoint of the body
	bounced to head height
	low horizontal flight to the midpoint of the body
	high flight in front of the face from a short distance
	low horizontal flight to the best hand
Difficult	long flight arc from a distance

This rank order of difficulty reflects the normal development with age and experience of the ability to monitor the flight of a ball.

Flight distance
1.5–2 m (simple) → 10 m plus (difficult)

PROGRESSIVE PRACTICE IN GAINING POSSESSION (CATCHING TECHNIQUES)

The ability to sit or kneel unsupported is an advantage in catching, but it will be necessary in some cases to manipulate the child into such a position. Foam-padded cushions with arm and back rests are valuable in establishing a straddle-legged sitting position at floor level. Without such apparatus the teacher or a helper may have to provide support by sitting behind the child to fix his feet firmly and hold his trunk vertical. If the helper also sits wide-legged behind the child, manual guidance can be provided until the learner begins to gain the 'feel' of the movement.

Low-bounce foam balls or cloth-covered playballs of 15–20 cm diameter are ideal pieces of equipment for the introduction of catching techniques. If vinyl soccer balls or playground balls are available, they tend to be rather hard and to bounce high; they should therefore be slightly deflated for easier handling. The weight of the object to be caught is an important factor in the early learning stages; if it is too heavy it is likely to upset the child's balance and if it is too light the child may find difficulty in shaping the hands and getting the feel of it on contact. As technique improves with practice, a wide range of other objects of varying shape, size and texture should be introduced to develop all-round catching skill. Beanbags, rubber quoits, smooth- and rough-surfaced balls, small balls, and high-bounce balls all form the basis of different catching games, and experience should be gained with all of them.

LEVEL 1

Trapping a rolled ball

1. In pairs, straddle sitting, facing each other approximately 1.5 m apart, roll the ball to each other with both hands. Stop the ball with both hands on top of the ball and thumbs behind the ball.
2. Same practice, but if difficulty is experienced in reaching for the ball, allow it to roll all the way and cradle it into the crotch with both hands.
3. Roll the ball with one hand but stop it with both hands.
4. Increase the speed of rolling the ball.
5. Roll the ball back and forward with both hands without stopping it first.
6. Increase the distance apart and use balls of varying sizes.
7. Change the position to high kneeling. Each child kneels on a mat 1.5 m apart. Roll the ball aiming between the partner's knees and stop with both hands.
8. Roll the ball with one hand but stop with both hands.
9. Roll and stop with one hand alternately.
10. Roll the ball back and forward with both hands without stopping it.
11. Roll the ball to either the left or right side of the partner so that he must judge the direction correctly to stop it. Point to or call the direction at first to give him a cue.
12. Increase the distance apart and the speed of the ball. Use balls of varying sizes.
13. Change the starting position to standing for ambulant children and experiment with different balls, increasing speed and distances.

LEVEL 2

Catching a bounced ball (17–20 cm foam ball)

1. Individual practice, straddle sitting. Holding the ball at head height allow it to bounce, then cradle it to the stomach with both arms.

2. While straddle sitting, throw the ball underhand with both hands up to head height, then cradle it to the body with both arms after it bounces.
3. Straddle sitting, facing a wall from 1 to 1.5 m distance. Throw the ball onto the wall and catch to the body after the bounce.
4. Increase the distance from the wall and allow more than one bounce if necessary.
5. In pairs straddle sitting 1.5–2 m apart. With both hands throw the ball one bounce to the partner.
6. How many times can you catch one bounce without dropping the ball?
7. High kneeling on a mat facing your partner from 1.5–2 m apart. Hold the ball at chest height and bounce once to your partner.
8. Hold the ball at head height and bounce once to your partner.
9. Ambulant children will perform all of the practices from a standing position as early as possible and progress to bouncing and catching on the move.

Teaching points
• Watch the ball all the way from your partner's hands.
• Move into the line of the ball as early as possible.
• Make a cradle using both arms with elbows tucked into the side.
• Cushion the ball in with both hands as it touches the body.

As the skill develops, children should be encouraged to progress from the cradle-catching position to reaching out with both arms, making an early contact on the ball with one hand either side (thumbs behind the ball), and drawing the ball in to the body to cushion the impact.

Catching a swinging ball
A suspended ball follows a fairly constant path and therefore provides good early training in judgement of ball flight. Airflow balls of various sizes are easily attached to beams, but if they are not available cloth or foam balls can be suspended in string bags.

1. Individual practice. Suspend a large ball from a beam or have an assistant hold the string so that the ball hangs at roughly chest height. In straddle-sitting position, swing the ball forward and back in line with the eyes. Touch the ball with one hand as it swings back.
2. Touch the ball with both hands as it swings back.
3. Trap the ball with one hand either side. Allow it to swing several times, judge the swing, then trap it.
4. Push the ball forward and catch on the return swing.
5. Use a smaller ball and try to catch in one hand, starting with a palm touch.
6. Repeat the practices from a kneeling position, shortening the string and adjusting the ball to chest height. (Wind the string over the beam to shorten.)

7. Repeat from a wheelchair or standing position.
8. Change the direction of the swingball to a left-to-right swing across the line of vision and repeat the sequence. (This may be too difficult for younger children.)
9. Lie the child on his back facing the ceiling, with the ball suspended above the chest and well within hand reach. Set the ball swinging in a circular motion around the child's head and repeat the process from touching to trapping.

Teaching points
- Watch the ball closely all the way.
- Raise the hands early.
- Decide *when* to move the hands in relation to the swing of the ball.

Catching beanbags
Progress from large beanbags to the standard size. Larger beanbags are not readily available, but they are easily made.

1. Individual practice. In straddle-sitting position, hold the beanbag in both hands and squeeze.
2. Balance the beanbag on the back of the hand, flick into the air gently and catch with the other hand. Change hands.
3. Toss into the air and catch with both hands.
4. Toss the beanbag to head height and catch with both hands. Make a cup with little fingers together.
5. Toss the beanbag into the air, clap hands once, and catch with both hands.
6. Toss the beanbag using different parts of the hand and arm and catch with both hands.
7. Repeat all practices from a kneeling position and, where possible, develop to standing position.
8. In pairs, straddle-sitting, facing each other with feet touching. Reach forward and hand the beanbag to your partner.
9. Move slightly further apart and hand the beanbag back and forward using both hands.
10. Move 1.5–2 m apart and slide the beanbag to each other along the floor. Stop with both hands.
11. Toss the beanbag in a low arc at your partner's stomach — never above chest height. Catch by making an elbow cradle and pull in to the stomach.
12. Toss the beanbag into your partner's lap, reach and try to catch in both hands (little fingers together and fingers pointing forward).
13. Repeat the practices from a kneeling position.

Teaching points
- Watch the beanbag closely before it is thrown.
- Extend the arms and place the hands (cupped) underneath the beanbag as early as possible.

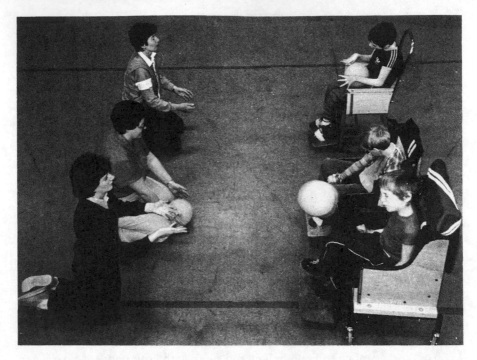

One-to-one assistance

- Allow the arms to give on contact.
- Cue for catcher — count one, two, three and throw.

LEVEL 3

Catching a large ball

In the early stages of learning, a ball of 17–20 cm diameter or greater should be used. The act of catching is almost entirely dependent upon the accuracy of throw; therefore severely disabled children will require assistance on a one-to-one basis from an assistant or an able peer. A major factor in the early stages of teaching handicapped children to catch a ball is to place them in such a position that the ball approaches from the front in full view of both eyes and from a trajectory so that the hands can also be in vision together with the ball. Because of poor proprioceptive feedback they need visual reinforcement concerning hand position. It appears that many children, even after a great deal of experience of playing with balls, never develop the facility to know where their hands are while they are tracking a ball and they always depend upon visual confirmation. This behaviour may be observed in older children as they move the head up and down in a catching task as if they were constantly cross-checking on the position of their hands and the ball.

1. Astride sitting, throw and catch. The feeder throws a ball with both hands, using an underhand action and aiming at a point between stomach and chest level. The receiver makes a 'basket' with elbows tucked in close, hands together with little fingers touching and palms uppermost. The ball should be caught with a cradling action of the forearms and squeezed in to the body. The throwing distance is important and should not be more than 1.5 m initially.
2. Increase the distance of the throw progressively while maintaining a low trajectory. Even severely disabled children should be able to learn to catch from a 3 m distance.
3. Individual practice. Astride sitting, throw up underhand with both hands and catch. Increase the height to which the ball is thrown.
4. Throw and catch from a kneeling position, as in practice (1).
5. Individual practice at throw and catch from a kneeling position.
6. In pairs, straddle sitting, 1.5 m apart. Using two hands, throw and catch with your partner. The pass will need to be a two-handed underhand or a two-handed push pass from the chest.
7. Individual practice of throw and catch, bouncing the ball off a rebound trainer (Figure 4.6). (The frame types with netting elasticated to the frame are ideal for use with handicapped children.)

Figure 4.6   Bouncing the ball off a rebound trainer

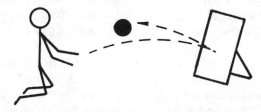

8. Individual practice of throw and catch off a wall. Starting positions and distance from the wall will need to be adjusted according to the throwing ability of the children. How many times can you catch a ball off the wall? Beat your record.

As skill develops, the catching technique should progress from the cradling action of arms and body to use of the arms only and eventually to use of the hands alone.

Assess the learning stages as follows:

1. Do the children focus attention on the ball and follow the flight?
2. Do they make a 'basket' with their arms ready to catch?
3. Do they cushion and 'give' with the arms on impact?
4. Do they need verbal cues? For example, 'I am going to throw the ball *now*!'

In many cases none of these stages occurs because the child shies away from the ball through inability to pick out its flight; also the child is frightened. The use of low trajectory and soft balls may ease the problem, but in the end many children will continue to show fear except when dealing with rolled or bouncing balls.

Once a child can successfully catch large balls delivered from a low trajectory, then practice should be amended to deal with higher trajectory passes. This technique is fundamental to participation in many games situations.

1. In pairs, throwing and catching a ball delivered from above head height. A two-handed underarm throw should be used from a 2 m distance. The ball should be aimed to land between head and chest height. Make a hand target for your partner to aim at — elbows out from the sides, palms facing partner with thumbs together, fingers pointing upwards.
2. In pairs, throw and catch using a two-handed chest pass aimed high. Reach for the ball and pull it in on contact, thumbs behind the ball.
3. In pairs, throw and catch, varying the height of the throw for a low cradle catch or a high two-handed catch. Catch low or high alternately and increase the distance apart.
4. Individual practice close to a wall using a two-handed push pass and high catch. How many consecutive passes can you make? Beat your record.
5. Chest pass in pairs. Pass, then move to a free position to receive the return. Call for the ball.
6. Cooperate with a partner. Which pair can make the highest number of passes and successful catches in 30 seconds? Count the catches.
7. Working in threes, pass the ball around first in one direction, then in the other.
8. Pass and move to a new position to receive the ball from the third player. Make sure you are in a free space, but watch the ball.
9. Cooperation and competition. What is the highest number of passes you can catch in 30 seconds? Beat your record. Which group of three can get the highest number?

Once children can successfully pass and catch in threes, they can be introduced to very simple group games and relays.

STRIKING SKILLS

Striking skills in physical education involve a variety of techniques in several different situations.

1. Hitting a small ball with a narrow bat, as in cricket, rounders, softball, croquet and golf.
2. Hitting a small object with a large bat as in badminton, tennis, table tennis, batinton, padder tennis and squash.
3. Batting a ball with the hand or fist as in volleyball or handball.

4. Repetitive batting of a ball to keep it under moving control as in dribbling a hockey ball, basketball or football.

A further variable within the situation occurs where the bat may be held in one or both hands according to the activity.

In all types of striking games the ball flight must be visually tracked from its source in order to predict where the point of contact will be; this visuo-spatial factor is a major problem requiring a high level of perceptual-motor ability. The motor aspects of performance depend upon the performer's ability to take up a preliminary stance, maintain a firm grasp on the bat handle and control the arc of the bat swing accurately and consistently. Provided that he can assess and predict the flight of the ball and perform the action of hitting, the vital factor in achieving success is the timing of the point of contact between bat and ball. The key points are:

1. when to swing the bat;
2. how to control the bat.

It has been stated previously that many handicapped children experience difficulty with the spatial and temporal aspects of ball skills, and this is particularly apparent as they attempt to learn striking techniques.

The development of striking skills in normal children seems less well ordered than with throwing and catching, and many movement patterns prevail. Initially, young children use a two-handed downward action as in hammering or beating on a drum. Later they use one hand in underhand and sidearm styles with no apparent body movement in the action and always facing square-on to the direction of their target. After the age of 4 years, one-handed batting with a sideways turn and some body action may be seen to develop. The more sophisticated two-handed batting style used in cricket and softball appears at highly variable times and depends very much upon pro-vision of opportunities and cultural circumstances.

In the early stages of learning, it is critical that children experience success and gain satisfaction from actually making contact with the ball in order to motivate them to continue practice. Success can be achieved if the normal stages of perceptual-motor development are taken into account and modifica-tion of the learning environment follows common-sense principles.

1. Stationary balls are easier to strike than moving ones. For the batter, the spatial and temporal elements in ball striking can be reduced according to the type of feeder service. For example, the problems of visual tracking are increased with small balls and are in ascending order of difficulty according to whether balls are stationary, rolled along the floor, bounced or held by the performer, bounced by a server, bounced off a wall and eventually thrown without bouncing.
2. It is easier to hit a large ball with a small narrow bat where the size of the ball allows for a wide margin of error.

3.   Conversely, it is easier to hit a small ball using a large bat with a narrow handle but light enough for ease of handling.
4.   Where children have arm and hand disabilities the bat must be light-weight with a slim handle. Solid-face bats are preferable to stringed rackets as the point of contact does not have to be so accurately gauged.

Throughout the presentation of a programme of bat/ball skills those children who cannot stand should be taken out of their wheelchairs and placed in a kneeling position. Initially, young children gain much enjoyment and benefit from play with a balloon.

LEVEL 1

Balloon activities
1.   In a kneeling position and with an underhand action, keep the balloon in the air by tapping it with one or two hands.
2.   Use different parts of the body to keep up the balloon — palm, back of hand, fist, elbow, head.
3.   Keep up the balloon using a table tennis bat.
4.   Keep up the balloon on one side of the body, knock it overhead and keep it up on the other side of the body.
5.   Keep the balloon up by tapping it from above shoulder height. This will encourage children to stretch and reach.
6.   Facing a wall in a kneeling or standing position, pat the balloon against the wall using an underhand action. Hold in the left hand and bat with the right to start the action.
7.   Pat the balloon repeatedly against the wall using an overhand action.
8.   Throw the balloon in the air and tap it towards the wall with an open-palm, overhand action.
9.   Keep the balloon up against the wall with both palms, as in volleyball.
10. In pairs, keep the balloon up in the air, tapping back and forward to your partner.
11. In threes, as above. How many successive taps can you achieve?

All of the above activities are self-challenging and the children can gauge their improvement by trying to beat their own record of successive contacts.

Progressive stages in learning striking skills
1.   Kneel facing a wall, turn sideways, then strike a large foam ball against the wall using a closed fist. Hold the ball steady with the non-striking hand on top, draw back the striking arm and aim at the centre of the ball just below the midpoint. To protect the hand the child should be placed on a mat. The ball may be teed up on a large beanbag.
2.   Increase the distance from the wall. Experiment with the position of the stationary ball — level with the front knee, in front, level with the rear knee. Focus on the point of contact on the ball.

3. Strike the stationary ball onto the wall using a variety of light bats. Stop the ball with the bat as it rebounds, replace it in position and repeat. Increase the distance from the wall.
4. Aim at a goal or large target marked on the wall.
5. Suspend a large soft ball at chest level in front of the child. Pat the ball forward using the hand. Stop the ball each time. Progress to continuous patting using either hand.
6. Suspend a medium-sized ball at chest height. Using a large bat, knock the ball back and forward with an overhead action.
7. Lower the ball to waist height and continue with a sidearm action. Turn to sideways kneeling. Ensure at all times that the child is positioned at arm's length from the ball.
8. Place a large soft ball balanced on a plastic cone at waist height or above. Using a narrow bat, strike the ball off the cone towards a wall. Retrieve and repeat. Increase distance from the wall.
9. Strike the ball off the cone, aiming at large targets drawn on the wall. Increase the distance or decrease the size of the targets.
10. Work in pairs or in a one-to-one situation. Roll a large soft ball to the child and have him bat it straight back. Kneeling sideways, using a narrow bat, roll the ball to arm's length distance from the child. Teaching points: watch the ball all the way; take the bat back early into a ready position; aim at the middle of the ball.
11. Progress by increasing the distance apart. Vary the speed of the ball or reduce the size of the ball.
12. Have the child aim to hit the rolled ball at targets in front, to the left and to the right.
13. Individual practice. Facing a wall and continuously rebounding. Vary the size of bat, ball, and distance from the wall. How many times can you rebound continuously?

LEVEL 2

Hitting bounced balls
1. Once the child is reasonably proficient at making contact with a stationary or rolled ball, it is a major step to progress to hitting bounced balls. In the first instance the child may set the bounce in motion himself or, alternatively, the ball may be dropped for him by a helper. The ball may be struck forward after one or two bounces as he learns to assess the bounce. Medium-sized balls and bats with a large surface area, like a padder bat, are recommended. The dropped ball should be struck at a wall target for easy retrieval.
2. One-to-one situation facing the batter. The ball is bounced several times for the child to hit up for a catch. Vary the size of the ball and the bat, increase the distance and reduce to one bounce only before striking.

3.   Rebound practice against a wall, using a variety of bats and balls and working up to one bounce rebounding. This type of rebound practice is best initiated using the fist against a large foam ball and progressing to bat/ball practice.

LEVEL 3

Striking a ball in flight

1.   Teach in a one-to-one situation. The feeder requires a level of skill necessary to produce an easy toss to the right place. Toss a large foam ball from no more than 1.5 m distance and dropping from less than head height. The child kneels sideways to the thrower and strikes the ball forward using fist or forearm. Alteration of the kneeling position allows the child to experiment with hitting sideways across the line or along the line of flight. Simple objectives, such as hitting at large targets or goals or hitting the ball up for catches, may be set to assess achievement.
2.   Progress by varying the use of airborne balls of different sizes and textures and adding variety in the use of hitting implements such as short hockey sticks, rounders bats or padder bats. In all practice situations involving an airborne ball, the quality of performance is dictated by the quality of service feeding in relation to the individual ability of each child.
3.   Devise simple partner and group games involving striking for accuracy and distance using targets, goals or catches. Most striking games are associated with aspects of fielding by other players, and these are described in the section on striking games.

Many practices for the acquisition of striking skills may be found in games texts, and those listed above have been placed in a sequential order of development merely as a guide to the selection of appropriate learning stages.

Throughout such basic practice it is essential to allow children time to experiment with ways of handling different implements and to discover certain fundamental principles involved in batting. They need to find ways of hitting straight, hitting along the ground, hitting in the air, hitting accurately and hitting for distance. However, in directed teaching it will almost always be necessary to observe the following key principles:

● establish a preliminary stance — for instance, sideways;
● check the quality of grip on the bat;
● pick up the bat early and prepare the backswing;
● transfer weight into the hitting action;
● focus on the ball right through the action;
● follow through after hitting.

In deciding when to make progress or how far to adapt the learning environment, the teacher must make an assessment of each child based on several factors:

1.   Can he focus his eyes on the ball?
2.   Can he monitor the flight of the ball?
3.   Does the ball flight require simplification?
4.   What is his most stable stance?
5.   Which implements can he handle easiest?
6.   Can he control the swing of the bat arc?
7.   Can he time the start of his forward swing of the bat? Does he swing too early or too late?

Based on such an individual assessment, the teacher is in a position to evaluate just how much assistance the child needs. This assistance will, as in other skills, vary from manual guidance and stabilizing support to the giving of verbal cues to prompt the timing of the bat swing. Such a checklist will aid the teacher in devising individual remediation programmes at the appropriate level.

Ambulant children (further development)
As far as possible, ambulant children should follow a typical primary school programme which will include all the activities listed above together with the greater challenge of increased locomotor possibilities. Many non-ambulant children with good hand control will be able to follow a programme of further skill development while moving around on their knees.

Individual: hands only

1.   Pat bounce a large foam ball on the floor with the favoured hand. (Use of soft fingers for control.)
2.   Bounce as high as possible, then as low as possible.
3.   Use the other hand, then bounce using each hand alternately.
4.   How many times can you bounce the ball with one hand? How many times can you bounce the ball using alternate hands?
5.   Pat bounce on the move and keep control of the ball. Avoid other children. Change hands.
6.   Pat bounce on the move around targets on the floor — hoops, mats, skittles, etc.
7.   Pat bounce on the move and change direction on a signal from the teacher.

BAT AND BALL: TWO HANDS

Two-handed batting is a sophisticated technique and must, of necessity, be taught late in the development sequence of striking skills. The two main actions are hitting downward along the line of the ball flight with an underarm action and hitting with a sidearm action across the line of the ball. Striking may be performed for distance or accuracy or both, but the batting action tends to be closely related to specific sports skills. The underarm action is relevant to hockey, cricket, golf, putting and croquet, whereas the sidearm action is relevant to softball, cricket, baseball and perhaps certain strokes in tennis. Amendments to teaching techniques are obviously best performed in relation to the specific needs of those activities, but a basis of generalized experience in batting two-handed forms a valuable introduction to the later techniques. Kneeling performers have less difficulty in handling shorter implements such as sawn-off hockey sticks or shorter plastic softball bats.

LEVEL 1

1. Using a plastic hockey stick, bat a large foam ball on to a wall and then retrieve. Balance the ball on a floppy beanbag to keep it stationary. Where necessary mark an X on the ball to indicate the best contact point.

Teaching points
(a) Two-handed chopping-axe grip on the handle, with left hand at the top (for right-handed players).
(b) Facing sideways, take up a preliminary stance at straight arm reach from the ball.
(c) Position so that the ball is level with the midpoint between the feet or knees.
(d) Swing the stick back from the shoulders and 'give' at the wrists.
(e) Swing down at the centre of the ball and hit from the wrist.
(f) Watch the centre of the ball at all times, even after the contact.
2. Using a plastic softball bat, hit a medium-sized foam ball onto the wall.
3. Using a hockey stick or golf putter, hit small stationary balls at targets for accuracy. A variety of balls and implements should be used to gain general experience. These will include airflow bowls, large pucks, bean-bags, medium-sized vinyl playballs.

Figure 4.7 Group game with one player batting

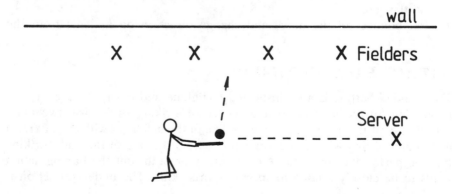

4. Organize into small group games with one batter and the remainder fielding or guarding targets (Figure 4.7).
    (a) The batter hits a stationary foam ball for catches.
    (b) The batter tries to hit the wall while the fielders prevent him.
    (c) The batter hits a rolled foam ball.
    (d) The batter hits a bounced ball.
5. Practise sidearm two-handed batting. Using a softball bat, hit a foam ball at the wall off a traffic cone. A Plasticine cup shape placed on the top of the cone allows balls of different sizes to be balanced. Hit the ball hard.
6. Hit the ball accurately off the cone tee to give catches to the fielders.
7. Hit an airflow ball suspended from a cord. Stop the swinging ball before hitting.

LEVEL 2

1. Hit a high-bounce foam ball onto the wall after it has been served one bounce by a feeder.
2. With a one-bounce serve, hit a high bounce foam ball for the fielders to catch.

LEVEL 3

1. Hit a variety of balls to the fielders after the ball has been tossed underarm full pitch.
2. Using a two-handed grip on a tennis racket, rebound a ball off a wall. Start with foam balls and progress to tennis balls. Move the feet quickly to take the ball after one bounce. Stay sideways to the direction of hit.

PARTNER WORK

1. Hit a large ball back and forward with a hockey stick. Stop the ball each time.
2. Aim at targets between pairs. Increase the distance. Progress to smaller balls.
3. Hit and stop with a partner while on the move. Try to be stationary when stopping the ball.
4. Partner passes the ball for the performer to shoot at a wall goal.
5. One partner guards a wall goal while the performer shoots for goal with a hockey stick. Make six shots, then change places.

   The method of teaching basic skills which develops progressively in a step-by-step sequence is built upon success. So long as the child enjoys the practice and the end result is always successful, motivation remains high throughout. The ultimate test of success, however, is the application of learned skills in a social play situation. The remainder of this book concerns methods of organizing play in cooperative and competitive games that the child will enjoy within limits consistent with the degree of handicap.

Several lesson plans are presented as examples of sound planning at the three levels of performance.

LESSON PLAN: LEVEL 1

INTRODUCTORY ACTIVITIES

These include general body management; postural control; gross bodily movement involving the development of spatial awareness in relation to the playing spaces and other children; and the opportunity for crawling, walking, running, dodging — with emphasis on stopping and starting, changing direction and avoiding other children. Non-ambulant children explore ways of moving around the floor, changing body shape and matching body shapes with other children. They move to the rhythm of music. These activities set the right atmosphere for the lesson and, according to the specific objectives, may be either vigorous or act as a calming influence.

SKILL TRAINING

This involves the practice of particular manipulative techniques, mainly individual but also in cooperation with a partner. Attention should be focused on one aspect of the skill and considerable repetition of practice in a variety of situations should be allowed — for example, rolling and stopping a large ball or aiming at targets.

FINAL ACTIVITY

This involves application of the skill training practised within a small cooperative group game. Games should be selected where the children perform individually but as part of a group — for example, circle target games.

SAMPLE LESSON: 20 MINUTES

Theme: aiming and throwing beanbags.

Objectives: eye–hand accuracy, development of throwing patterns.

INTRODUCTORY ACTIVITY

Floor work on individual mats — stretching, curling, rolling. Curl up tight around a beanbag — stretch tall with beanbag in fingers. Alternate side lying, kneeling, and back lying. Side rolling — beanbag held at different levels.

SKILLS PRACTICE: INDIVIDUAL

Establish high-sitting position on crash mat, peto table, etc.
1. Throw beanbags overhand down a channel 1 m wide.
2. Throw overhand down into a large hoop.
3. Increase distance of hoop. Beat your score at each distance.
4. Aim beanbag down into large shallow boxes.
5. Aim beanbags to knock down a skittle 1.5 m distance.
6. Progressively increase distance of skittle. Count your hits and beat your score at each distance stage.

FINAL ACTIVITY: TARGET BEANBAG (Figure 4.8)

Organize high-sitting around large target board. Count the group score each time. All throw on command at the *red* area, at the *white* area, and finally at the *blue* area.

Figure 4.8 Target beanbag

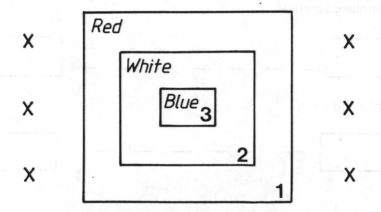

SAMPLE LESSON

Theme: ball rolling in pairs.

Objectives: eye–hand coordination and head control.

INTRODUCTORY ACTIVITY

Head and arm movement to music. Establish sitting position. Look at the ceiling, look at the floor. Turn head right and look at the wall. Turn to the front. Turn head left and look at the wall. Establish a sequence. Arms to the ceiling, hands to the floor. Stretch tall, curl small. Arms out to the front, arms out to the sides. Follow a rhythmic sequence.

SKILL PRACTICE

Establish position — sitting, kneeling, prone lying over wedges. Use large soft and hard balls. Figure 4.9 shows the first three stages of practice; Figure 4.10 shows the fourth stage and Figure 4.11 the fifth.

Figure 4.9   Rolling the ball

1. Roll to partner and stop.

2. Roll along a channel.

3. Roll along a line.

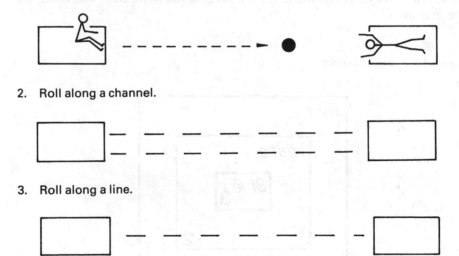

Figure 4.10   Aiming a skittle

4. Aim at a skittle.

FINAL ACTIVITY (Figure 4.12)

Circle skittle-ball — knock down all the skittles.

Figure 4.11 Rolling ball between skittles

5. Increase distance apart (vary texture of ball).

6. Roll ball between two skittles.

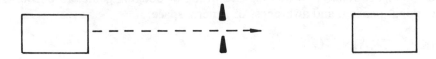

Figure 4.12 Circle skittle-ball

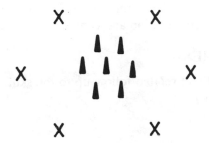

LESSON PLAN: LEVEL 2

INTRODUCTORY ACTIVITIES

General warm-up for all children, involving gross body movement. Simple tag games or dodging games encourage sensible use of space. Establish good control by stop/start activities to the command of the teacher. Warm-up activities may be centred around an object to stimulate further reinforcement of individual skill — bouncing a ball, off a wall, bat and ball movement, roll and chase, etc.

SKILL TRAINING

Practice of skills in twos or threes. Link up practice of techniques which are related in the playing of games — passing and catching, batting and catching, aiming and dodging. Practice adapted techniques based on individual ability in all skill areas. Introduction of limited competitive situations — individual and partner, group drill sequences.

FINAL ACTIVITIES

Individual and partner games.
OR Group games of a low organization nature.

LESSON PLAN: LEVEL 3

INTRODUCTORY ACTIVITIES

General warm-up for all children, involving moving, stopping and changing direction. Dodging and tracking activities with a partner to develop awareness of space relative to others. Group tag or dodging games to encourage marking, passing, and awareness of general space.

SKILL TRAINING

Practice of techniques related to control over an object in flight in pairs or small groups. Practice of skills closely related to the specific techniques of lead up activities for striking games, net games and larger group games. Introduction of tactical understanding in realistic game rehearsal situations. Greater emphasis on cooperation and competition in small groups.

FINAL ACTIVITIES

Group games as a direct related follow-up to the skill training session.

REFERENCES

Arnheim, D.D. and Pestolesi, R.A. (1978) *Elementary Physical Education*, C.V. Mosby, Saint Louis, Minnesota

Cotton, E. (1970) Integration of Treatment and Education in Cerebral Palsy, *Physiotherapy*, April, pp. 143–147

Cratty, B.J. (1969) *Motor Activity and the Education of Retardates*, Lea & Febiger, Philadelphia

Department of Education and Science (DES) (1965) *Planning the Programme*, HMSO, London

Mauldon, E. and Redfern, H.B. (1969) *Games Teaching. A Heuristic Approach for the Primary School*, McDonald & Evans, London

Means, L.E. and Applequist, H.A. (1974) *Dynamic Movement Experiences for Elementary School Children*, Charles C. Thomas, Springfield, Illinois

Oliver, J.N. and Keogh, J. (1967) Helping the physically awkward, *Special Education*, Vol. 56, pp. 22–25

Schurr, E.L. (1975) *Movement Experiences for Children*, Prentice-Hall, Englewood Cliffs, NJ

Vodola, T.M. (1981) *Developmental and Adapted Physical Education: Low Motor Ability Project Active*, C.F. Wood, Bloomfield, NJ

Chapter 5
INDIVIDUAL AND PARTNER ACTIVITIES

The beauty of individual and partner games is that they can be enjoyed at any level of performance. Provided that two players or two pairs of approximately equal ability are matched together, they can enjoy the fun of playing a good game with a realistic opportunity for fair competition. This is true for two normal sportsmen playing their weekly game of squash or golf at their own level; it is equally true when two disabled sportsmen of matched disability play each other. Well-chosen individual and partner activities allow competition between disabled persons who are well matched, without the danger of their developing feelings of inferiority because they might spoil the game for others. When the matching up of pairs is not so close, then it is feasible to operate a handicap system as in normal golf to provide equal opportunity for winning.

The type of activities available for play on a partner basis vary from very simple children's games suitable for use in physical education to those more sophisticated games that can be enjoyed on a lifelong basis in a friendly social setting. The decision-making element in games playing is considerably reduced when only two or four persons play within a restricted environment; therefore all partner games tend to be of a simple nature. Depending on the environmental demands, these games will also vary from simple, discrete, single response activities to more complex activities involving spatial and temporal judgements, thereby allowing a wide scope for selecting an activity appropriate to a range of disabling conditions.

As children develop skill and acquire the various basic techniques, they feel the need to try out their new-found technical competence against someone else, and partner activities provide for this necessary early experience of competition. Competition against another person is the earliest form of competitive or cooperative social experience and may be introduced as soon as the child is seen to develop an awareness of other players. Normal children begin to show the need for partner work from as early as 6 years old, and between the ages of 6 years and 8 years this is a feature of mainstream physical education. The activities in this chapter have deliberately not been related to age; instead, they are related to difficulty of performance. The experienced teacher will select activities appropriate to the age and ability of the children. Activities have been presented which do not need much loco-motor ability nor a great deal of fetching and carrying. All these games may be modified to emphasize either cooperation with a partner or competition against others, as necessary.

BEANBAG AIMING GAMES

Many simple aiming games can be adapted for playing with beanbags. Bean-bags are most useful for severely handicapped children because they do not bounce away from the playing area, they can be thrown or slid along the floor, they tend to stop where they land, and they may be gripped with ease by children with severe hand impairment. Because the beanbags slide along the floor after landing, the player does not have to judge bounce or parabolic flight to be successful and need only judge force, distance and horizontal direction. Thus the factors which contribute to force of throw and accuracy in the horizontal plane can be determined and learnt without the child needing to be concerned with control of the vertical angle. Throwing patterns may be of any type and from the most suitable stable starting position — either from a wheelchair or from the floor. It has been found that many severely disabled quadriplegic children are able to throw beanbags accurately from a back-lying position on the floor with the feet pointing at the target. An overarm throw forward is used with the feet acting as a guide for the direction of throw.

For severely disabled children the difficulty of moving from one end of a court to the other can be a problem at the end of each throwing sequence. Under normal circumstances beanbags must be collected, and the slow move-ment of players interferes with the continuity of the game. This is simply solved if targets are set up at each end of the rink or court, and in a game of doubles (or small teams of three or four) the partners play from opposite ends.

Figure 5.1   Targets set up for a game of doubles

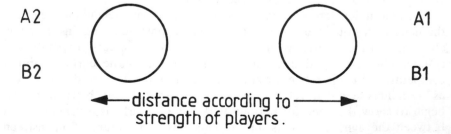

A1 and B1 throw alternately at their target then count the score. A2 and B2 collect the beanbags, then throw at their target in the same fashion. Play continues with the A players adding together their scores until the winning score is reached.

Singles can be played in the same way for players with locomotor problems, but this does interfere with the tactics of the game. The game simply becomes an aiming activity without the tactical element of throwing beanbags in such a position as to block the opponent from teaching the target.

To guarantee successful performance the length of court, the size of target, and the size and weight of the beanbags can be modified to suit the strength of the player.

BEANBAG SHUFFLEBOARD

Figure 5.2   Regular, closely spaced targets in beanbag shuffleboard game for four
players

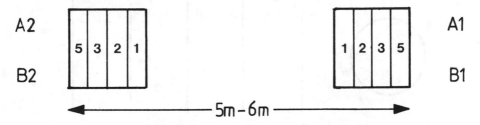

In this game (see Figure 5.2) A1 and B1 have four beanbags each (different colours). They throw alternately with their score depending upon the lane in which the beanbag stops. A2 and B2 collect the beanbags and repeat the sequence. The winning pair are the first to reach an agreed score (e.g. 50 points).

Figure 5.3   Arrangements of small, widely spread beanbag shuffleboard targets

Figure 5.4   Beanbag shuffleboard targets arranged in lanes of decreasing size

As skill develops the distance may be increased and the targets made smaller or more widespread. Examples are shown in Figures 5.3 and 5.4.

TARGET TOSS

Figure 5.5   Target toss: circle with lines drawn at 1 m intervals to mark position of players

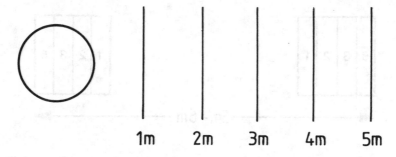

A circle of between 50 cm and 1 m in diameter is drawn on the floor with throwing lines set at 1 m intervals from the circle (Figure 5.5). Each player throws four beanbags at the circle from the 1 m line. One point is scored for each beanbag stopping within the circle. All players move back to the 2 m

Figure 5.6   Target toss for two teams

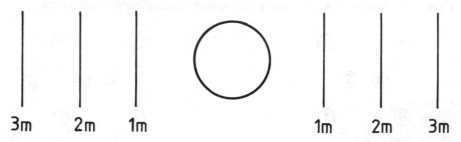

throwing line and repeat the sequence, and so on until a round is completed. The winner is the player with the highest score at the end of each round. Distance limits can be set according to the strength of the weakest player.

The game can also be played with the target situated between two teams (Figure 5.6). Each uses a different coloured beanbag to aid scoring.

The game can be made progressively more difficult by changing the target to a hoop, tyre, bucket, wall target or low netball ring.

LINE TARGET (Figure 5.7)

Figure 5.7   Line target

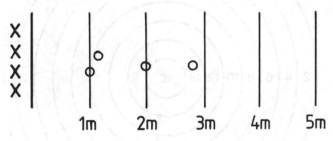

The game is played as singles, doubles or in small teams. Each player throws four beanbags, aiming to land on the first line. Once this is achieved he aims at the second line and so on in ascending order until the fifth line is reached. At this stage each player continues aiming at the lines in descending order until all have been marked. Winners may be the first to complete the sequence or to have the most lines marked within a given time.

A mobile player is needed to return the beanbags to the start line.

LADDER TOSS (Figure 5.8)

Figure 5.8   Ladder toss

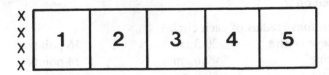

The rules are as for line target except that beanbags must be thrown into each square in correct sequence. The progressive nature of the game helps the children to judge correct distance and the necessary force required.

TARGET BEANBAG (PRECISION THROW) (Figure 5.9)

This is an international field event, with standardized rules, for the severely disabled cerebral palsied athlete.

Figure 5.9   Target beanbag

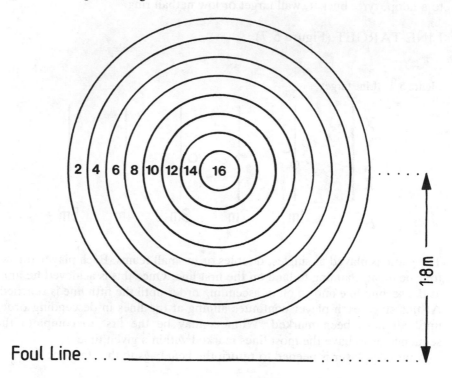

1. The competitor throws six beanbags at a target consisting of eight concentric circles at a distance of 1.8 m from the centre.
2. The target is best made from a cloth fixed to the floor with lines pre-painted on it.

   Dimensions (radius of each circle)

Bullseye centre	20.3 cm	16 points
2nd ring	40.6 cm	14 points
3rd ring	60.9 cm	12 points
4th ring	81.2 cm	10 points
5th ring	101.5 cm	8 points
6th ring	121.8 cm	6 points
7th ring	142.1 cm	4 points
8th ring	162.4 cm	2 points

3. All six throws are counted. When a beanbag lands across a line, the circle containing the larger part of the beanbag counts. Where this is too difficult to determine, then the lower score counts.

Target beanbag

TARGET BALL (Figure 5.10)

Played as singles or doubles. The object is to knock a large ball out of a hoop.

Figure 5.10   Target ball

A large foam ball is placed inside a hoop on the floor. Each pair of players is stationed behind a throwing line and is armed with six beanbags. The players throw the beanbags in any style and score one point each time they knock the ball out of the hoop. Beanbags are collected and redistributed after each round.

TARGET HOOP

The rules are similar to those for the above game, except that no ball is used. The object is to knock the hoop along the floor until it touches the opponents' line to score one point.

TARGET BOARD (Figure 5.11)

A light wooden base of 1 m square is divided into smaller squares painted different colours. The squares are separated by strips of narrow wooden beading tacked to the board to prevent the beanbags from sliding across the board.

Figure 5.11   Target board

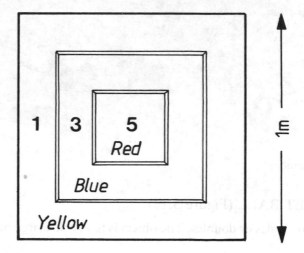

Players aim to throw beanbags into a designated colour on each round of throws. The game can be played in many ways; it can be either cooperative or competitive.

TARGET BOARD (VERTICAL) (Figure 5.12)

Simple target boards can be made with holes cut in the wood through which children throw beanbags. Any piece of board 1 m × 0.5 m can be used. The

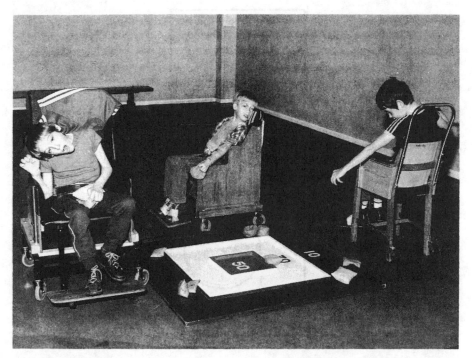

Target board

board may be leant against a wall or a hinged strut fixed to the back so that the target leans at an angle of 45°.

Each hole has the score marked above. Throwing lines may be marked on the floor at 1 m intervals from the board. Each player throws an agreed number of beanbags from each line with the first to reach 21 points winning that round.

The holes cut in the board should be of different sizes and shapes to vary the degree of difficulty.

ROLLING HOOP (Figure 5.13)

This is quite a difficult game and children need to be quite skilful, as the target is moving. The children line up in two parallel lines facing a partner, with the lines roughly 6 m apart. The teacher and an able helper stand facing each other in the gap between the end of the lines, as in the diagram. Each player has one beanbag.

The teacher rolls the hoop between the two lines. As it passes, each player tries to throw his beanbag through the hoop. The beanbags are collected,

Figure 5.12   Target board (vertical)

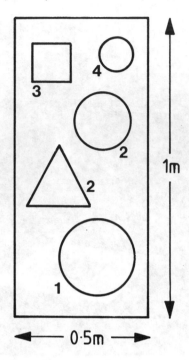

then the hoop is rolled back once again. One point is scored for each beanbag through the hoop, with the winning pair having the highest combined score after a given number of 'rolls'.

An old car tyre produces a better game for more disabled children as it can be rolled more slowly, remains stable and is not knocked off course when hit.

After every four rolls of the hoop or tyre, each pair should change places with another pair to ensure that they have the same chance for an early or late turn to throw.

Figure 5.13   Rolling hoop

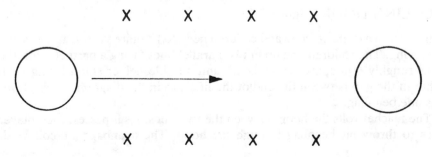

BEANBAG GOLF (Figure 5.14)

Figure 5.14   Beanbag golf

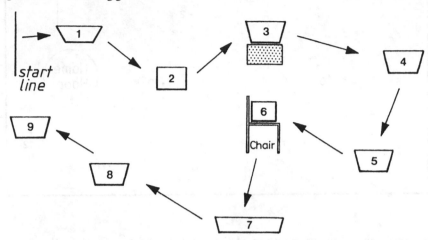

A series of baskets or buckets, numbered in sequence from 1 to 9, are placed around the room at varying distances, thus making a course. Players start at number 1 and throw a beanbag at the first basket. Their next throw is taken from where the beanbag lands and so on until the beanbag lands in the basket. Players then proceed to the next 'hole'. Every throw is counted towards the total taken to complete the course. The lowest scorer is the winner. The holes may be made more difficult or less difficult by varying the distance, varying the size of the basket, or raising some baskets above floor level.

BEANBAG CROQUET (Figure 5.15)

Pairs of skittles or cones are set up around the room to act as the croquet wickets. The aim of the game is to throw a beanbag through each pair of skittles around the course in sequence and be the first player to finish by throwing into the home hoop. Players spin for starting order, then take alternate turns to throw. Each player takes one throw unless the beanbag passes through the wicket, when a second throw is allowed immediately. If a player hits his opponent's beanbag, he is allowed one further bonus throw.

NETBALL GOLF

Numbers from 1 to 9 are marked on the floor at varying distances from a netball ring 1.5 m high. Players start at number 1 and throw a beanbag until they score through the ring. They then proceed to each number in the

Figure 5.15   Beanbag croquet

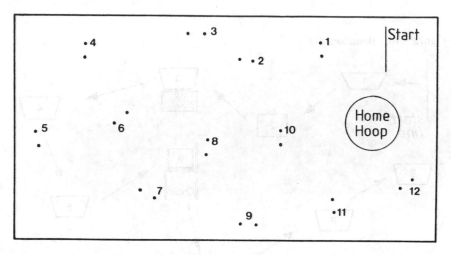

sequence, counting the number of throws required to complete the course. The player wins who completes the course of nine numbered spots with the least throws.

The degree of difficulty is controlled by the distance of the spots from the ring and by the size and weight of the beanbag.

Many variations can be invented by changing the target (tyre, basket, hoop, etc.).

BEANBAG NUMBERS GAME (Figure 5.16)

Mark a numbered grid on the floor.

Each player throws three beanbags at the grid from behind the start line. Each beanbag must land in a separate square. If two bags land in the same square, only one counts. The winner scores one point for the highest score after each round of throws.

BEANBAG BOWLS

This game may be played as singles, doubles or as a rink competition with similar rules to lawn bowls. A white beanbag substitutes for the jack and each team uses a contrasting colour of beanbags. Each player has four beanbags.

RULES

1.   Players spin for first delivery. The winner throws the white beanbag down the rink. The beanbag may be thrown in any manner or slid along the floor. The jack is then centred.

Figure 5.16   Beanbag numbers game

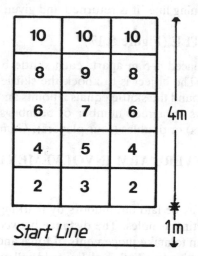

2. The first player then throws his beanbag as near to the jack as possible.
3. Thereafter, players throw in alternate sequence until all beanbags have been delivered. That constitutes *one end*.
4. Points are scored for each beanbag nearer to the jack than the opponents' nearest delivery. Where the two nearest opposing beanbags are equidistant from the jack, then the end is declared null and void.
5. The team winning an end has the privilege of throwing the next jack.
6. The winner is the first to achieve 21 points or the best score from an agreed number of ends played.

Where players of mixed disability are involved, the skill factor may be equalized by restricting the length of the rink to the distance thrown by the least able competitor. Lines drawn at 5 m and 7 m simplify this procedure.

Figure 5.17   Target skittle

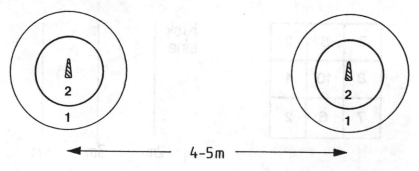

All beanbags past this point become null and void. When the jack is thrown beyond this restraining line, it is returned and given to the opponents.

TARGET SKITTLE (Figure 5.17)

Two skittles are placed 4–5 m apart, each skittle being surrounded by two concentric circles. The object is to knock the skittle over and earn 3 points. The inner circle around the skittle equals 2 points and the outer circle 1 point. Each player throws an agreed number of beanbags in turn. Games can be singles (two players) or doubles (four players). Game up is 30 points.

GAMES FOR SEVERE ARM INVOLVEMENT

INDOOR PUT

A putting green may be laid out indoors by marking chalk circles of roughly 15 cm diameter acting as holes. The distance between holes ought to vary to compel the children to make judgements of force and distance. Wooden discs are a useful alternative to a ball, which would roll away out of control. Discs should be flat wooden blocks of 10 cm diameter and 4–5 cm thickness. Plastic hockey sticks or shinty sticks may be used to strike the disc. Scoring is exactly the same as in normal golf or put with the players counting the number of strokes to complete a nine-hole course.

Severely disabled players who are unable to use their arms but have some foot control can kick the wooden discs around the course.

DISC SHUFFLEBOARD (Figure 5.18)

This is played according to the normal rules for shuffleboard, except that a wooden disc is kicked towards the target from either a standing or a sitting position. Wheelchair competitors should have the footrests removed to allow for greater freedom of leg and foot movement.

According to the degree of leg disability of the players, the kicking-line

Figure 5.18   Disc shuffleboard

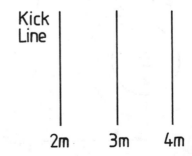

distance should be agreed beforehand. For the sake of continuity, each player should kick three discs in turn at the target. A game consists of an agreed time period, an agreed total number of kicks, or the first player to score an agreed total number of points (e.g. 50).

Many of the simple aiming games using beanbags can easily be adapted for children with severe arm involvement by substituting discs which can be kicked at various targets.

DISC CROQUET (Figure 5.19)

This is an adapted form of croquet played indoors with a wooden disc which is struck with a plastic hockey stick. The wickets are formed from pairs of skittles arranged as in the diagram. The wooden disc may be of any suitable size (recommended size: 8 cm diameter × 4 cm thick).

Figure 5.19   Disc croquet

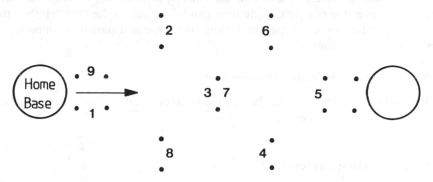

A chalk circle at each end of the court represents the home base.

METHOD OF PLAY

The object of the game is to drive the disc through all the wickets in the correct sequence. The first player or pair to complete a full round is the winner.

The game is started with a disc placed on the home base being hit through the first pair of wickets. Each player is allowed one hit. After passing through every wicket, a player is allowed a further hit at the next wicket in sequence until he misses. The sequence of playing wickets proceeds from home base, through the centre pair of wickets, to left side wicket, to centre wicket, to right side wicket, through the centre pair of wickets to second home base, and return on the opposite route, as numbered in Figure 5.19. As an alternative to aiming at a wicket, any player may aim to hit an opponent's disc. After such a hit he may place his own disc alongside the disc just struck and take a second shot. By so doing he may knock his opponent's disc away into a more difficult position while deflecting his own disc into a favourable position to aim more directly at the next wicket in sequence. The game thus develops into a match of tactical gamesmanship.

The game may also be played by foot kickers in electric wheelchairs.

ACTIVITIES WITH QUOITS

QUOIT-ON-A-ROPE

Two children each hold one end of a skipping rope which is threaded through a rubber quoit. A great deal of arm and shoulder movement may be stimulated as the children cooperate to move the quoit in a variety of ways. The quoit may be swung from side to side, round and round in a circular motion, and up and down in a wavelike action to move the quoit along the rope from end to end.

If a coloured braid is knotted to the rope approximately 30 cm from each end, an interesting competitive activity can take place as the children flick the rope attempting to move the quoit along the rope and past their opponents' braid to score a point.

QUOITS PEGBOARD (Figure 5.20)

The game is similar to quoits horseshoes, except that the quoits are pitched onto a numbered pegboard.

Figure 5.20   Quoits pegboard

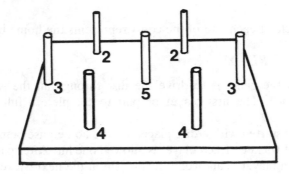

If the pegs are screwed onto a light wooden base, the game can be made more difficult by hanging the pegboard on a wall.

QUOIT HORSESHOES (Figure 5.21)

The object is for players to pitch rope or rubber quoits over a peg set in a wooden base. A point is scored for each quoit to ring the peg. Distance limits should be set according to the strength of the players. The game may be organized in ways appropriate to the mobility levels of the players.

Figure 5.21   Quoit horseshoes

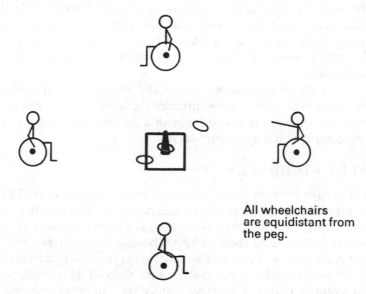

All wheelchairs
are equidistant from
the peg.

The quoit may be pitched in any manner.

VARIATION (Figure 5.22)

Figure 5.22   Variation of quoit horseshoes

Pairs may play best to a given number of ends or play to a given poin target.

WALL GAMES

These are games where a ball is struck or thrown onto a front wall in such a way that an opponent cannot make a good return back to the wall. All wall games can be simply adapted to suit most degrees of disability and are ideal for small groups of mixed ability where integration is easily possible. The major considerations in adapting wall activities are to reduce the size of the playing area, to use lightweight equipment and high-bounce balls, and to modify the rules to allow for a greater range of performance techniques. Mobility factors are reduced anyway as the ball always rebounds within a limited area towards the players and little fetching and carrying is necessary. So long as the service and method of return is appropriate to the limited ability of the players, children of all disabilities can successfully take part in these activities.

As with all similar games, a carefully chosen developmental sequence should occur when children first practice the techniques needed for individual play; they then learn to cooperate with a partner and finally, when they are ready, competition may be introduced.

WALL CATCHBALL

The objective is to cooperate with a partner to keep the ball in play longer than any other pair. A large playground ball or high-bounce foam ball is used. The first player bounces the ball on the floor so that it rebounds off the wall. This service ensures a short but high bounce for the receiver. The second player is allowed one bounce before catching the ball. He then serves onto the wall in turn. One point is awarded for each successful catch after one bounce. After a dropped catch or a second bounce the pair begin counting again from zero.

No floor markings are necessary at this stage. As skill develops, the ball must be thrown onto the wall without first touching the floor.

GROUP WALLBALL

The same game may be developed as a cooperative group game for participants of mixed ability, using three or four players in a team. Restriction of space to a court area of 4 square metres encourages the players to work out angles of rebound from the wall to assist their team mates in making a successful catch. A further development is to make the players catch the ball and return to the wall in strict rotation. With several groups playing, the team with the highest number of consecutive catches wins.

WALL NEWCOMBE (Figure 5.23)

Two, four or six players can take part. Court size will vary according to the number of players and their mobility. A volleyball or similar ball is used.

Figure 5.23   Wall Newcombe: court markings for four players

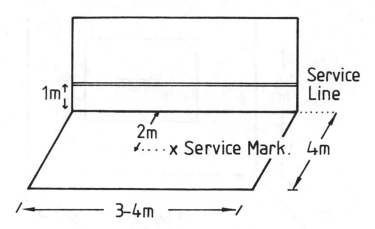

In a game for 2 v. 2 players, the pairs spin for service.

The server positions himself on the service mark and throws the ball onto the wall above the service line so that it rebounds into the court area. Service is illegal if it strikes the wall below the service line or rebounds out of court. After the service the receiver must catch the ball successfully either after one bounce or on the full and throw the ball back to the wall above the service line.

SCORING

A point may only be scored by the serving team. When the server loses a rally or serves illegally he concedes service to the opposition. A point is scored when a player fails to make a clean catch, allows more than one bounce, fails to return his throw accurately to the front wall or knocks the ball out of court. A match is best of 1, 3 or 5 sets. First team to 9 points wins a set. Players in each team serve in strict rotation. Each player continues serving until his service is broken.

The size of the ball obviously dictates the skill demands on the players and use of a tennis ball produces a fast game of one-handed catch and throw for more skilful children. For more seriously handicapped children, a shorter and narrower court reduces the degree of difficulty and they may play successfully from wheelchairs or from a kneeling position.

TARGET WALLBALL (Figure 5.24)

This may be played as either a cooperative group game or a competitive team game.

Figure 5.24   Target wallball: court markings

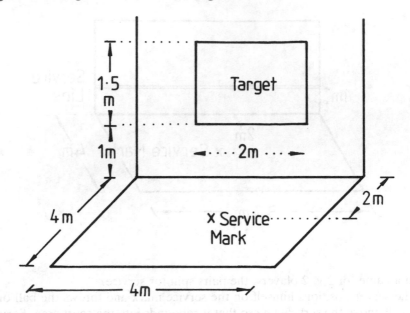

In a cooperative game for four players using a volleyball or similar ball, the server throws the ball against the target marked on the wall so that it rebounds and lands within the court area. Other players within the group must catch the ball within the court area either after one bounce or on the full and return it to the target. No player may play the ball twice in succession. An infringement occurs when the ball is not caught successfully, fails to hit the target, bounces twice, or rebounds out of court. The group with the highest score of consecutive catches is the winner.

The game may also be played between teams of two or three players on the same court, with scoring rules similar to wall Newcombe.

WALL HANDBALL (Figure 5.25)

With suitable adaptations the game may be played as singles, doubles or triples. A volleyball or similar ball is used.

The object of the game is for the server to hit the ball against the wall so that the receivers cannot return it back to the wall. The server positions himself on the service mark, drops the ball and, after it bounces, strikes it with the hand, fist or arm so that it hits the wall and rebounds within the court area beyond the service line. The receiver then tries to strike the ball back on to the wall to rebound within the court and *over the service line*. The receiver may hit the ball after one bounce or on the volley. Use of the service line

Figure 5.25   Wall handball: court markings

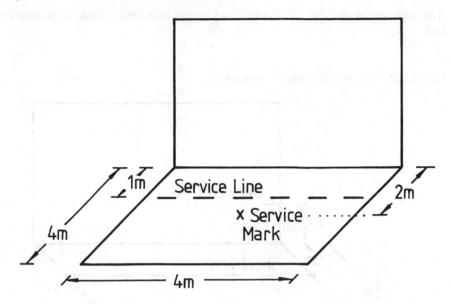

prevents play from developing into too many short drop shots requiring speed and agility for recovery. The game then carries on in sequence until one side commits a foul.

SCORING

Points scored only when serving. The receiving side regains service after winning a rally. A set consists of 9 points (or any agreed number).

RULES

1. The server must make the service rebound into court beyond the service line.
2. In a game of three a side, no player may strike the ball twice in succession.
3. The ball must be struck cleanly with hand, arm, or crutch (or walking stick).
4. No player may intentionally impede an opponent trying to play the ball.
5. After accidental interference, a let is called and the point replayed.

Many variations of this game exist using different bats and balls and children can be encouraged to invent similar games of their own.

SHORT-WALL TENNIS (Figure 5.26)

The equipment consists of plastic short tennis bats and a foam high-bounce ball.

Figure 5.26   Short-wall tennis: court markings

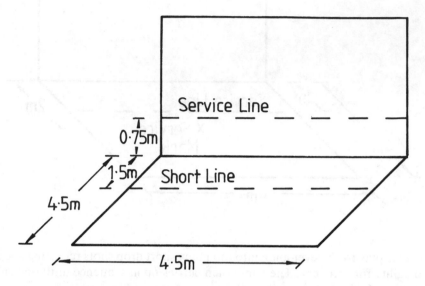

The size of the court may vary according to the degree of skill and mobility of the players. The game may have two or four players. The players spin for service. The server stations himself behind the short line and serves the ball onto the front wall above the service line so that it rebounds beyond the short line and inside the court. The service may be struck in any manner, either forehand or backhand, on the volley or after one bounce. A service is illegal if:

1.   the ball strikes the wall or floor below the service line;
2.   after striking the wall, the ball rebounds directly out of court or lands in front of the short line.

SCORING

A player may only score a point when he is serving. When the server loses a rally or serves illegally he concedes service to his opponent. A point is scored when a player fails to make a good return to the wall above the service line, hits the ball out of court, or allows the ball to bounce twice before his return.

Where a player is accidentally obstructed from making a shot by his opponent, or is hit by the ball, then a let is called and the point is replayed.

A match may be best of 1, 3 or 5 sets. The first player to 9 points wins a set.

DOUBLES

Pairs of mixed disability may play doubles with the less mobile player covering the front part of the court. Players may volley the ball onto the wall without waiting for a bounce. Service is taken in rotation as in badminton, with each individual continuing to serve until a rally is lost. Partners need not return the ball alternately; the nearest player in the pair may return the ball at any time.

The game may also be played as a form of one-wall squash using a variety of bats and balls according to skill level.

CORNER WALL GAMES (Figure 5.27)

Many adaptations of wall games can be played at a more advanced level utilizing the corners of a gymnasium. The corners need to be clear of fixed apparatus and numerous variations of wall games can be invented, all requiring very little space.

Figure 5.27   Corner wall games: basic court markings

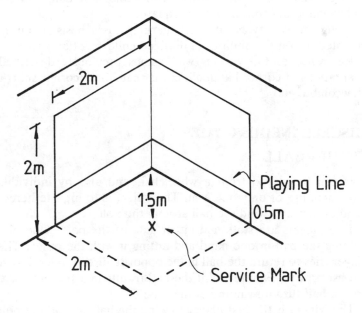

The skill, mobility and speed factors inherent in these games can easily be controlled by altering the size of the court area, amending the type of service, and choosing playing apparatus appropriate to the ability levels of the participants.

BASIC RULES

1. Played as singles or doubles.
2. The server bounces the ball on the service mark and strikes it onto a wall above the playing line so that it rebounds within the court area. For catching games the ball is thrown from the service mark.
3. The service is a fault if the ball fails to strike the wall above the playing line or rebounds out of court.
4. The receiver must return the ball onto either wall, above the playing line, so that the ball rebounds within the court area.
5. The receiver thereafter must return the ball after only one bounce or on the volley.
6. Players may rebound the ball off both walls as a tactical play, provided that it lands within the court.
7. Scoring may be as in badminton or table tennis, according to local rules.

Use of the playing line ensures that the ball rebounds within reach of less mobile players and too much short play is avoided.

An alternative method of play allowing more varied game tactics uses a service square of 75 cm with no playing line. The ball must strike two walls and rebound beyond the service square.

Using the two types of court markings as a basis, many games may be invented to suit the abilities of disabled children of all ages.

Reference to the various wall games previously described will suggest adaptations of corner handball, corner catchball, corner short tennis, corner Newcombe, etc.

MISCELLANEOUS GAMES

TETHERBALL

This can be played from a wheelchair and also by individuals limited to functional use of only one arm. The object is to hit a tethered ball with the hand or arm and wind the ball around the pole.

Two players are stationed either side of the pole. One player serves by holding the ball in one hand and hitting it with the other. Thereafter, each player tries to return the ball in the opposite direction by striking it hard with the fist or arm. Failure to hit the ball results in a free hit for the opponent, after a half-turn unwinding of the rope.

The winner is the first player to wind the ball around the pole completely.

Severely disabled children may be allowed to play the game on a throw-and-catch basis. The rope needs to be arranged as a guy line so that it can be changed in length to suit the players, with the ball at chest height.

A variation of the game exists, known as swingball, using a tethered foam ball and plastic padder bats.

GOALKEEPERS

There are many skills that can be used to produce a simple game of scoring or saving goals. Two simple marked goals are set up at a suitable distance apart (4–5 m). Goals should be approximately 3 m wide, and in certain games a mat can be provided for the goalkeeper to kneel or lie on. Players try to score a goal by pushing, throwing or hitting a ball at their opponents' goal. A match can consist of 5 minutes for each half. A scratch line should be drawn 1 m from each goal, and the ball must be shot from behind that line.

The apparatus should be varied to produce opportunities for the practice of different skills. Hockey sticks, rounders bats, padder bats, airflow balls, foam balls and vinyl footballs can all be used to maintain interest.

CARPET BOWLS

Sets of small bowls are available from several manufacturers, and the game is an excellent lifelong leisure activity for all handicapped people. Any large carpeted room is suitable, and special roll-out mats are available for use in gymnasia or dining halls.

Wheelchair users with good arms face down the rink, remove armrests, and bowl by leaning sideways out of the chair. Children with balance or body-control problems perform best from a high-kneeling position. Severely disabled players can perform well using a short length of plastic guttering as a chute to roll the bowls. On a short playing area, use of a chute may produce too fast a delivery speed, but this can be reduced by sticking a thick layer of foam at the bottom end of the gutter to slow up the bowl before it leaves the chute. Coloured wooden croquet balls produce a cheap alternative game.

CURLING

Indoor curling is now available in miniature sets under the brand name Unicurl, with a roll-out mat providing the appropriate surface. The sets are expensive but produce a fine leisure activity for a wide range of disability.

A cheap alternative is to use wooden discs coloured on one side and polished on the other so that they slide easily along a gymnasium floor.

WHEELCHAIR BOCCIA (Figure 5.28)

This game is now part of the international games for cerebral palsied athletes. The form of play is similar to bowls, except that the apparatus consists of small sand-filled leather balls of two distinct colours, plus a white target ball. Each ball weighs 275 grams. These balls are now available commercially, but the game can also be played with tightly packed beanbags.

The game may be played as singles, doubles or as a triples team game.

Figure 5.28   Wheelchair boccia: court layout

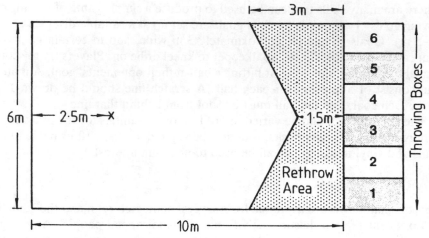

RULES (TRIPLES)

1. Each team consists of three wheelchair players. Each team receives six balls and each player must throw two balls. Each set of six balls must be of a different colour to distinguish between teams.
2. The teams are placed in alternate throwing boxes — boxes 1, 3 and 5 for one team; boxes 2, 4 and 6 for the other team.
3. A match comprises the best of 6 rounds (or an agreed number of rounds).
4. At the end of a round all team balls ending up nearer to the target ball than the nearest ball of the opponents will receive *one point per ball.*
5. When two or more balls from different teams are equidistant from the target ball (and are the nearest balls to it), each team is awarded one point per ball.
6. In the event of a tie after 6 rounds, a further round or rounds will be played on a sudden-death basis.

METHOD OF PLAY

1. Teams spin for the privilege of starting. The team winning the toss positions in throwing boxes 1, 3 and 5.
2. The player in box 1 begins by throwing the target ball. The ball must land within the court. If the target ball lands outside the court, it is placed on

the cross. All balls, including the target ball, landing within the rethrow area may be retaken immediately.

3. The starting player then throws the first ball at the target ball. The ball may be propelled in any manner, including by the use of artificial aids (chutes, etc.). After this first play, the opposing team captain may select any of his players to throw at the target ball in an attempt to beat the previous ball. Thereafter, the team with the ball nearest to the target ball has the option of continuing to throw, with the captain deciding the order of throw by his team members. The captain may elect to pass the next throw to the opposition players at any time, but if they produce a best throw the privilege of deciding the throwing order passes to them.

4. At the end of the first round the score is marked, the balls are redistributed and play recommences with the player in box 2 taking the target ball.

5. Any team ball landing outside the court or being knocked out is declared null and void.

The rules for singles and doubles are exactly the same, with the target ball throw alternating between players.

Tactics are simple: the team captains decide the order of throw according to the angles of throw by their players, and they decide whether to shoot at the target ball or place team balls to block the opponents' route to the target.

TARGET FRISBEE

A large circle is drawn on the floor with start lines set back from it at 1 m intervals. The players start at the 1 m mark and take one throw each, scoring one point if the frisbee lands fully within the circle. They then move back to the 2 m mark and repeat the sequence. If no score is made from a particular mark, the throws are repeated until one player scores. The winner may be decided on an agreed total of points.

An alternative form of play is to draw three concentric circles scoring 3 for the centre, 2 for the middle and 1 for the outer. Players throw three frisbees each from an appropriate distance to form one round of play. A game may be decided on an agreed number of rounds or on a points total.

DISTANCE FRISBEE

This is a simple field event with competitors throwing from behind a restraining line and marking distance from the point at which the frisbee first grounds.

BATINTON (Figure 5.29)

The game is suitable for mobile or paraplegic players with good arms. It may be played as singles or doubles. Rubber-tipped batinton shuttles and lightweight cork-faced bats should be used.

Figure 5.29   Batinton: court approximately 2.5 m × 9 m

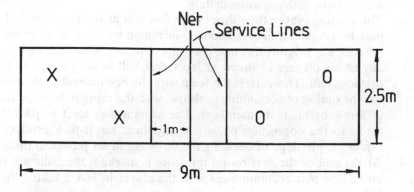

The court may be of any size and can be adapted to suit the needs of the players.

The net should be set at approximately 1.5 m. A service line is drawn parallel to the net at 1 m distance. Mobile players should cover the back court and less active players cover the front court.

RULES

1. Partners spin for service. There is a choice of side or service.
2. The service is struck from behind the service line and must land within the opposite court beyond the service line.
3. Standing players must serve underhand, but wheelchair or kneeling players may serve overhand.
4. Each player makes five consecutive serves; then the opponents take their service turn in rotation.
5. A point is scored if the shuttle lands within the court, is hit out of court or into the net, or is hit twice on either side of the net.
6. Scoring as in table tennis with 21 points winning a set. Game is best of three sets.

Many games described in this section are net games. They are, of course, suitable for playing as singles or doubles and could just as easily have been classified as individual or partner activities.

Experienced teachers will appreciate that the ideas within this chapter relate more specifically to children with fairly severe movement problems. There is, indeed, a vast array of games which can be played with little or no modification by children of mild to moderate handicap. Many of these games may be played either indoors or out of doors and provide worthwhile opportunities for lifelong leisure interest. These include: ten-pin bowling, table tennis, croquet, lawn bowls, crown bowls, boule, lawn darts, put, pitch and put. It should be remembered, too, that many leg-affected people can play golf.

In addition, there are table versions of many of the games listed in this chapter. Although these games cannot in any way be classified as active, they do stimulate arm and finger movement, linked with fine digital control; they can also provide hours of sheer fun. Wooden or plastic checkers can be substituted for the larger-scale equipment; they can be flicked and controlled by finger or ruler and kept within the table-top playing area by a wooden rim fixed around the edges of the table. A close look at the categories of games listed here should suggest miniature table versions which can be easily adapted.

Chapter 6
GROUP GAMES

The group games listed in this chapter are simple, informal games involving minimal organization. There are few formal rules and little equipment is required. They may all be played in a fairly limited space. Many of the rules will tend to evolve from the play of the children themselves and can be easily adapted to a large variety of environmental situations or to any number of players.

Group games provide good opportunities for primary-age children to practise their recently acquired personal skills in a small social setting without too great an emphasis on the competitive element in play. The emphasis should be placed on pure enjoyment of play, use of simple techniques, and, of course, depending on the locomotor ability of the children, a great deal of physical exercise can be gained. Provided that groups are always kept relatively small, all children can take part fully, regardless of their disability. Once children have learnt to perform simple games techniques it is important for them to apply these techniques in groups working with and against others of similar inclination. Socially, group games are a logical extension of work previously done with a partner, and active cooperation with others should be encouraged. In classes of very mixed disability there are excellent opportunities for children to involve their more disabled friends in an active situation by adapting techniques and rules to suit the ability level of all of the players.

In a minor games lesson for upper juniors, once a level of personal skill has been achieved, most of the lesson should be devoted to playing games in which all children can take part.

The games in this chapter have been arranged according to the skill level required and the degree of activity necessary. Several standard set formations which simplify organization and performance have been used.

The teacher should stress fun, activity, fairness, and the encouragement of skill.

CHASING GAMES

These games are useful in the warm-up phase of any lesson.

BRITISH BULLDOG (Figure 6.1)

All the children line up on the start line, except for one player who guards the centre. On the signal 'Go!' the children try to cross the centre area to reach the opposite safety line without being tagged. Any player tagged by the centre player joins him in the middle. The game continues until all players are caught, with the last player tagged being declared the winner.

Figure 6.1   British bulldog

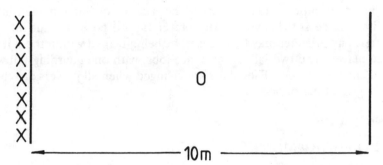

For less mobile children, a foam ball may be thrown to tag players.

CHINESE WALL (Figure 6.2)

A safety line is drawn at each end of the playing area. The object is for the players to cross from one safety line to the other without being tagged by a

Figure 6.2   Chinese wall

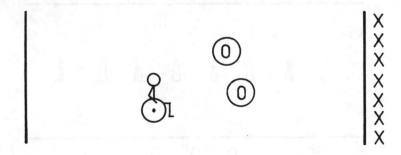

large foam ball. Three defenders guard the central space. Defenders who are walkers are restricted to remain within hoops 3 m apart, but wheelchair defenders may move to chase the attackers. When a defender calls 'Go!' the attackers must immediately try to cross the space. Defenders have one large foam ball with which they try to hit the attackers. No walker may leave his hoop except to retrieve the ball. Defenders may pass the ball between themselves to make hits easier. Those tagged remain in the centre and become extra defenders for the next turn. As the number of defenders increases, they must start at least 3 m from the nearest defender. (Walkers remain restricted to stand in hoops.)

PRISONER RELEASE

Jail consists of a large semicircle marked at one end of the playing area.

Two jailers attempt to catch the rest of the class by touching them or hitting them with a large soft beanbag. Any player tagged goes straight into jail. Thereafter, any prisoner may be released by being tagged within the jail area by a free player. The two jailers can share jobs, with one guarding jail while the other catches players. The jailers are changed when all players are caught or after a given time period.

AIMING GAMES

LINE BOMBARDMENT (Figure 6.3)

Each team lines up behind its restraining line. Different coloured skittles (i.e. red and yellow) are set up alternately in a line between the two teams. The object of the game is for each team to knock down its allotted coloured skittles before the opponents. The team to knock down its own skittles first is the winner.

Figure 6.3   Line bombardment

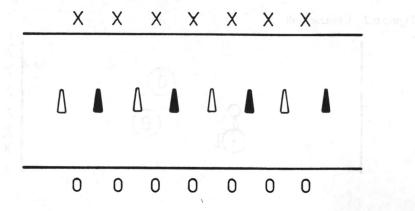

A player on one team throws or rolls the ball from behind his line at the skittles of his team. The ball is then thrown back by a player in the opposing line. If a player knocks over one of the opponents' skittles, this remains down and counts for the opponents.

CIRCLE ROLL-BALL (Figure 6.4)

Figure 6.4   Circle roll-ball

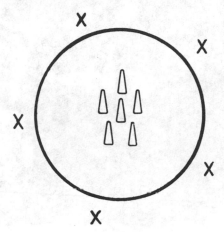

Groups of five or six players are spaced around a circle. Several plastic skittles are placed in the centre of the circle. One player rolls a ball at the skittles, attempting to knock them down. The ball is then passed to the next player in sequence until all of the skittles are down. The first group to knock down all the skittles is the winner.

TARGET ROLL-BALL (Figure 6.5)

The class is divided equally into four teams, each positioned along the side of a square, the size of which depends upon the number of players. A small goal formed by two cones is set up in the centre of each side of the square. A 10 cm playball is placed in the centre of the square. Each player is armed with a small ball. Each team tries to drive the playball through any other team's goal by hitting it with the small balls, which must be rolled along the floor. After a goal the playball is replaced in the centre and the small balls shared out. All players must throw from behind their own line, no player may be positioned within the goal, and goals may only be saved by a rolled ball, not by any part of the body. If the playball crosses a team line outside the goal, it is replaced in the centre for a restart.

Circle roll-ball

Figure 6.5   Target roll-ball

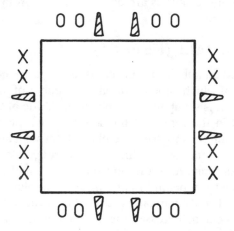

Beanbags may be used by severely disabled children with grasp problems, but the beanbags will need to be constantly retrieved from the central area by mobile players.

MOVING TARGET (Figure 6.6)

The class is divided into two teams with each team taking up position in lines facing each other.

Figure 6.6   Moving target

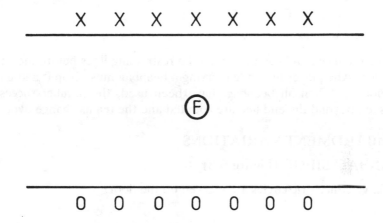

A football is placed between the teams and each player holds a tennis ball or a similar ball. On a signal, each team tries to drive the football past the opponents by hitting it with the tennis ball. A point is scored when the football rolls past a team line. The football is replaced in the centre and the tennis balls shared out ready for the game to recommence. Loose balls may be collected throughout but must be thrown from the team line. The football may not be touched in any way except by a thrown ball.

The game can also be played by four teams arranged on each side of a square.

RUNNING-THE-GAUNTLET (Figure 6.7)

The class is divided into two teams of 'runners' and 'hitters'. The hitters line up in two parallel lines approximately 10 m apart and are armed with two foam balls. The runners line up behind the start line, with a large number of beanbags. The runners each attempt to carry a beanbag to the end line while the hitters try to hit the runners below the waist with the foam balls. All balls

Figure 6.7   Running-the-gauntlet

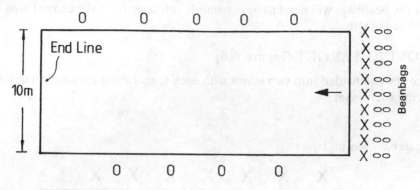

must be retrieved and passed behind the restraining lines before they can be rethrown. Any player hit while carrying a beanbag must drop it and go back for another. When all beanbags have been used, the number successfully deposited beyond the end line are counted and the teams change over.

BOMBARDMENT VARIATIONS

BEANBAG SIEGE (Figure 6.8)

Two large concentric circles are marked on the floor.

Figure 6.8   Beanbag siege

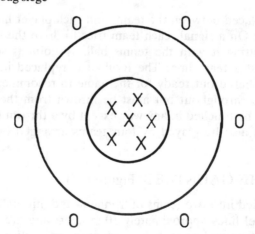

One team occupies the centre circle and the other team spreads around the outside circle. The outside team lobs a very large beanbag into the centre circle using an underhand throw while the inner team tries to stop it landing on the floor by catching it or deflecting it outside the circle. A point is scored when the beanbag lands on the floor within the centre circle, when it is returned to the outside team. After a given period of time, the teams change places.

Depending upon the level of ability of the children, and the size of the inner circle, two beanbags may be used simultaneously.

OVER-THE-NET BOMBARDMENT

There are two teams on a short badminton court with a 2 m high net between them. Each team starts the game with six large beanbags. The aim is to throw the beanbag over the net and into the other court. At the end of a set period (e.g. 3 minutes) the team with the least number of beanbags on its court is the winner. Beanbags landing out of court or passing under the net remain there until the end of the game period, then count against the throwing team. A match may be played for any agreed number of sets.

BOMBARDMENT (Figure 6.9)

The class is divided into two equal teams. Each team guards a goal line across the width of the playing area. The two goal lines should be approximately 12 m apart. The objective is to score goals past the opponents' goal line while guarding one's own goal line. Large foam balls are struck with the fist.

Figure 6.9   Bombardment

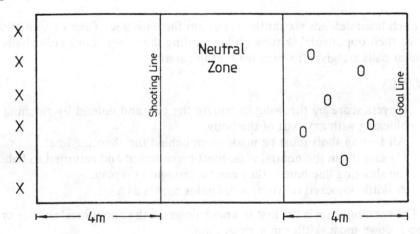

Each team starts with an equal supply of foam balls (three or four). At a given signal, the teams start bombarding their opponents' goal with balls. Loose balls must be returned to behind the shooting line before they can be brought into play.

The team scoring the most goals within a given time wins.

The game may also be played at a more advanced level by throwing light vinyl playballs.

SKITTLE BOMBARDMENT (Figure 6.10)

The playing area is divided into two shooting areas and a central zone.

Figure 6.10   Skittle bombardment

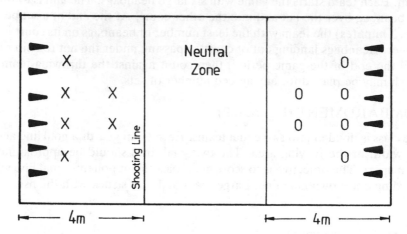

Each team defends six skittles set up on the base line. Teams try to knock down their opponents' skittles while guarding their own. Four volleyballs or similar balls are given to each team at the start.

RULES

1. Players score by throwing or rolling the ball and defend by catching or blocking with any part of the body.
2. All scoring shots must be made from behind the shooting line.
3. Loose balls in the neutral zone must be collected and returned to behind the shooting line before they can be brought into play.
4. A skittle knocked down by a defender counts as a hit.

The winning team is the first to knock down all the opponents' skittles or to knock down most skittles in a given time.

BOMBARDMENT (VARIATION) (Figure 6.11)

Two goals are set up with gym benches laid on their side at each end of the gymnasium. Several benches are laid together to make a wide goal of some 8 m.

Figure 6.11   Bombardment (variation)

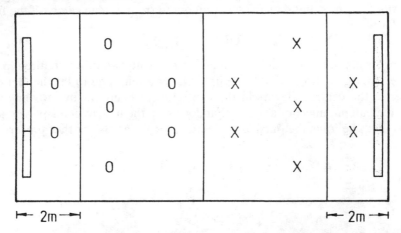

A zone line is marked 2 m from each goal, within which only the goal-keepers may play. Two goalkeepers are named in each team and they should be kneeling or wheelchair players only. Wheelchair goalkeepers may use a hockey stick to extend their reach.

Players on each side are restricted to play in their own half between the centre line and the goal zone.

At the start each team has an equal supply of large foam or vinyl playballs (four or five each). On the signal to start they throw, roll or bounce balls to score goals by hitting their opponents' benches. Players may move anywhere within their own half to retrieve balls, and balls may be thrown in from any position in their own half. All loose balls within the end zones must be retrieved and brought into play by one of the goalkeepers. Goalkeepers should be changed at the end of each time period.

Many variations in rules exist to allow for individual disabilities and throwing regulations may vary within each team (e.g. certain players may be allowed to carry the ball up to the centre line before shooting).

DODGEBALL VARIATIONS

ALL-IN-DODGEBALL

The game is played with a large beanbag or large light ball. A mobile player begins the game by trying to hit other players below the waist with the ball. Each player thus caught puts on a coloured braid and joins forces in catching the remainder. After the second player is caught, the catchers may not run with the ball but must interpass to move nearer to players they intend to hit. Wheelchair players with poor arms should be pushed by runners, but both players must be tagged before they are both caught. The last player to be caught is the winner.

A useful variation is to allow players to defend themselves by striking the ball with their fists, but they may be caught out from a clean catch off the fist.

CIRCLE DODGEBALL (ROLLING)

Five or six children kneel or sit around a circle with two other children in the centre. A large ball is rolled by a circle player attempting to hit the feet of a player in the centre. Players in the centre avoid being hit by moving away from the ball but may not use their hands to stop the ball. When a player is hit by the ball, he joins the outside circle and is replaced by another player.

Circle dodgeball

IRISH CRICKET

One player is armed with a light bat and the other players attempt to hit him below the waist with a foam ball. No player may run with the ball in his possession, so passing is required to get near the striker. The striker may move anywhere he wishes and may also protect himself with the bat. Any player hitting the striker with the ball or making a clean catch from a hit off the bat takes his place. The new striker is allowed to move 2 m from the ball before the game recommences.

Irish cricket

BOX DODGEBALL

Two lines are marked approximately 6 m apart and parallel to each other, and a circle of 1.5 m in diameter is drawn halfway between the lines.

The group is split half on one line and half on the other, with one child standing or sitting inside the circle (Figure 6.12). The object is to hit the centre player below the waist with a large foam ball while he avoids the ball without moving outside the circle. When he is hit or moves outside the circle

Figure 6.12   Box dodgeball with centre player within a circle between teams

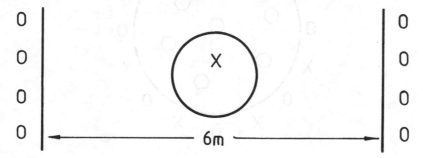

he is replaced by another player in turn. Two balls may be brought into play to speed up the game.

Wheelchair players try to spin their chairs to shield their legs away from the ball.

The game may also be played with the centre player operating within a 1 m lane between the two teams (Figure 6.13).

Figure 6.13   Box dodgeball with centre player within 1 m lane between teams

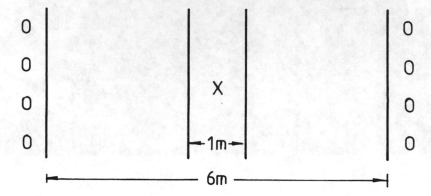

TEAM CIRCLE DODGEBALL

The players divide into two equal groups. One team forms a large circle while the member of the other team spread themselves within the confines of the

Figure 6.14   Variation of team circle dodgeball

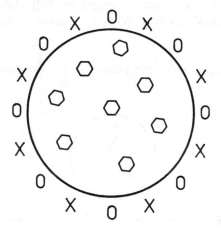

circle. The circle players attempt to hit the players within the circle below the waist by throwing a foam ball. Players within the circle dodge and move to try to avoid being hit but cannot leave the circle or use their hands to stop the ball. Loose balls are retrieved by members of the circle but must be passed out to the circle before they can be thrown. All hits below the waist are counted, and the teams change places after a set period.

VARIATION *(Figure 6.14)*

Players are divided into three groups with one group scattered inside a circle formed by the other two groups (Figure 6.14).

Players in the outer circle try to hit the team players inside with a foam ball. Players who are hit join the outer circle and help them. The last player left within the circle is the group winner.

THREE-COURT DODGEBALL (Figure 6.15)

A large foam ball or soft cloth-covered ball is safest to use.

Figure 6.15   Three-court dodgeball

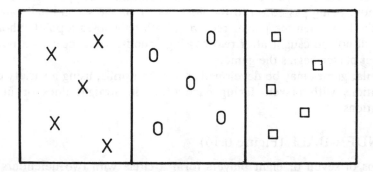

The playing area is divided into three courts.

The class is divided into three equal teams with one team in each court. The objective is for the teams in the outside courts to throw the ball and hit players of the team in the centre court. A point is scored for each player hit. The ball may be passed among the attacking players to bring it nearer to the centre court and make it easier to hit the central players. After a given period of time, each team takes a turn in the centre court. The team against which the lowest number of hits is recorded wins.

Rules may be amended to allow less mobile players in the centre court to defend themselves with their hands. Only hits on body or legs register.

SIMPLE BALL GAMES
CHASE-THE-BALL

Players are arranged in a large circle spaced about 2 m apart. Players may stand, kneel or sit according to their disability. Two balls are started at opposite points on the circle and passed quickly around the circle in the same direction until one ball catches up with the other. Any player being 'caught' with both balls is awarded a point, and the game restarts with the first ball being given at least three places' start around the circle. The player with the least points at the end of the game is the winner. Passes used should be appropriate to the individual ability of players and for severely disabled children two large beanbags may be substituted.

VARIATION

A fairly large number of players (nine or more) form a circle. For practice in speed of handling, large beanbags should be used when younger children are playing. A nominated player is handed the beanbag ball which is named after him (e.g. Tom's ball). He starts the ball being passed around the circle. When the ball returns to him he starts if off again, counts the next two passes, then starts off a second ball after the first. Any ball that is dropped must be picked up before being passed on to the next player. If the second ball catches up with the first, then the player receiving both balls loses a point. Should the first ball not be caught after two passing rounds, Tom receives a point and another player begins the game.

Similar games may be developed as two-ball drills, using a variety of floor formations with players facing each other in straight lines or in zigzag formations.

WANDER-BALL (Figure 6.16)

Groups of seven or eight players form a circle with two defenders in the centre. The aim is to pass a large ball or beanbag across the circle while the two defenders attempt to intercept it. If a defending player touches the ball or a player while in possession of the ball, he moves out and, in rotation, is replaced by another player. More handicapped defenders may be replaced after a time period. Players should be encouraged to pass the ball quickly through gaps and make feint passes to create gaps; they should not be allowed to pass above head height.

KEEP-THE-BALL-IN

The group of players should all kneel in a closely knit circle. The object is to push, roll or punch a large foam ball out of the circle past other players while preventing it from being knocked past oneself. With a large group two balls may be used simultaneously.

Figure 6.16   Wander-ball

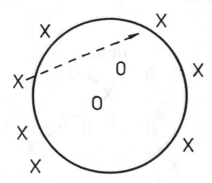

TEAM KEEP-THE-BALL-IN (Figure 6.17)

Players are divided into two teams with one team kneeling or sitting around one half of a large circle and the other team occupying the opposite half circle. Each team tries to punch or roll a large foam ball out of the opposite half circle past its opponents. A point is gained for each ball that passes the opponents below head height. Balls may not be thrown but may bounce across the circle.

Figure 6.17   Team keep-the-ball-in

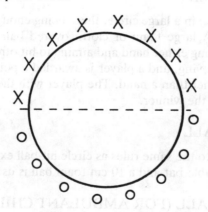

Two or more balls may be used at once if the skill level is sufficiently high.

A similar game may be played by ambulant children, with the ball being kicked or hit with a crutch below waist level.

CIRCLE PASS-OUT (Figure 6.18)

The object is for the thrower in the centre of the circle (3 m radius) to pass the ball to the players outside the circle while the guards inside the circle try to

Figure 6.18   Circle pass-out

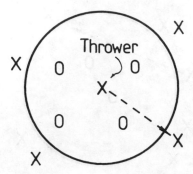

intercept the ball. The ball must be passed out below head height, otherwise any form of pass may be used. Each successful catch is scored and the ball returned to the centre thrower. After a given period of time, the two teams change places.

This can provide a useful opportunity to teach marking by the guards and finding space by the outside players. If necessary, the outside players may be restricted to remain within 2 m of the circle to ease the marking problem for the guards.

CIRCLE HIT-BALL

Players stand or kneel in a large circle, there being enough players to prevent gaps in the circle. A large foam or cloth-covered ball is batted across the circle, the players using either hand and aiming to hit others in the circle. The ball must be kept moving, and a player is awarded a point if the ball touches some part of him other than a hand. The player with the lowest score after a set period of time is the winner.

CIRCLE BAT-BALL

The game is played to the same rules as circle hit-ball except that each player is armed with a suitable bat and a 10 cm foam ball is used.

CIRCLE KICK-BALL (FOR AMBULANT CHILDREN)

Players are arranged standing in a circle formation. One player is given a foam football, which is placed on the ground in front of his kicking foot. Play commences when the ball is kicked towards other players in the circle. Players may catch the ball to defend themselves, then place it on the ground ready to kick. A point is scored if a player is hit anywhere other than on the hand or foot or if the ball goes between the legs outside the circle. The player with the lowest score at the end of the game is the winner.

Non-ambulant children can take part by kneeling and using a bat to strike the ball or protect their body.

HIT-THE-KNEES

The group form a large circle with each child half a metre away from the next. All the children take up a high-kneeling position and face the centre. The object is, while guarding oneself, to roll or bounce a large playball so that it hits another player on the knees or thighs. No player may attempt to hit the child to his immediate left or right on the circle. After a set period of time, the player with the least hits scored against him is the winner.

CRAB KICK-BALL

Two teams sit on one of two parallel lines approximately 5 m apart. The object is to kick large foam balls past the other team. All players must sit on the floor, feet pointing at the opposing team, hands on the floor. Depending on ability, more than one ball may be in play simultaneously. A ball may be blocked by the feet or any part of the body except the hands. Use of the hand to prevent a score (except by accident) results in a point to the other team.

TOWER-BALL

Players form themselves into a large circle about 4 m in diameter. A large skittle is placed inside a small circle in the centre (diameter 1 m) and one child defends this skittle. The defender may use any part of his body to protect the skittle but may not infringe the circle. Players in the outer ring try to knock over the skittle and may pass the ball to each other to move the defender, or they may shoot directly. Attacking players must not shoot from within the circle of players, and loose balls must be passed out of the circle before a shot may be taken. When the skittle is hit, the defender is replaced by another player.

GUARD-THE-CAPTAIN

Arrange the group in a large circle around a small mat (1 m × 2 m) located in the centre. Two players are picked out as the captain and his guard. In a mixed ability group the captain should be the most disabled of the pair.

The captain takes his place on the mat (standing, kneeling or in a wheel-chair) and the guard patrols the perimeter of the mat. The circle players try to hit the captain with a large soft ball while the guard protects him by blocking the ball with any part of his body. The guard may not touch the mat, and loose balls must be returned to the circle to be thrown. If the captain is hit, he is replaced by another player from the circle. The game can become a fast passing game if the circle players are taught to pass the ball around or across to move the guard out of line.

POISON-BALL

The class is divided into two parallel lines facing each other at a distance apart appropriate to their passing ability.

The teacher turns his back to the teams and signals 'Go!'. On the signal, a ball is passed back and forward between the teams until the teacher calls 'Stop!'. Whichever team has the ball loses a point to its opponents. The game should continue for a given period of time or up to a set number of points.

The type of pass to be used can be nominated beforehand to suit the ability of the children. Deliberate poor passing should be penalized by loss of a point, and one child can be nominated as referee to observe that no cheating occurs.

GUARD-BALL (Figure 6.19)

Two parallel lines are drawn on the floor approximately 4 m apart, or cones may be used to mark the corners of the playing area.

Figure 6.19   Guard-ball

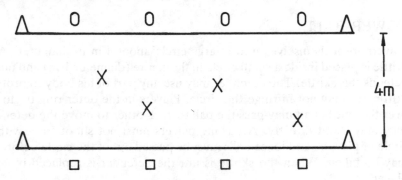

The class is divided into three equal teams with one team positioned between the lines and the other two teams each stationed outside one end line. The players outside the lines try to pass a large ball back and forward between the team players in the centre. Any form of pass is allowed, but the ball may not be passed above head height. One point is scored each time the ball passes successfuly through the team guarding the centre. Teams change roles after a given time period. The winning team is the team with the least points against it.

ISLAND-BALL (Figure 6.20)

This is a static passing game. Two or three defenders attempt to intercept a ball or large beanbag while it is passed around the remaining players. The

Figure 6.20   Island-ball

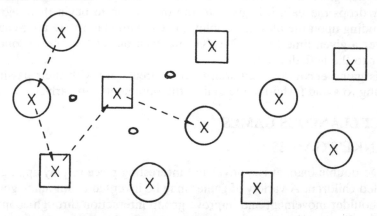

standing or kneeling players are each restricted within a hoop, and wheelchair players are placed on small mats. When a defender intercepts the ball or touches an 'island' player when in possession of the ball, he changes places with either the passer or the touched player. Islands should be placed 2 m apart to keep passing simple, and players need to be encouraged to pass quickly and make feint passes.

At a reasonable level of skill, players who fail to catch the ball are replaced and become 'chasers'.

CIRCLE NETBALL (Figure 6.21)

Two netball rings are spaced over 10 m apart. The two teams are arranged as above with each player positioned inside a hoop (or circle if in a wheelchair). X1 starts by passing the ball to the player in the adjacent circle and so on until the ball reaches X2, who is allowed one shot at the netball ring to score. The

Figure 6.21   Circle netball

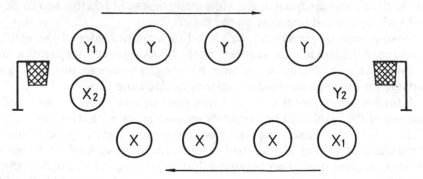

ball is then given to Y1, who repeats the sequence until Y2 has a shot. If any player drops the ball, it is given to the opposition to begin their sequence. Depending upon the players' mobility, each team may rotate after each shot or after a given time (e.g. X2 to X1 and each player then moves one place nearer to the netball ring).

This game encourages children to take great care with their passing and catching to avoid forfeiting the ball to the opponents too early.

MISCELLANEOUS GAMES

BLANKET GAMES

A large double blanket is a novel and interesting piece of play apparatus for disabled children. A variety of games may be invented to stimulate good arm and shoulder movement and improve group interaction through cooperative activity. Teams of four players stationed at each corner of a blanket can engage in a good range of play activities.

BLANKET WAVING

The children kneel at each corner and pick up the blanket with both hands. The most efficient grasp is with the hands in the pronated position, palms facing the floor. By simultaneously raising their arms the children can make the blanket fill and balloon up into the air. A steady rhythmical raising and lowering of the arms will cause the blanket to rise and fall. The children may then be encouraged to experiment at producing varying patterns of flow with the blanket. Alternate raising and lowering from each end will produce ripples and waves and the children will be encouraged to try out different forms of timing the lift from corner to corner, side to side, and in individual sequence. There are interesting possibilities for young children to synchronize their movements to different types of music or singing chants.

BLANKET TOSS

A large ball is placed in the centre of the blanket and each group tosses the ball in the air and catches it again. How many times can you toss and catch the ball without the ball bouncing on the floor?

Small groups of players can be placed on opposite sides of the blanket. They throw the ball into the blanket and the blanket group tries to toss a catch to the other side, and so on. A large beanbag produces an intriguing game suitable for the most disabled of children to catch and toss.

A further development is to have each team of four trying to toss a ball up and out of the blanket to be caught by another group with its blanket.

If the blanket is raised and stretched rather more tightly, the children can experiment at rolling a large ball in different ways around or across the blanket. A great deal of cooperative effort can be engendered in this way, as the children work together to produce a predetermined pattern of ball rolling.

The use of a low net allows for further variation as two groups try to toss a ball over the net for the other group to catch in the blanket. Obviously this net game allows for a wide range of cooperative activity; alternatively it may be a competitive adapted form of simple volleyball.

ARCHBALL ROUNDERS VARIATION (Figure 6.22)

The area of play is marked by two parallel lines 10 m apart. The class is divided into a batting team and a fielding team. The players in the batting team line up one behind the other on the end line, with all of the fielders positioned behind the restraining line.

Figure 6.22   Archball rounders variation

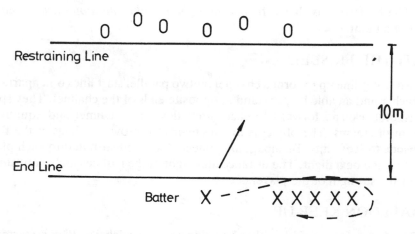

The first batting player starts on the end line and throws (or kicks) a volleyball into the playing area, then attempts to move around his own team line as many times as possible before he is out. He counts one run for each time he passes both end men in his team.

The player who fields the ball remains still while his team mates form a line in front of him. The ball is passed along the line overhead to the back player who then calls 'Stop!' and the batter is out. The fielders must remain behind the restraining line until the ball is thrown by the batter. The batter's score is then counted; he joins the far end of the line and is replaced by the next batter in turn.

After all the batters have had their turn the teams change places.

TEAM FRISBEE (Figure 6.23)

Two courts are marked at an appropriate distance apart. Each team occupies a court. The aim is to score a point by grounding the frisbee in the opponents' court. Players attempt to catch the frisbee or deflect it out of court.

Figure 6.23   Team frisbee

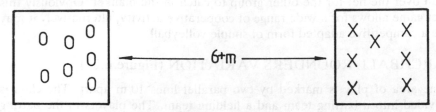

Loose frisbees may be collected at any time but must be thrown from within the team court. A frisbee which is dropped by a defender but lands outside the court does not score. Stray frisbees do not count against the thrower.

The basic rule is that a frisbee must *land within the opponents' court* to score a point.

HIT-THE-FRISBEE

Two teams line up to form a channel on two parallel start lines 6 m apart. The teacher and an able helper stand at opposite ends of the channel. They spin a frisbee back and forward to each other down the channel and equidistant from the teams. The object is for the teams to throw beanbags at the flying frisbee to score hits. Beanbags are collected and redistributed to each player before the next flight. The distance and flight of the frisbee can be adjusted to suit the strength of the players.

BALLOON KEEP-UP

The players form a circle either kneeling or in wheelchairs. Play is started by one player tapping a balloon into the air. The object is for the players to keep the balloon in the air as long as possible. No player may tap it twice in succession.

VARIATIONS

1. If the balloon hits the floor or is tapped too hard and goes outside the circle, the last player to touch it is awarded a point. At the end of the game the player with least points is the winner.
2. Each group is given a target some distance away into which the balloon must be tapped. The size and height of the target will vary according to the ability of the children (basket, low netball ring, etc.). One player starts by tapping the balloon into the air, then the whole group cooperates in trying to keep the balloon up while manoeuvring it towards the target. If the balloon touches the floor or misses the target, the group must start again.

Teachers should be aware of the dangers of hyperacoustic children being frightened by a bursting balloon.

These variations are suitable for young children (4–6 years) or severely disabled children.

TOWER BUILDING

This is a static bowling game. Six players sit or kneel in a circle inside which six wooden blocks are placed on end in various situations.

The first player rolls a large ball, trying to knock over a block. If he succeeds, that block is placed in the centre of the circle and becomes the first brick in the tower.

The next player attempts to hit a block; if he is successful, this is placed as the second brick in the centre tower.

The game proceeds until all blocks are on the tower. The next player in the sequence then rolls the ball, attempting to knock down the tower to win a point. If he fails, the attempt is passed to the next player. No player may break down the tower until it is complete.

FILL-THE-BOX

All the children sit within a marked circle, which has a box placed in the centre. The teacher scatters beanbags all over the room. On a signal the children collect the beanbags and fill the box as quickly as possible. Each child may only collect one beanbag at a time.

A large class should be divided into small groups, each with a box, and compete for the highest number of beanbags collected.

POISON SKITTLE

Groups of four children kneel in a small circle on a mat with a plastic skittle in the centre. The children then all join hands. The aim is to pull other players' hands and arms onto the skittle to knock it down while resisting for oneself. Each time the skittle falls a point is awarded against the player responsible.

To compete in this activity children must have good arms and be capable of holding a balanced kneeling position.

RELAYS

In the normal school setting, relay activities are games in which groups or teams of children compete against each other. Each child performs some prescribed motor skill over a clearly defined course, with each team member taking his turn until the whole team has finished. A relay race is a test of speed and accuracy under competitive pressure, with each child contributing to the total team effort. Although children may derive a great deal of enjoyment from relays, and they can be used to heighten motivation to perform, I suggest that the highly competitive element should be reduced or eliminated for most disabled children because increased excitement may often hinder skill learning. This is particularly true for certain types of cerebral palsy. The stereotyped movement patterns and drill formations which make up relays can be used more effectively to set up skill learning situations where cooperation with team mates is of paramount importance. The key factor for the teacher to consider is for which qualities of performance he should award points. If the speed factor and racing element are reduced, then greater emphasis can be placed on quality of performance in terms of skill, accuracy and team cooperation. If a competitive motive is desired, points can be awarded not necessarily to the group that finishes first but to the group that plays with good style and produces fewer errors. In this way the children may be stimulated to greater concentration in trying to link together several sequences of techniques without making errors of judgement. Where the emphasis is placed on quality of movement rather than on speed, the children must exert greater self-control in helping others within the group to perform successfully, be patient in waiting for their turn, and concentrate on getting a sequence of events correct within the rules controlling the activity.

Relays organized in this way provide a useful reinforcement to simple skills recently acquired by placing the skills in the context of an enjoyable game.

A number of principles should be considered before a series of relay formations are used within the games programme:

1. Select simple, already well learned skills appropriate to the level of skill required. Group formations should be organized to preclude the necessity for running or too much movement.
2. Ensure that the size of the groups is small (six or less) to give all children the maximum opportunity to participate.
3. Place the most severely disabled children in the middle of a group so that they are not involved in the excitement of starting and finishing.
4. Clearly establish the objective of any relay before starting. Carefully explain the emphasis on points allocation and the criteria for success (number of successful tries, first finished, etc.). If a winner is required, lay down clear targets for achievement.
5. Starting formations and finishing positions must be clear. Stress any penalties for failing to complete a sequence (dropping a ball, giving a poor pass, etc.).
6. In selecting groups of players match them up for size, ability and disability where possible (e.g. two wheelchairs, one crutch or sticks, two kneeling players, plus one runner).
7. On first introducing a new formation, be prepared to proceed through the sequence of skill pattern and player's movement in slow motion until the pattern is clearly understood.

8. Once a formation has been set up, use the same arrangement for several different relays to save time spent in organizing the children into groups and to reinforce their understanding of that formation by repetition.

In dealing with younger children in the junior school, emphasis must be placed on quality of performance in beating their own group score without reference to other groups. Points may be awarded, by whatever criteria, each time improvement is observed. Older children enjoy competition much more and, provided that fairness is clear to all, winners and losers may be recognized.

There are many relay formations that can be organized to produce good practice conditions without too much running involvement. These are now described in more detail.

FILE RELAYS

This is probably the simplest form of relay formation for skill practice, and it can be adapted in many ways. One player at a time works with the next player in line, starting as soon as the previous player has completed the course. The winning team is usually the one which has all its players over the finish first, but in a less competitive situation the rules may be changed to emphasize accuracy and quality of performance in gaining points scores.

The degree of physical activity involved in a file relay is controlled by the size of the group and the length of the course to be covered. Groups of four or five children ensure an adequate frequency of practice, and the course distance should be adjusted in accordance with the locomotor problems of the children. Adapting these two variables can produce a game ranging from a very static situation geared to accuracy to a highly active race with fitness objectives.

Several file relays are illustrated. These can easily be adapted for a range of skill practices and modified to become quiet or vigorous activities.

BATON RELAY (SHUTTLE FORMATION)

The players line up as shown in Figure 6.24.

Figure 6.24   Baton relay (shuttle formation)

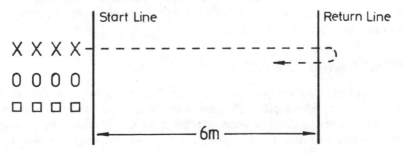

All teams line up behind the start line. The first player in each file moves as fast as possible to the return line and back, hands a beanbag to the front player, then moves to the back of the file. Each player performs in sequence until the team finishes.

VARIATION 1

Each player carries a beanbag and drops it into a basket on the return line.

VARIATION 2

While covering the course, each player performs a simple skill, like bouncing or dribbling a ball.

VARIATION 3

Each player dribbles a ball by bouncing, drops it through a low netball ring, collects the ball and returns to pass to the next player in line.

BEANBAG POTATO RACE (Figure 6.25)

Figure 6.25   Beanbag potato race

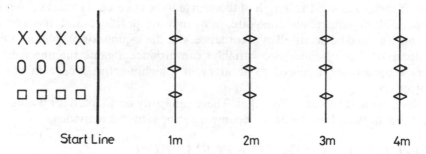

Beanbags are placed on each of four lines spaced apart. The first player moves forward and collects all of the beanbags in any order, returning to hand them to the next player. The second player returns the beanbags to their original position and races back. The third player collects the beanbags, and so on until each player has had a turn.

LINE RELAY (Figure 6.26)

Player No. 1 passes an object back through the team in a prescribed manner until it reaches the back player. He races to the front of the team and sets off the sequence once again. The winning team is the one in which the players are the first to finish in their original positions without dropping the object.

Figure 6.26   Line relay

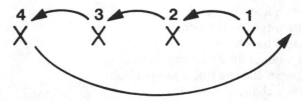

VARIATION (Figure 6.27)

At each end of the file, place a receptacle. One should contain several objects, such as beanbags or small balls. Player No. 4 picks out an object and passes it through the teams to No. 1, who aims at the empty receptacle. Player No. 4 then picks out another object and repeats the procedure until the rear container is empty. Players then change places to take turns at front and rear of the file. Points may be awarded for accurate aiming and deducted for dropping the object, thus ensuring that the children take greater care in handling and passing.

Figure 6.27   Variation of line relay

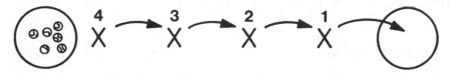

The size of receptacle and the distance from the front player may be changed to increase the challenge as the children improve.

TARGET RELAY (LINE FORMATION)

The class is organized into small groups of four or five, each arranged in single file facing a target. The player at the front of the file has one throw at the target and then moves to the rear of his file. The sequence continues until all players have taken their throw, and an agreed number of rounds can be played. If a ball is used, one player stands near the target and returns the ball to the next player in sequence. The retrieving player takes his turn at the end of each round.

Each team counts the number of hits on target and keeps a running total.

The apparatus used, the distance from the target, the size of the target, the height of the target, and the style of throw used should be adjusted to the ability of the children to guarantee successful performance.

Suitable activities include:

- beanbag into a hoop on the floor;
- beanbag into a tyre on the floor;
- beanbag into a basket;
- beanbag at a target drawn on the wall;
- beanbag thrown above a line 2 m up a wall;
- ball rolled at a chair;
- ball bounced into a basket;
- ball tossed into a basket.

CORNER SPRY (Figure 6.28)

The players in each group are placed in file behind a line facing the leader, who is positioned approximately 3 m from the centre of the line. The leader, X1, passes a ball or beanbag to the first player in the line (X2), who immediately passes it back. The object is then passed to the next player in sequence (X3) and so on until it reaches the last player in the line (X5). The last player with the object moves out and replaces the leader, who moves into the line at X2, and the whole line moves along one place. The passing sequence then continues until each player has had a turn as leader and all players have returned to their original starting positions. Points may be awarded for the first team to finish or to each leader who completes a passing sequence without the object being dropped.

Figure 6.28   Corner spry

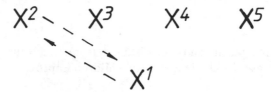

Any wheelchair player unable to change places easily may be wheeled into his position as leader. The type of object and style of pass used can be adjusted to the ability within each group.

SHUTTLE RELAY (Figure 6.29)

Teams of six players are divided into two half-teams in file facing each other.

The even numbers are placed in file behind one start line with the odd numbers placed behind another. The No. 1 player in each file moves as fast as possible to the opposite start line and starts off the No. 2 player by passing an

Figure 6.29   Shuttle relay

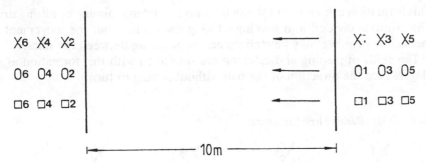

object such as a beanbag or ball. Player No. 1 then moves to the back of that file. The sequence continues until all the players have completed the course.

In the interests of fair play, the teams should be matched in ability at each phase. For example, all the No. 1 players may be wheelchair racers, the No. 2 players may be in electric chairs, the No. 3 players may be walkers, and so on. If an object is passed to start off each runner, the relay may be run as a cooperative effort not to commit errors, or as a competition to see which team finishes first.

OBSTACLE RELAY (STAGES 2 AND 3) (Figure 6.30)

Each player in turn completes an obstacle course until the whole team finishes. The obstacles chosen should be appropriate to the disabilities of the children.

Figure 6.30   Obstacle relay

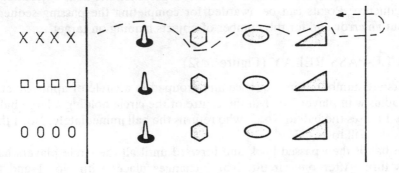

Skittles, traffic cones, small ramps, flat sticks and hoops can be arranged in a variety of ways to make an obstacle course.

PARALLEL LINE FORMATION (Figure 6.31)

This formation can be used for any throwing, catching, aiming or hitting drill. The group is divided into two lines facing each other, but the movement of the ball or beanbag may be straight across or zigzag between the lines.

The skills of passing and catching are simplified with this formation as all players face the direction of the ball without having to turn.

Figure 6.31   Parallel line formation

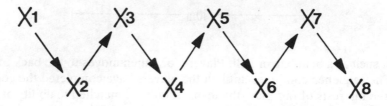

VARIATION 1

If greater movement is required at a more advanced level, the formation can be used as a pass-and-follow drill. Two players are stationed at the start point, one behind the other. The first player passes the ball and follows it to replace the position of the receiver. With two players in the start position the formation remains constant.

VARIATION 2

A target is placed 2 m from the last player. Six objects are placed beside the first player. Player number 1 starts by passing the object across the files until it reaches the last player, who aims it at the target; then the next object begins the sequence. Points can be awarded for completing the passing sequence without an error and for the number of objects landing on target.

CIRCLE-PASS RELAY (Figure 6.32)

Players are numbered in sequence and grouped in a circle of approximately 3 m radius with player No. 1 in the centre of the circle holding a large ball.

No. 1 passes the ball to No. 2, who returns the ball immediately. No. 1 then passes the ball to No. 3.

The ball is then passed back and forward until all the circle players have had a turn. After one circuit, No. 2 changes places with No. 1 and the sequence continues until all players have had a turn in the centre. When the last player finishes he holds up the ball to indicate a team finish.

The relay game may be played using a steady progression of passing styles

Figure 6.32   Circle-pass relay

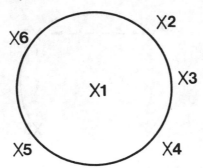

appropriate to the age and ability of the children. They may range from rolling to bouncing and throwing. Initially the sequence may begin with large beanbags, but as skill develops balls of different textures and size should be introduced.

With younger children the different groups should not compete against each other and speed of play ought not to be emphasized. Accuracy of throwing and catching is more important, and the challenge could be to see which teams complete a sequence without making an error.

CIRCLE-BALL RELAY

Players are organized in a circle formation with a 2 m space between players. One player starts with a ball or beanbag and passes it to the next player who shouts 'One!' as he catches it. The ball is passed around the circle with each player calling the number of his consecutive catch. If the ball is dropped, the count starts again.

The winning team may be the first to an agreed total (e.g. 25) or the team with the highest count after a set period of time.

TARGET RELAY (CIRCLE FORMATION)

Players are arranged in a circle with a target in the centre. Each player makes one throw at the target; the ball is then returned to the next player in sequence, and so on.

PASS-AND-FOLLOW RELAYS

These relays are useful in encouraging skill in throwing and catching, allied with supporting moves by all players. Several formations may be used, but only two are described.

1. Players are arranged in a square with two players at one corner (Figure 6.33).

Figure 6.33   Pass-and-follow relay: formation 1

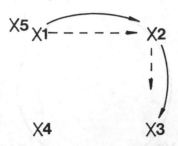

Player No. 1 starts by passing to No. 2, then moves quickly after the ball to replace No. 2. No. 2 then passes to No. 3 and follows after the ball.

The winning team may be the first to achieve a set number of passes or the team that achieves the highest number of passes without error in a given time.

Mixed ability groups may play together if allowance is made for different types of pass and the form of locomotion within any one group.

2.   Players are arranged in a circle with one player in the centre and two players in file at the starting point (Figure 6.34).

Figure 6.34   Pass-and-follow relay: formation 2

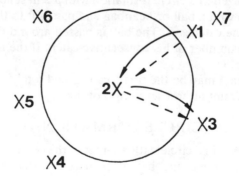

Player No. 1 starts by passing to No. 2 in the centre of the circle. He then follows quickly to replace No. 2. No. 2 then passes the ball to No. 3 and replaces him. No. 3 then passes the ball to No. 1 who is now in the centre and again follows his pass.

This formation stimulates a great deal of concentration in order to gain the correct sequence. The children will need to be drilled in slow motion throughout the sequence until they understand the movement pattern. The main points to teach are: always follow your pass immediately and always pass the ball through the centre player before it is next passed to the outer circle.

Accuracy and correct movement patterns must be achieved. The speed factor only interferes with learning if it is introduced too early. Award points to a team that makes no catching errors and gets the sequence correct over one round.

TEAM PASSING VERSUS TEAM RUNNING (Figure 6.35)

One team is positioned in two parallel facing lines about 2–3 m apart. The other team runs a relay race around four cones while the first team makes as many passes as possible before all the runners have completed the course. Teams then change places and the team making the most passes wins. All passes should be loudly counted.

Each runner must be tagged by the incoming runner before he may set off around the course. Wheelchair players, including electric chair users, should wheel the course under their own power.

Figure 6.35   Team passing versus team running

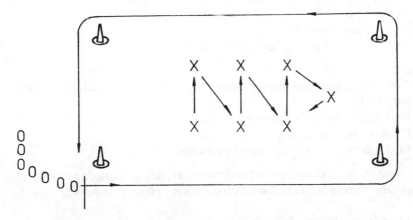

The passing team must pass in sequence to players in the opposite line and may be standing, sitting or kneeling. Any form of pass is allowed and either a large ball or beanbag can be used.

TEAM SCORING VERSUS TEAM RUNNING

There are many variations of this type of relay, depending upon the levels of skill and mobility of the players. The basic points of organization are as follows:

1.   One team scores points by aiming at targets continuously.

2. The opponents complete any type of slalom course in turn until all the players in their team have finished.
3. The players in the aiming team complete their score when the last running or wheeling player crosses the finish line.
4. The teams then change places and attempt to beat their opponents' score.

The score of the aiming team will depend upon the accuracy of its players and the time allowed, which is controlled by the speed of the opponents.

VARIATIONS

Aiming team

Stage 1
1. Aim beanbags into a hoop — circle formation.
2. Aim beanbags into a large box.
3. Throw beanbags through a netball ring 1–1.5 m high — semicircle formation.
4. Aim beanbags at a wall target.

Stage 2
1. Throw large beanbags through a ring 1.5 m high.
2. Throw large foam balls into a box.
3. Throw plastic balls into a box.
4. Throw plastic balls through a netball ring.

Stage 3
1. Pass a large beanbag to each other in a set formation, either circular or in parallel lines.
2. Pass a large ball in sequence any style.
3. Pitch quoits onto a peg at floor level.
4. Pitch quoits at a wall-mounted pegboard.

At each stage of development it is necessary for at least one mobile player continually to return the apparatus to players behind restraining lines.

Running team (Figure 6.36)
Although the word 'running' is used, players will cover the course under their own power in a manner appropriate to their normal mode of locomotion.

Course (c): each player in turn moves around the front player, around the back player, then returns to his own place.

Course (d): each player moves around the four cones in turn. As the runner passes cone 4, the next player starts.

Obviously the length and type of course will be varied according to the mobility of the children. Two courses of differing length may also be used simultaneously for runners or wheelchair players. So long as the two teams are equally balanced by ability, many such variations may be used within a single game.

Figure 6.36   Courses followed by team runners

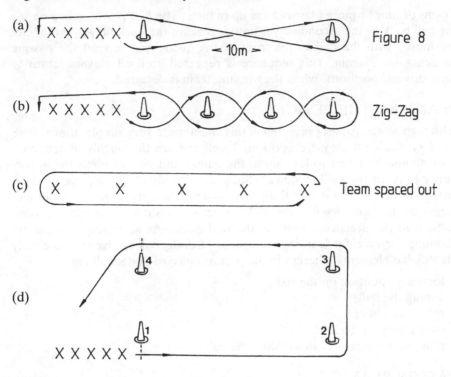

CATCH-AND-SIT (Figure 6.37)

Four or five players stand or sit in a close line one behind the other facing a leader who holds a ball. The leader is 2 m from the first man in line. The leader throws the ball to the first player, who returns it and then sits down. The sequence is repeated to the second player, and so on. When all players have passed the ball the leader places it on the ground and moves to the back of the queue; then the first player replaces him as leader. The sequence is repeated until all players have had a turn as leader; the team completing the sequence first is the winner.

Ambulant and non-ambulant players may be mixed through the teams, but non-ambulant players obviously are sitting or kneeling throughout.

Figure 6.37   Catch-and-sit

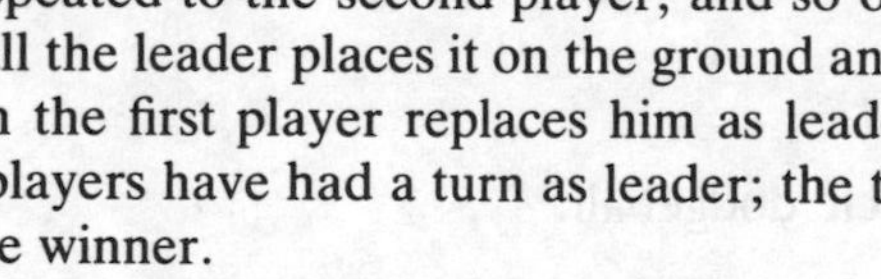

$$X^L \quad X^1 \ X^2 \ X^3 \ X^4$$

$$\longleftarrow 2m \longrightarrow$$

LINE PASS

Teams of four or more players form up in lines. The first player in line passes the ball back to the second player until it reaches the back player in the line. He moves with the ball to the front of the queue and sets off the passing sequence once again. This sequence is repeated until all players return to their original positions, when the winning team is declared.

PLANNING THE LESSON

Although all the games presented in this chapter are very simple, they will be more enjoyable if they are performed well and are thoroughly understood. Care should be taken to lead up to the games and give children the opportunity to learn the skills required. Such learning should take place in small groups to reinforce the social aspects, and the activity should contain elements of the game itself if the children are to positively transfer the skills learned in the practice activity to the real game. As an example of careful planning for efficient learning, the game of dodgeball is given. The clearly identifiable elements inherent in the performance of dodgeball are:

focusing attention on the ball;
aiming the ball;
rolling the ball;
controlling the ball;
gross motor activities in avoiding the ball.

LESSON PLAN

Introductory activity
All-in dodgeball

Skills training
1.   In threes, cooperative practice in rolling and stopping.
2.   Pig-in-the-middle. Avoid ball by rolling, spinning chairs, etc.
3.   Competition. First 3–20 consecutive passes or number of passes in one minute.

Final game
Several games of circle dodgeball.

Teaching points
● Pay attention to the ball carrier.
● Keep the ball within the circle.
● Move away to be opposite the ball carrier.
● Possibility of the circle players either passing, feinting or dummying.

Further development of this approach can logically lead to three-court and four-court variations of dodgeball.

Chapter 7
TEAM GAMES

When children reach the stage of playing together and working as a group towards a common cause, games of a much more skilful nature should be introduced. From the age of 10+, children tend to be much influenced by the cultural and social environment of their peers and wish to imitate their sporting heroes. At this stage of social development, team games may be introduced at a fairly simple level of performance. The selection of suitable informal game situations may be greatly influenced by a developing interest in the major traditional team games with which the children can identify. Although participation in the major games will always be beyond the capacities of many handicapped children, there are great opportunities in informal team games for them to perform in an identifiable context. Where the skills of a group of handicapped children develop to the point where team games can be played, in whatever adapted form, it is critical that they learn the techniques, rules and tactics of each situation. At the very least, an understanding and knowledge of game tactics in sports which are part of our cultural heritage will produce handicapped adults who are well informed spectators.

When children are ready to play team games it is important in our lesson planning to be aware that they appreciate much more the practical application of their learned techniques to the real game situation. Throughout this chapter the emphasis is on providing small-sided simple games which retain the essential elements of the major games and act as a cognitive bridge or lead-up stage to the more traditional games. Most of the activities may be played on a mixed basis. At secondary and adult level the restriction would be in activities involving body contact, where differences in weight and strength between males and females could increase the injury factor. No restrictions are needed on females playing contact games in single-sex teams.

The modern approach to the teaching of team games recognizes three divisions into which games may be categorized: invasion games, net games, and striking games. Although the specific techniques of different games within each category may show wide variations, there are common tactics involved in each grouping that require understanding and need to be taught. A successful programme of games teaching carrying through from the last two years in the primary school to the secondary school will include adequate courses in all three areas of team games. Each of the three areas has been presented in a progressive scheme from the simple to the more difficult.

INVASION GAMES

Depending on the children's ability levels, these games can normally be taught in simple form from the age of 9 or 10 years onwards. The vast majority of major games played in normal schools are of the 'invasion' type where one team retains possession of the ball to invade the territory of the opposing team to attack a goal or target to score. Typical of these activities are soccer, rugby, netball, hockey and basketball, all of which require a high standard of mobility and skill. Adapted forms of these games, suitable for presentation to handicapped children, are described in the next chapter. This section deals with teaching minor games of a free ball-passing nature, based on simple rules and minimum organization, which can be played by handicapped children of mixed ability. Minor team games differ from the major invasion games only in their lack of sophistication, changed playing environment and informal rules. In the normal school situation these are small-sided games which allow maximum participation and activity and have deliberately adapted goals and boundaries. In the special school only the size of teams and playing rules are likely to change. The general principles of play which govern performance and lead to the development of understanding of tactics remain constant.

Once children reach the age of 10 or 11 years, it is important that games lessons should be organized and structured so that team games can be played. Unlike the junior school situation where each class tends to go for physical education as a small mixed-class unit, in the senior school the numbers in class should be large enough to allow team games to be played. This probably means that the boys and girls from several senior classes are grouped together for games sessions. Obviously within such a group there will be a wide range in handicap and perhaps in age, depending upon the size of the school population. Many of the games can be played with the sexes mixed. Some years ago it was felt that mixed ability was a hindrance to good teaching, but experience in teaching team games has shown that this can be an advantage both in the direct and indirect outcomes of the work. Socially and psychologically it is good for the slightly older and more able children to accept some responsibility for the enjoyment of the younger children by helping and encouraging them in their play. Older children accept responsibility for preparing equipment, storing equipment, dressing and undressing the more handicapped youngsters and getting them to and from physical education classes. During team games there will be some severely handicapped children who are involved in the game merely by their physical presence on court, but it is vital that they should feel part of the proceedings even if their active participation is somewhat minimal. Involving such children in the practical experience of being part of a team is entirely the responsibility of the more able players, helped by rule modifications. Thus, in a class of very mixed ability the less motor-handicapped players act as a catalyst bringing everyone into the action. Provided that opportunities exist elsewhere within the curriculum for the more able-bodied to shine in their own right, they are often happy to play a role as feed players for the more disabled. Mixed ability teaching in this instance allows everyone to take part in games performance of a high standard.

Even with the severely disabled players an understanding of the principles of play and tactics must be emphasized. Good understanding may compensate for lack of locomotor ability. Children with locomotor problems who read the game situation well can move into space early and give themselves more time to take up supporting positions.

All the invasion games in this section have common factors in their tactical make-up, and the common principles should be taught in a structured way to help the children develop understanding and tactical awareness. Too often these minor games are presented merely as a fun activity and they are much more than that. The children ought to be making cognitive decisions within the game based on sound understanding of tactics rather than merely performing physical movements. The similarity between many ball-handling games and the major game of basketball is a classical case. A severely handicapped child playing skittle-ball, who understands the nature of tactics and techniques, may improve his chances of enjoying his role as a better-informed spectator at a national basketball match.

Throughout a progressive scheme of work seeking to develop cognitive understanding of tactical awareness, many simple concepts can be practised in small group situations, then transferred and reinforced in invasion games of the minor game type. The following information is presented in the hope that it will assist teachers to present simple tactics to children in all invasion-type ball-passing games.

PRINCIPLES OF PLAY

The principles of play are those common elements of team play which, when thoroughly understood, play an important part in the continuing development of young players.

ATTACK

1. *Team possession*. This is achieved by a combination of good-quality passing and adequate support at the correct distance and at the correct angle.

2. *Support*. Whenever a player has the ball, team mates should understand where to position themselves to be of help to that player. This may be in depth behind the ball with time and space available for safety, at a wide angle to the side of the ball, or in front of the ball behind defenders.

3. *Creating space*. By spreading out from side to side and end to end once possession of the ball is gained the attacking team demands the defenders to guard larger areas of space, thereby leaving more room for individual players to operate. Space may also be created by quick movement of the ball and running or wheeling behind the defending players.

DEFENCE

Defenders should attempt to deny the attacking team possession and reduce the space (and time) in which they play.

1. *Pressurizing*. This involves standing close to the player with the ball, without causing physical contact, and preventing that player from playing the ball forward or scoring. A good position between the attacker and the goal may force him to play the ball away from goal or into narrow angles.

2. *Marking*. This involves positioning close beside an opponent to prevent him receiving the ball from a pass. The opponent must be kept in view at all times and the defender must be on line between the attacker and his own goal.

3. *Cover*. To cover another defender means to take up a position behind that player so that if an error is committed the attacker with the ball is still faced by another defender.

4. *Concentration*. On occasions, the defending players will deliberately withdraw towards their own goal to set up a tight block of defenders around it, thereby increasing the number of players in front of the target area and considerably reducing the time and space in which the attackers are allowed to play.

The above concepts are a considerable oversimplification of game tactics but adequate to establish a core of tactical understanding by physically handicapped children of both sexes. Many other principles of play involve speed factors and these are considered to be inappropriate complexities. To provide stimulating opportunities for playing team games it must be stressed that understanding the principles of play is just as important as technical competence in manipulating a ball; this is not always understood by teachers of handicapped children. Understanding cannot be achieved quickly and teachers must be prepared to take one theme at a time in a related manner and work for years to accomplish these objectives in helping children to achieve competence in playing team games related to the principles of play and understanding of game tactics. In simple form, the two most vital factors involved in the understanding of team play are:

1. *Keeping possession of the ball*, achieved by good-quality passing which is accurate and of the appropriate speed, good support from the correct distance and angle, and through the ball player looking up and being aware of supporting players.
2. *Winning the ball*, achieved by close pressurizing of the ball carrier, close marking of the supporting attackers and adequate covering of players who are pressurizing the ball.

PROGRESSIVE TEACHING OF INVASION GAMES

It is assumed that before passing games are introduced to the programme children will have acquired the basic techniques of passing and catching to a competent level. These skilful games need to be introduced gradually, and preliminary training should be given in the fundamentals of team-passing skills. The simplest form of organization for small-sided teaching situations is to use a form of coaching grid (Figure 7.1). The grid, quite simply, is an area

Figure 7.1   Coaching grid

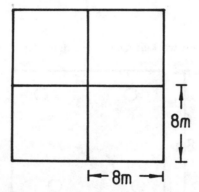

of the gymnasium or playground divided up into squares of different sizes which form the restrictive boundaries within which a group of children play. If a grid is not actually prepared, lines on a badminton or netball court can be used to designate specific sizes of play area. For ball-handling activities, for example, 8 m or 10 m squares are very suitable. The grid area provides a simple solution to the problem of organizing a fairly large class into small groups and allows the pursuit of meaningful learning activities in a reasonably small space. Furthermore, it produces real games in a simplified form which can be used as a basis for fruitful teaching.

The teaching of skilful team passing games is based upon the principle of 'opposed practice'. This means that in order to make children more skilful they must practise in situations which are not artificial but closely related to a real game and containing as many elements of the real game as possible. All team passing games include:

supporting players;
opponents;
targets, direction, and objectives.

It is essential that a good practice includes each of these elements, although the balance between them may be reduced to increase the chances of success. If we are attempting to make children skilful, then it is necessary here to remember what is meant by skill. There is a clear distinction between technical competence and skilled performance in games. Technique may be seen to be the ability to perform a particular action in isolation from the game, as in two children passing a ball between them. Genuine skill is the application of that technique within the actual game when, for example, those two children are attempting to pass the ball between them and opponents attempt to intercept. In the latter case the players are forced to make tactical decisions in relation to their reading of the game situation and if errors are committed these may not be the result of poor technique but of misreading the environmental factors.

Figure 7.2   Four players working against one defender

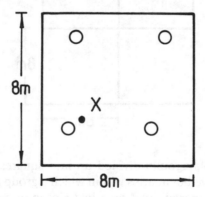

In Figure 7.2 four players are working against one defender. They are practising for improvements in the skill of passing, keeping possession and supporting each other. The objective is for the four players to build 10 consecutive passes without dropping the ball, allowing the defender to touch it, or letting it go out of the area. The balance of numbers may be changed according to the ability or mobility of the players, but the attackers ought to have adequate numerical superiority to achieve success in their objective. Where larger numbers are involved, a greater grid area can be produced by increasing the number of squares used. In this way, the teacher faced with a class of 24 children in a small gymnasium could accommodate four groups playing 5 v. 1 or 4 v. 2, each in a quarter of the space available.

It must be emphasized that the grid is only a learning device and the quality of learning is totally dependent on the skill of the teacher in observing and analyzing the problems that the children face in their practice. In order to develop understanding, the teacher needs to analyze the causes of breakdown in performance and provide accurate feedback to the children. It is inadequate merely to say 'That was a poor pass' and relay irrelevant information to the players. A much more sound teaching procedure demands that the teacher pinpoints the cause of the mistake and offers an alternative, successful, solution to the problem. For example, where a breakdown occurs in the 4 v. 1 situation quoted, this may be caused by any number of factors:

1. The catching technique may have been inadequate.
2. The pass may have been too strong or too slow for the catcher to cope with.
3. The passer may not have delivered the ball at the right time — for instance, too early or too late relative to the defender.
4. The receiver may not have taken up a good supporting position or he may not have moved into position quickly enough.
5. The technique of the pass may be inadequate or the passer may not have looked up to check the exact whereabouts of his support at the moment of passing.

The teacher must become skilled at assessing these factors and make the children aware whether errors are caused by faulty technique, making the wrong tactical decision, or poor visual awareness of the situation. Small-sided games with unequal numbers may thus be used to reinforce the practice of techniques and simultaneously develop understanding of the principles of play in simplified situations. It can be seen that the presence of one or two defenders, although heavily outnumbered, creates a situation where attacking players must make correct tactical decisions while having more time and space than in the real balanced game. Although there are opponents present, there is a good chance of successfully achieving an objective.

The following brief programme is merely an example of a progressive scheme of work steadily increasing in complexity as skill and understanding develop. The time spent on the programme obviously depends upon the technical competence of the children and their level of handicap, but it is likely that one lesson per week for at least one term will be necessary to produce effective results.

THE DEVELOPMENT OF OPPOSED PRACTICE IN TEAM PASSING

1. 4 v. 1 in one grid area (Figure 7.3). Achieve eight good passes and change the defender, or change at interception. Work for quality passing, good

angles of support in wide positions, and calling for the ball. No running with the ball. No physical contact by defender.

Figure 7.3   4 v. 1 in one grid area: supporting angles

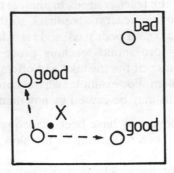

2. 5 v. 1 for more handicapped players.
3. 5 v. 1 skittleball (Figure 7.4). The defender guards a skittle which stands within a circle of 3 m diameter. He may not enter the circle. The five attackers pass the ball around the circle until they catch the defender on the wrong side of the circle, when they attempt to knock it down. This adds a specific directional objective to the passing practice.

Figure 7.4   5 v. 1 skittleball

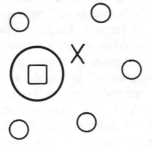

As a variation, the circle may be enlarged with the defender playing within the circle, thus encouraging greater speed of passing.
4. 6 v. 2 in two grid areas (Figure 7.5). Change the defenders after a set time period ($1\frac{1}{2}$ minutes). Attackers count the highest number of passes before interception. Defenders score for the number of interceptions in the time

limit (or defender changes after each interception). Work for good supporting positions all around the ball moving into space and encourage the use of a pass which goes between the two defenders. Show the value of moving into the gap between and behind the defenders. Stress the importance of timing the release of the pass before the defender can get too close to the ball, and encourage speed of passing. Establish the rules of no running with the ball and no physical contact. Defenders wear coloured braids.

Figure 7.5   6 v. 2 in two grid areas

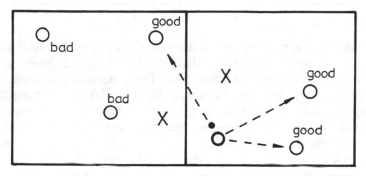

5. 6 v. 2. Introduce direction to the practice to encourage movement into space. Six players attack two defenders along a channel of two grid squares, attempting to work the ball towards the end line. A point is scored if a player receives the ball on the end line.
6. 8 v. 4. Eight players keep possession against four defenders in half the gymnasium (Figure 7.6). Count the number of consecutive passes for the attackers and interceptions for the defenders for a set period of time, e.g. 2 minutes. Defenders wear coloured braids. Change the four defenders. Encourage the defenders to pressurize the ball, mark players close to the ball, and ensure the fourth defender seeks to cover behind the other three.

In the scheme of work above, the numerical balance between attackers and defenders is only presented as a guideline at different progressive stages. The discerning teacher will obviously adapt the space and the unequal numbers to suit the abilities of the children.

Throughout the development of work of this kind, children should be constantly encouraged to 'play to strength'. In other words, they develop an awareness of individual limitations and abilities and use the most appropriate method of passing to the more disabled players in a manner which simplifies the catching process by using either a bounce pass or a rolled pass.

Figure 7.6   8 v. 4: good defending

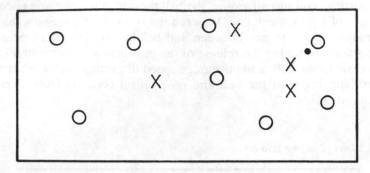

In all invasion games and in practice situations the most disabled children must be positioned in such a way that they have relatively free use of their arms and can operate from a stable base. Thus, athetoid and ataxic children and many arm-crutch users of unsteady balance play more efficiently from kneeling positions on the floor. If they are severely disabled, they may be designated as 'safe ball' players and function within certain modified rules quite separately from the others. Once a 'safe ball' player has the ball in his possession only a player on his side may take the ball from him. Severely handicapped children in wheelchairs or on the floor, who are unable to pass because of hand and arm impairment, may have the ball handed to them or rolled to them; they become valuable team members as safe ball-handlers until they can be supported by more mobile players. They cannot be directly challenged, but defenders may intercept the ball before it reaches them, thus encouraging even the severely disabled to move into space to receive the ball, however slowly. Defenders may not infringe the personal space of 'safe ball' players by standing over them; a further useful rule is not to allow defenders within one metre of a 'safe ball' player when he has the ball in his possession.

CONSECUTIVE TEAM PASSING

This is a free ball-passing game between two equally balanced teams; it forms the basis of most team passing games. Teams may be of any size and with a large class two such games can be played simultaneously in different halves of the hall. The objective is to pass a light football with the hands to team mates for as many passes as possible before the opponents win the ball. Each pass is loudly counted by the whole team. At the end of a set period of time the team gaining the highest number of consecutive passes is the winner.

To encourage maximum participation by all players and to discourage the more able children from dominating the game a 'no pass back' rule may be introduced. Any catcher may not immediately and directly return the ball to the passer. This means that if A passes to B, then the ball must be played to a third player C before it may be passed back to A. In this way very disabled players must be used within the team pattern to relay the ball back to the more skilful players so that the disabled players fulfil a role within the team.

RULES

1. No running with the ball.
2. No physical contact or tackling.
3. No standing over a wheelchair or floor player.
4. Any infringement results in a free pass to the other team.

In a simple passing game of this type, without goals, the principles of play which govern the understanding of tactical performance in all team games can be taught in depth. The children must learn to see the relationship between concepts learnt from grid work (support, possession, creating space, tight marking, etc.) and their application to the team game. Exactly the same terminology used in the major team games should be used in minor games of this type to help develop a tactical vocabulary.

COURT TEAM PASSING (Figure 7.7)

This is a variation on consecutive team passing and is much less strenuous. Each team is split into two halves with each half-team in a separate court. The teams form up in pairs, matched by ability, with equal numbers of pairs in each half-court. Once a player has been assigned to a half-court, the centre line must not be crossed. The pairs mark each other.

The aim of the game is to make three consecutive passes between members of the same team in one court to score one point. After three successful passes, the last player in the sequence must pass the ball across the centre line to a team mate in the other half. If the ball is held for longer than 5 seconds, a

Figure 7.7   Court team passing

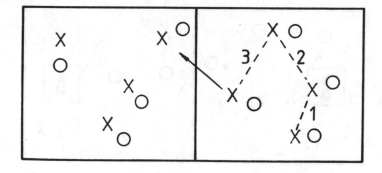

free throw is awarded to the opposition. The pass across the centre line does not count and may be intercepted by the opponents.

It is important that pairs are evenly matched by handicap; the two halves of the court may also be used to divide the class into an active court and a court for the more handicapped players. Normal rules for consecutive team passing should apply to control running and physical contact.

Very severely disabled children can play this game on the floor using a large beanbag.

SKITTLE-BALL

The game is played by two equal teams and the aim is to knock down the opponents' skittle to score a point. Each team guards a skittle standing within a circle or standing in the centre of a gym-mat. The game begins with a ball being bounced between two players in the centre.

RULES

1.   No running with the ball.
2.   No tackling or physical contact.
3.   No infringement of personal space for wheelchair and floor players.
4.   No direct return passes.
5.   'Safe ball' rule for the severely disabled.

     A free pass is awarded for infringement of the above rules.

6.   No defender or attacker allowed within the circle (or on the mat). Penalty is a free shot at the skittle for a defence infringement or a free pass for an attack infringement.
7.   After a score the defending team recommences play with a throw from in front of its skittle.

Figure 7.8   Skittle-ball played in two halves with unequal numbers of attackers and defenders

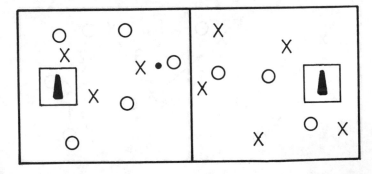

Wheelchair or electric wheelchair players can be placed as guards covering the space in front of the skittle, but they must not roll into the legs of standing or floor players.

In the early stages of learning skittle-ball and as a logical follow-up from skills learned on the grid practices, the game may be played in two halves with unequal numbers of attackers and defenders (see Figure 7.8). Each team plays with perhaps five attackers and three defenders who may not cross the halfway line, thus ensuring a high-scoring game.

After a score the defending team starts with a throw from the centre line.

POST-BALL

This game is a variation of skittle-ball using a badminton stand or portable netball stand as the target on the mat.

Using the same rules of play, there are an infinite variety of invasion games that can be played where the only variable is the final target to be attacked.

CAPTAIN-BALL

This game is played to exactly the same rules as skittle-ball, but the objective is to score by passing the ball to the captain, who sits or kneels on the opponents' mat. Wheelchair players or floor players thus play a critical role as the target for their team. No infringement of mat space is allowed by either team, and no defender may place his arms above the Captain. The Captain should be replaced after a set period of time at both ends of the court. One point is scored each time the captain makes a successful catch from any kind of pass. With large classes, two mats may be placed together at each end and two Captains operate together to increase the target area for the teams.

END-LINE CAPTAIN-BALL (Figure 7.9)

Played to the same rules as captain-ball, this game allows the captain more freedom of movement and demands better awareness of marking by the defenders. The captain is a mobile wheelchair player operating behind an end line which is off limits to all other players. The captain is allowed to wheel to any position behind the line in order to take up a better position to receive the final scoring pass. After a score the game restarts with a defence free throw.

To reduce the overall degree of movement the game may be played on a two-court basis with attackers and defenders restricted to their respective front and back courts.

CAPTAIN BASKETBALL

Played as a variation on captain-ball, but the role of captain becomes more critical. A portable netball ring approximately 1.5 m high is placed in front of the Captain's mat. One point is scored for a pass to the Captain and a further

Figure 7.9   End-line captain-ball

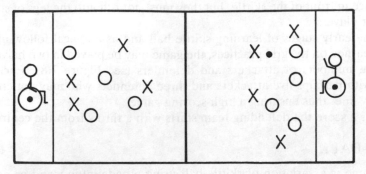

Figure 7.10   Captain basketball

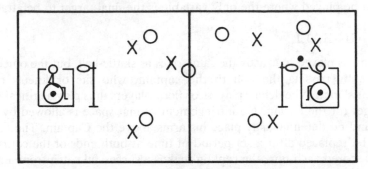

point is scored if the Captain can throw the ball through the ring. If he fails, the defenders restart play with a throw from in front of the mat.

HANDBALL (Figure 7.11)

The aim is to keep possession of the ball by passing and to score goals in the opponents' goal. The pitch size may vary depending on whether the game is played indoors or on the playground, but in a hall or standard gymnasium the full area can be used. A size 4 plastic football is recommended.

RULES

1. Goals should be 3 m × 1 m, but five-a-side soccer goals may be used.
2. A half circle is drawn around the goal and only the goalkeeper is allowed in that area.
3. No tackling or physical contact.
4. Only two paces or two wheel pushes may be taken when in possession of the ball (or the game may be adapted to no running).

5. The ball may not be held for longer than 5 seconds.
6. Goals must be thrown in or batted with the hand from outside the circle.
7. After a goal, either the goalkeeper or a defender throws the ball into play from within the circle.
8. A defensive infringement into the circle results in a penalty throw from the edge of the circle.

Figure 7.11   Handball

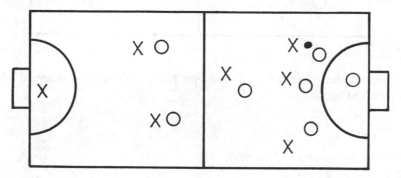

The role of the goalkeeper is important and a floor player may kneel on a mat within the goal or an electric wheelchair may operate in a forward and backward direction across the face of the goal with the goalkeeper holding a plastic hockey stick to extend his reach.

As a tactical manoeuvre, the defenders must learn to retreat before the ball and set up a concentrated zone around their circle. Conversely, the attack must be developed quickly and on a wide front.

A variation which prevents rough play from developing and encourages quick passing involves the 'touch' rule. All mobile players may be dispossessed by being touched while in possession of the ball. The ball must be passed immediately after a 'touch' and no goal may be scored by a player who has been touched. The rule would not apply to wheelchair or floor players.

PERMIT NETBALL (Figure 7.12)

There are two teams of seven players with five attackers and two defenders in each half. Mobile attacking players must stand with at least one foot within a hoop on the floor and wheelchair players may move freely without the ball. The five attackers must make five consecutive passes to gain a permit for a shot at the netball ring, while the two defenders try to intercept.

Only one shot is allowed, after which the ball is given to the team in the other half of the court. If the defenders intercept the ball, they pass to their

Figure 7.12   Permit netball

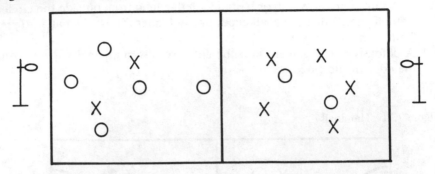

attackers in the other court. Defending players should be changed after a given period of play.

SCORING

1 point for a permit (5 passes).
2 points for a basket.
1 point for a successful pass by a defender into the other court.

FLOOR HANDBALL (FIST-BALL)

Two equal teams attack each other's goal; the objective is to score a goal by batting the ball into goal using only one hand.

All players kneel or sit to equalize some of the mobility problems and the ball is propelled with the open hand or clenched fist. A football-size foam ball (high-bounce) or a cloth-covered ball should be used. Wheelchair-bound children should play in goal.

RULES

1. Goals 3 m × 1 m with a restraining circle around the goal.
2. No infringement of the circle.
3. Stopping, dribbling and batting must be performed with one hand at a time.
4. The ball must not be caught or held at any time except by the goal-keepers. Goalkeepers may throw the ball into play.
5. After a goal the game is restarted with a hit from the front of the circle.
6. Any infringement results in a free hit to the opponents. At a free hit the opponents must retreat 2 m from the ball.
7. Dribbling players must have one hand or part of the body below the waist (other than the feet) in contact with the floor.

This is a most active game and must be played on a non-abrasive surface. Players need to be encouraged to pass the ball quickly and often and the usual principles of play apply.

STICKBALL

Two teams attack and defend goals 2.5 m × 1.5 m. A very light football or foam ball is used and all players use walking sticks, crutches or plastic hockey sticks to dribble, control or shoot at goal. Players may be ambulatory or in wheelchairs and the only rules are for safety. Free hits are awarded if sticks are raised above waist level and a penalty is awarded if a player is struck with a stick. This can be a rough game and the teacher must maintain strict control. To protect the goalkeeper a defence circle should be drawn around the goal as an off-limits area to all other players.

Stickball

CRAB FOOTBALL

This is a football game played in a small area from a sitting position. The children sit on the floor with both hands behind them. They may move anywhere on hands and feet with bottoms raised from the floor or may shuffle on their bottoms. Goals are scored by kicking or heading the ball into the opponents' goal. Only the kneeling goalkeeper may handle the ball.

THROW–HEAD–CATCH

This soccer training game is very popular with older handicapped pupils of mixed ability. Two teams attack and defend goals which are 3 m × 1 m high. The goalkeeper should be kneeling on a mat or sitting in a wheelchair. A football-size high-bounce foam ball produces a safe and painless game. Goals are scored when the ball is headed into the goal.

METHOD OF PLAY

The game starts with a bounce at the centre, then proceeds in the following manner: a player throws the ball for a team mate to head, after which it is caught. Opponents may only intercept a thrown ball with their head. After a header any player may catch the ball. Failure to head the ball after it has been thrown by a team mate gives possession to the opponents.

Goalkeepers may well be players who can catch but have limited throwing ability. In this case, balls thrown out by goalkeepers may be caught by fellow players, but the next pass must result in a header.

Accuracy of passing, very close support play, and tight marking form the essence of this game. Even very disabled children play this game aided by mobile players who feed the ball on to the head of kneeling or wheelchair performers. Because of the limited speed of ball movement even very handicapped players can cover much ground to support the ball handler. Players of very limited mobility should be positioned in final attack or defence positions from which they can still play a vital role.

THE SEVERELY DISABLED

Throughout this chapter it has been demonstrated how the severely disabled can be integrated with their less handicapped peers on a mixed ability basis. In a situation where handicap groups are relatively homogeneous, it is still possible to involve the severely disabled in the performance of team games by suitable adaptation of the playing conditions. It matters little whether we are dealing with physical handicap, educational subnormality, dystrophy, or neurological impairment — the principles remain the same. The greatest problems are lack of mobility, poor balance, inadequate hand and arm control, limited visuo-motor capacity and lack of strength. Provided that children can be safely removed from their wheelchairs and placed on the floor, many of the games described above can be played indoors or on a grass area outside. If the speed and mobility factors are removed from the games, then the children can play. The principles of play which govern the understanding of tactics in team passing situations remain the same, but the techniques involved need to be amended.

In general terms, the court size must be smaller, the targets need to be bigger and lower, and a large beanbag may be substituted for the ball. A

Throw-head-catch pratice

bcanbag does not bounce, it is easily grasped and it can be thrown or slid around the floor, thereby remaining within the playing area of the children. Use of two-court, four-court, or more playing areas reduces the space to be covered and limits the distance over which a beanbag has to be passed. The example quoted below is only one specimen of a team game adapted for the severely disabled, but by substituting a different target or objective a very large number of variations may be developed.

BUCKET-BALL

The object is to score a point by throwing a beanbag into a large bucket guarded by the teams. The bucket stands in a circle or on a mat, and players may not infringe the circle. The court is divided into four areas with two players from each team operating within each area (see Figure 7.13). No player may move outside his area, so a series of 2 × 2 grids are set up. The beanbag may be passed between two players within a grid any number of times while they move to support until the beanbag can be transferred to a player of the same team in a grid nearer the bucket.

RULES

1. No moving with the beanbag in possession.
2. No physical contact except by accident.

3. No moving outside the grid.
4. No player may infringe the circle. If a shot misses the bucket, the teacher gives the beanbag to the nearest defender.
5. Any pass may be intercepted, but the defender must beware of physical contact.
6. Any form of pass or shot is allowed.

In this game general movement is well controlled and, by using a beanbag, all play is at floor level.

Figure 7.13   Bucket-ball: court divided into four areas

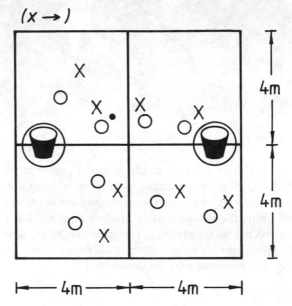

Obviously the number of grids may be changed and the number of matching pairs competing within each grid may be varied. The final target may be a table top, a tyre, a hoop, a very low netball ring or any other suitable object, but the game basically remains the same.

An alternative to this grid play is to form channels within which each set of matched players must remain (see Figure 7.14).

Movement is restricted to small areas and simple principles of play are more easily understood by the children.

The channels may be changed to zones across the court, again reducing the amount of space to be covered by players.

The ball or beanbag must be passed into the adjacent zone to ensure

Figure 7.14   Bucket-ball: court divided into three channels

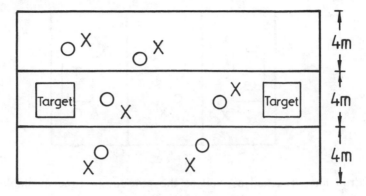

maximum participation by all players. After a given period, players in an end zone rotate with the mid-court zone players.

PLANNING THE LESSON

There are basically two types of lesson plan in common use which both satisfy principles of sound skill acquisition according to the age and ability of the children. The type of lesson plan used will depend upon the stage that the

Heading at goal

Figure 7.15   Bucket-ball: court divided into three zones

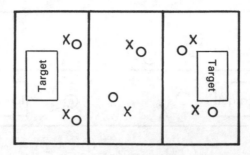

children have reached as well as the amount of time available. Younger children will benefit from a progressively structured lesson where practice in skills proceeds from the simple to the more complex and all parts of the lesson are seen to be related to a common theme. On the other hand, older children may gain greater understanding of the principles of play in a lesson which begins with a simple team game, followed by a technique practice session based upon deficiencies noted during game performance, and then finishes with a game to reinforce learning as in whole–part–whole teaching. Examples of both types of lesson plans are given in both a specific and a general way.

UPPER JUNIORS

Introductory activities
A vigorous warm up involving movement centred on specific cooperative skills using balls or other small play objects. Tag or chasing games involving group or team cooperation.

Skill training
Group practice of specific games skills with more formal teaching of sound technique. Practice should be closely related to the techniques and tactics involved in the performance of group games, invasion games, net games or striking games. Much of this work should be cooperative, aiming at the consolidation of efficient techniques in small groups of three or four. Limited opposed practice should be introduced in 4 v. 1 and 5 v. 2 situations to establish the cooperative principles of team play.

Small-sided games
Simple group games and small-sided team games should be played on a competitive basis. The understanding of games tactics should be taught and reinforced. Social cooperation within the competitive set up should be emphasized.

Recapitulation
End the lesson on a question-and-answer recapitulation to reinforce the level of understanding of the main tactical principles learnt.

OLDER CHILDREN

Introductory activity
Vigorous warm up.

Small-sided games
Organize into small-sided games, perhaps emphasizing sound use of one particular technique and one tactical concept. Carefully observe performance and analyze those deficiencies in play which prevent full enjoyment. Although tactical play might be reasonable, some technical deficiency may prevent further development. Highlight the deficiency and establish the need for practice.

Skill training
Organize group and individual practice that is clearly related to the use of a specific technique or tactic within the game. Teach the technique in a formal manner, ensuring that children understand *why* they are practising.

Small-sided games
Return to the games playing situation and reinforce the use of that particular technique or tactic within the game. If necessary, apply restricted conditions upon the game to ensure that maximum opportunity for practice occurs.

Recapitulation
By question and answer, reinforce the element of understanding that has been practised and learnt.

TYPICAL CLASS LESSON PLAN: UPPER JUNIORS

Aim: to provide opportunities for the acquisition of a range of games skills pertinent to invasion games.

Objectives: by the end of the lesson the children will be able to
- work cooperatively in a grid, sharing one ball while participating fully in game-skill activities;
- take a full part in a game of 4 v. 1 passball, utilizing skills learned in the lesson.

Lesson 1: 30 minutes	*Teaching points*
Introduction: gross motor activity.	
All-in-dodgeball.	Reinforce precise area of activity.
	Use four grids. Start two catchers.
	Quality passing.

Cooperation in a grid
Skills:

1. Throwing and catching in pairs.	Teach technique. Increase distance apart.
2. Pass, then move to a corner.	Be still in possession, then move.

3. Pass, then move to a space between other players.

Lively movement after passing. Find a gap to receive a pass.

Cooperation and competition

4. Highest number of passes in 30 seconds.
5. Ditto but as a pass and move.

Pass to strength. Teach responsibilities of passer and receiver. Teach 'ball out of play'.

Final game

Introduce 4 v. 1 in grid (see Figure 7.16).

No stealing the ball.
No moving in possession.
Teach angles and space.

Figure 7.16   4 v. 1 in grid

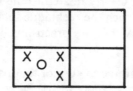

TYPICAL CLASS LESSON PLAN: JUNIORS

Objectives: by the end of the lesson the children will be able to
* perform a bounce pass in a competitive practice;
* participate fully in a game of captain-ball.

Introductory activity	*Teaching points*
1. In pairs. Bounce pass to partner.	Teach, demonstrate and use bounce pass.
2. Pass, then move.	Pass, then find a space.

Skill training

3. In fours. Pass and follow drill.
4. Play 4 v. 1 (or similar).

Make a good angle to receive. Hold ball only 5 seconds. Correct supporting distance.

Final game

Small-sided captain-ball.

Teach use of space, movement 'off' the ball, calling for the ball, no physical contact.

TYPICAL CLASS LESSON PLAN (WHOLE–PART–WHOLE)

Objectives: by the end of the lesson the children will be able to
* understand the principles of marking;
* participate fully in a game of skittle-ball.

Introductory activity	*Teaching points*
1. Dodge and mark.	Stay with your partner. Time start of movement, change pace.
2. Free and caught.	Be honest when tagged.

Introductory game	
3. Small-sided skittle-ball.	Mark tightly when ball is lost. Stay between player and skittle. Find space when possession is gained. Establish the need for working and getting free. Demonstrate good marking.

Skill training	
4. 2 v. 2 passball.	Stay with your opponent.
5. Consecutive team passing 4 v. 4.	Player more important than the ball. Get free. Stay with your opponent.
6. Games of single skittle-ball 3 v. 1.	Defender focuses on the ball. Attackers pass quickly to unbalance the defender.

Final game	
7. Small-sided skittle-ball.	Reinforce marking. Show examples of good guarding. Encourage attack to pass quickly.

NET GAMES

Many active games with simple rules can be played on a court area with a net between the teams. Several factors determine the amount of vigorous activity and skill required to participate successfully in net games. In general terms, an object is thrown or batted over the net and aimed at the floor in the opponents' court. The height of the net governs the flight time of the object and dictates the overall speed of the game: raising the net slows down the tempo of a game more in keeping with the slower motor responses evident in physical handicap. The composition and size of the object used obviously affects the speed of flight and may simplify the handling and striking procedures, as a large, light and overinflated ball will travel more slowly in flight and will be easier to catch or hit. The size of the court area on each side of the net controls how much ground has to be defended: a smaller court cuts down the area to be covered by each player. Having larger numbers in a team also reduces the total area to be covered and the range of movement needed from any individual player; courts can be zoned into various sized squares covered by players of different locomotor ability.

Net games produce an ideal cooperative or competitive game situation for teams of very mixed ability and handicap as the children can play together in a united team effort regardless of the degree of handicap. Generally, during net games the more handicapped players should cover the front court from sitting or kneeling positions while the more mobile players guard the larger spaces in the rear court.

The basic tactics of all net games are simple and similar in nature. They involve accurate placement of the ball into open spaces on the opposite court; the creation of space by moving opponents around their court to cope with the changing direction and length of the service; anticipation of the intentions of the opposition; and good tactical covering of the court space to guard the floor.

Provided that a sound programme of skill training has been presented, most children at the upper end of the junior school ought to have acquired the fundamental techniques of catching, throwing and batting which form the basis of playing net games. Although the selection of material will depend upon the appropriate level of ability of individual children, net games can usually be introduced into the games programme in one form or another from the age of 9+ years.

NEWCOMBE (Figure 7.17)

The court size should be approximately 4–6 m wide and deep on each side of a net or beam 1.5–2 m high, but a badminton court can be used. An attack line should be drawn across the court and parallel to the net some 2 m from it to distinguish front court and back court players. Six or more players cover each court. The size of court may be increased to allow larger numbers to play. A light vinyl football or volleyball is used. The object of the game is to throw the ball over the net and land it on the opponents' floor space.

METHOD OF PLAY

Teams toss for service or side of court. The service is thrown over the net to land in court and any player may catch it. With less disabled players, the ball must be returned by a throw from the catcher from the position in which he catches the ball. Play continues until a point is scored when the ball hits the floor within the court, hits the net, or is thrown out of court. Play is restarted by the team that lost the point throwing the ball back over the net. A match may consist of an agreed points target (i.e. 15 points per set) or an agreed time period of two equal halves (i.e. 2 × 7 minutes).

When teams of mixed handicap levels are competing, certain adaptations may be allowed to gain maximum participation for all. No mobile back-court player may return the ball from in front of the attack line. In the event of a back-court player catching the ball in front of the attack line, he must pass the ball to a handicapped front-court player for return, or pass the ball back behind the line for another back-court player to return. Only one such pass should be allowed in any rally. If a disabled front-court player with poor arm

Figure 7.17   Newcombe

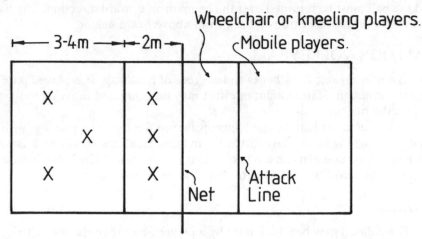

control is able to catch but not throw the ball over the high net, then that player is allowed to pass the ball overhead into the home court for a mobile team mate to throw the return.

Severely disabled players who cannot catch may bat the ball into the air to be caught by a team mate.

BEANBAG NEWCOMBE

In the introductory stages the above game can be played with a large beanbag of approximately 250 g weight, which is easy for the severely handicapped to grip and catch.

TENNIS QUOIT

This game is similar to Newcombe, except that a rubber quoit is used. The quoit must be thrown underarm from below the waist.

ONE-BOUNCE NEWCOMBE

Played with a large foam ball, this game is ideal for the very disabled competitor from a wheelchair or from a kneeling or lying position on the floor. The net should be lowered in accordance with the throwing power of the players. The rules are similar to Newcombe, except that the ball is allowed to touch the floor once on either side of the net.

MEDICINE-BALL NEWCOMBE

This game is suitable for older children with good strong arms. It is played over a 2 m high beam with a 2 kg medicine ball. It develops explosive strength in arms, shoulders and back. One pass is allowed on either side of the beam and the ball must be returned over the beam in an upward direction. The ball may not be dropped or thrown back from above beam height.

BALLOON VOLLEYBALL

This is a useful game for all ages and degrees of handicap. It is played purely for fun, although a fair amount of effort may be generated in trying to reach and hit the balloon.

Any size of court may be used appropriate to the numbers playing, with a rope or net strung across the court at 1.5 m high. Sidelines should be drawn to mark the court boundary, but a back line is not essential. The balloon should be served by a toss and hit from a mark 2 m back from the net.

RULES

1.   The balloon may be struck once by a player other than the server to help it over the net.
2.   The balloon may be played five times on one side of the net before being returned, but no individual may make two successive hits.
3.   In the event of the balloon striking the net, play should continue.
4.   No player may reach over the net to play the balloon.
5.   The players in the serving team continue serving until they lose a rally, as in volleyball.
6.   Points are scored when a balloon is not returned within five hits, is hit out of court, or is allowed to touch the floor.

Teachers should be aware that hyperacoustic children ought not to play this game because of the panic caused when a balloon bursts. A similar game requiring quicker responses can be played with an inflated football bladder, but the net should be raised slightly.

TEAM SOFT TENNIS

This is a form of team tennis using a small high-bounce foam ball and plastic padder bats.

The size of the court will depend upon the degree of mobility and the skill of the players, but a badminton court is suitable using a 1 m high net (or higher appropriate to the players' ability).

METHOD OF PLAY

Players divide into two equal teams (six or more a side) and spread out to cover the court space, with the most disabled at the front. The game is played like tennis, with the players hitting the ball over the net into the opposite court so that the opponents cannot return it. The server must serve underhand either by bouncing the ball first or by striking it with an underhand action from a toss. A serving base should be marked 3 m from the net.

RULES

So long as the ball continues bouncing it may be returned over the net. It is dead when it rolls along the ground, is hit out of court or into the net. According to the problems faced by players, they may not have to return the ball first time but may be allowed to combine a sequence of hits to save a difficult ball. No player may hit the ball twice in succession. If the net is high enough to prevent setting up a smash, up to three hits may be allowed on one side of the net.

SCORING

The first team to achieve 21 points wins a set.

The simplest way of organizing serving is for each player (who is capable) to serve three times and then to change over; this is similar to the sequence in table tennis.

A similar game may be played as a form of hand tennis using a larger foam ball struck with the hand, but players need to be more mobile to reach the ball without the aid of a bat. This game works better with older players.

TEAM BATINTON (Figure 7.18)

This game is similar to badminton, except that a rubber-tipped batinton shuttlecock and cork-faced lightweight batinton bats are used. The batinton 'bird' flies much faster than a badminton shuttle and follows a normal parabolic flight curve. Although the flight is faster, it is easily predictable, and from experience it appears that handicapped children with good arms find the rubber-tipped shuttle easier to hit.

Four a side can comfortably play on an area half the width of a badminton court with the normal 1.5 m high net (see Figure 7.18). In this way two games of four a side can be accommodated on a badminton court.

RULES

1. The shuttle is served underarm from behind the service line over the net and into the opposite court past the service line.
2. The shuttle may be struck twice by either team, but no individual may hit it twice in succession.
3. Points are scored when the shuttle lands on the floor, goes into or under the net, or is struck out of court.
4. Each set consists of 21 points and scoring takes place as in table tennis.
5. Each player serves five times in succession, then service changes over.

This game is suitable as vigorous exercise for moderately disabled children, but paraplegic children with good arms have been found to cope well in the front-court position either kneeling or in a wheelchair. The cork-faced bats are light and little technical ability is required to hit the shuttle hard. Basically the game is like badminton played to table tennis rules, but the shuttle may be struck twice on one side of the net.

Figure 7.18   Team batinton

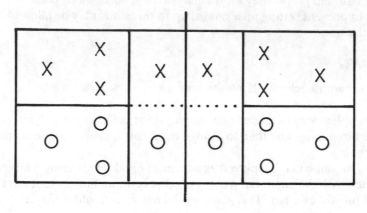

As in all team net games it is important for the flow of the game that players are taught to call early so that other players do not interfere with the shot to be played.

FOUR-SQUARE VARIATIONS (Figure 7.19)

The playing area of 4 m × 4 m is divided into four squares with a player in each square. Gymnasium benches can be set up as low nets.

Based on this formation, a wide variety of net games may be played with a range of ability levels. In the early stages of learning, all games should be based on principles of cooperation. As skill increases, group collective scores should be used with the four players working together to achieve a common goal. With older children of relatively matched ability, individual competition may be organized.

BASIC RULES

1. An object is served by bouncing, batting or throwing over the bench into an adjoining court, either in strict rotational sequence or at a later stage in any direction.

Figure 7.19   Four-square variations

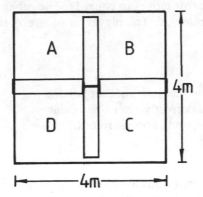

2. After the first service the receiving player must keep the ball in play and redirect it into the next square in the sequence.
3. The object must not hit the bench and must land within the confines of the appropriate square.

These three simple rules can be adapted to govern a wide variety of simple games.

DEVELOPMENTAL SEQUENCE

1. Cooperation from square to square — any number of hits.
2. Throw large beanbags from a kneeling position. Count the group score before a drop occurs.
3. Bounce a large ball from square to square. Catch after one bounce and pass it on.
4. Bat a large ball with the fist or hand. Start with two bounces, then reduce to only one.
5. Use a short tennis bat and foam tennis ball. Build up to a one-bounce sequence.
6. Play over a net 0.5 m high. How many consecutive hits can the four of you make before a mistake? Hit the ball so that the next player has an easy shot within reach. Can you beat your best total score? Can you hit the ball up into the air?

COMPETITION

Using any of the above skills at the appropriate ability level, the object of the game is to stay in square A as long as possible. The player in square A always starts the service sequence. The game then continues with each player trying to redirect the ball into any of the other three courts. After a mistake or a foul shot, the player in error moves to court D. The other players each move one square nearer to square A. The player in square A then restarts the service sequence.

FAULTS

1.   Failure to hit the ball into another square.
2.   Failure to serve correctly after one bounce.
3.   Balls which land on the lines are out.

HAND TENNIS

This game is played on a court approximately 10 m × 5 m with a 1 m high net. Up to four players a side may play, according to degree of mobility. Players attempt to bat a light beach ball with their hands over the net and into the opposite court. Points are scored when a ball is hit out of court or into the net. Able players play a one-bounce rule, but for the less mobile two bounces may be allowed. The ball must be struck by the hand or arm and may not be held. Under certain circumstances the ball may be struck more than once on one side of the net to work it nearer to the net.

PLANNING THE LESSON

Because of the need for technical competence to participate in net games, the best form of lesson plan for disabled children is a gradual build up of techniques related to the game. Unlike in many other games, the skills involved in playing over a net tend to be highly specific to serving in an upward direction and coping with a steeply falling projectile. These skills, therefore, need to be rehearsed *in situ*. Throwing and catching in invasion games can be easily adapted to general situations, but this is less likely in net games. Unless the handicapped child can throw, hit or catch in the court and net situation, he cannot participate at all; therefore, a progressive sequence of specific technique teaching is essential. The easily isolated basic skills of net games are:

1.   Serving over the net.
2.   Playing rallies.
3.   Moving opponents around the court to create space.
4.   Defensive covering of the court space.

Elements of each of these skills should be taught in a net games lesson to improve both tactical understanding and technical competence. Prior to the setting up of a competitive game, most net games lend themselves easily to cooperative practice in making rallies. Through practising the basic skills in a cooperative manner, the children may well be able to invent their own versions of games suited to their talents.

LESSON MATERIAL

Cooperation
In pairs:
1. Throw and catch a beanbag over a low net. Increase height.
2. Throw and catch a ball after one bounce.
3. Bat and rally a foam ball over a low net.
4. Practice serving over the net to a partner.

Cooperative/competitive
1. First pair to make 10 successive catches or hits.
2. Most hits in a rally of 30 seconds.
3. Highest successive number of hits.

Competition
1. Throw ball over the net; score if opponent misses the ball after one bounce. Restrict individual space.
2. Hit over the net within reach of partner; score if he misses or hits into the net.

In fours, 2 v. 2 (very narrow courts)
1. Throw and catch over the net. Practice a front- and back-court formation. Cooperate and alternate length of throw to front and back player. Players take turns at positions. Teach technique of throwing and catching.
2. Hit and rally over the net using front and back formation. Judge strength of hit to front and back player.
3. Cooperative/competitive. Each group of four cooperates to achieve longest rally.
4. Competitive 2 v. 2 after an easy service.

Groups 4 v. 4
Repeat as above but lay emphasis on the need to alternate the rally from front to back and side to side. Teach defending players to support each other closely in case of an error while still covering the court space.

LESSON PLAN

Introductory activity
Warm up by rallying over the net continuously in pairs.

Skill training
Introduce a new technique as a cooperative activity in pairs, progressing through to a cooperative/competitive small-group activity.

Final game

Organize a series of net games on a team basis. Teach the basic rules and reinforce both the related techniques and tactics taught in the skills training section.

STRIKING GAMES

All striking games which are played on a team basis involve the techniques of:

1. striking a ball;
2. fielding the ball and dismissing the strikers;
3. scoring runs by running between bases.

Before striking games are introduced to children it is essential that some mastery of these basic techniques has been achieved at an early learning stage. Provided that some proficiency has been demonstrated, a wide range of striking games can be adapted for play by handicapped children. There is a great danger that many striking games can produce long periods of inactivity while fielding, because usually only one or two players are involved in batting. Care should be taken to modify the games in several ways to ensure maximum all-round participation. Where possible, the normal 'one-life' innings of a striker should be amended, and in many games played on a small-sided basis the batsman can join the fielders after being given out.

The basis of inventing new games or of adapting established games for handicapped children revolves around a close inspection of the three main areas of skill involvement.

1. Simplify the type of service delivery to be struck and modify the playing equipment.
2. Restrict the total area of playing space and simplify the methods of dismissing the striker.
3. Adapt the method of scoring runs to allow for the limited locomotor ability of the runners.

BUCKET ROUNDERS (Figure 7.20)

The batter strikes a volleyball with his fist and attempts to run or wheel a circuit of the two cones before the fielders can retrieve the ball and drop it in the bucket.

The game can be played in two ways. In the first, batters are never out and a time period is played before the teams change over. An alternative is for batters to be either caught out or run out until the whole team is out, when the teams change roles.

A simple alternative for severely disabled children is to substitute a bean-bag throw instead of a hit ball. Any number of variations can be invented by changing the type of ball used and utilizing different kinds of bat to suit the ability of the players.

Figure 7.20   Bucket rounders

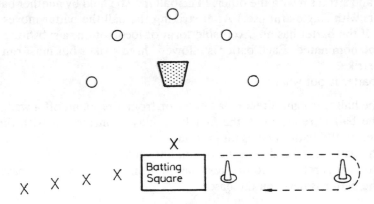

FIST-BALL ROUNDERS (Figure 7.21)

The pitch is laid out with a batting square and four bases (cones) in the shape of a diamond. The distance between bases may vary according to the size of the hall and the locomotor ability of the children. The game is played with a volleyball or cloth-covered football, which is struck with the fist.

Divide the players into two equal teams, a fielding team and a batting team. Players on the batting team bat in strict rotation throughout the game. The fielding team spreads out to cover the playing area, with the more handicapped players stationed at the base cones and inside the diamond.

Figure 7.21   Fist-ball rounders

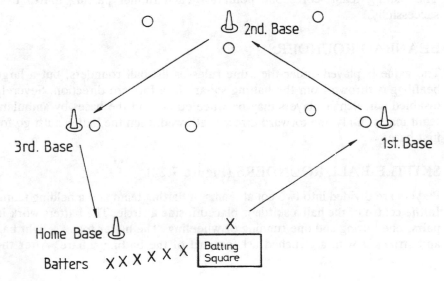

The first batter takes up position in the batting square, holds the ball in one hand and strikes it with the other. (The ball may be held by another batter for players with single-arm use.) After striking the ball the batter moves to first base. If the batter has no acceptable form of locomotion, a substitute runner may be nominated. Each batter is allowed three strikes but must run on the third strike.

A batter is out when:

1. the ball is caught direct by a fielder or from a rebound off a wall;
2. the ball is returned to the first base player, in contact with the base, before the batter makes his ground;
3. the batter is tagged with the ball in between bases;
4. the ball is returned to the next baseman, in contact with the base, while the batter is between the bases.

Runners who are at bases on the diamond must not start before the batter strikes the ball.

Base runners are out when they are:

1. hit by the batted ball;
2. tagged with the ball by a fielder when off base;
3. caught on a base by an incoming runner and tagged with the ball by a fielder (only one batter may occupy a single base);
4. forced to run to another base and fail to arrive before the baseman receives the ball.

An innings is over when all players in the batting team have been given out.

SCORING

The batting team scores one point for each runner passing fourth base successfully.

BEANBAG ROUNDERS

The game is played under the same rules as fist-ball rounders, but a large beanbag is thrown from the batting square in a forward direction. Severely disabled wheelchair players may be wheeled around the bases by ambulant team mates. Only one forward throw is allowed, then the batter must go for first base.

SKITTLE-BALL ROUNDERS (Figure 7.22)

Players are divided into two equal teams, a batting team and a fielding team. In the centre of the hall a skittle is placed inside a circle. The batters work in pairs, one hitting and one running or wheeling. The batter tosses a light ball and strikes it with a clenched fist forward of the batting square. After the

Figure 7.22   Skittle-ball rounders

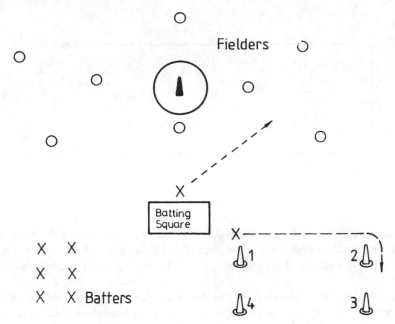

strike, the partner tries to score a run by running around the four base cones. The striker moves forward into the circle and attempts to defend the skittle. Fielders retrieve the ball and try to knock down the skittle while remaining outside the circle. If the skittle is hit down before a run is completed no score is counted, but if the runner completes the circuit of cones before the skittle is knocked over then a 'rounder' is scored. The defending batter may not completely shield the skittle with a body block. When each pair of batters has had two tries and changed places, the teams change over.

DANISH LONGBALL (Figure 7.23)

PLAYING AREA

The pitch is marked with two parallel lines, a front line and a back line approximately 10 m apart. Where suitable lines are not available, the four corners of the playing area may be marked by skittles or cones.

The object of the game is to score runs by batters getting to the back line and back without being out.

THE GAME

The players in the batting team line up at one side and behind the front line, with one batter positioned ready in the centre and behind the front line. The

Figure 7.23   Danish longball

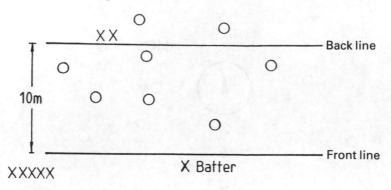

fielding team covers the space between the two lines and behind the back line. This batter holds a volleyball in one hand and strikes it with the other, his fist clenched. Very disabled players may have the ball held for them by another player.

After striking the volleyball the batter must run or wheel to the back line. A disabled wheelchair player may be pushed by an ambulant team mate after fisting the ball. That player may remain safely behind the back line as long as necessary until he decides that another batter has hit a ball that is good enough to give time to return to the front line to score a run. No restriction is placed on the number of batters safe behind the back line, but a team may not run out of batters at the front line.

A batter is out if:

1.   the ball is caught by a fielder in the air or off a wall;
2.   touched by a fielder in possession of the ball anywhere within the playing area between the two lines;
3.   hit by a thrown ball below the waist while he is within the field of play.

Any number of batters may be given out following one strike and according to the rules above. Batters may be given out for deliberately obstructing fielders who are already in position and, conversely, fielders without the ball may not get in the way of a batter running between the lines.

The whole batting team is given out when no batters remain behind the front line and all the players in the fielding team run behind the front line before the last batters can return from their safe positions behind the back line, or if a fielding player bounces the ball behind the front line.

Games may last any number of innings depending upon the time available.

Very severely disabled children with total arm involvement but with some kicking power in one foot are allowed to kick the ball from a stationary position and are then pushed in their wheelchairs by other players.

LONGBALL ROUNDERS

The game is played according to the rules of longball, but a 10 cm foam ball or playball is struck with a light narrow bat. The batter tosses the ball or drops the ball on the bounce with one hand and then strikes it with the bat. Very disabled players may strike a stationary ball from the ground or from a batting tee (e.g. balanced on a plastic cone).

This game is much simpler than the usual game of rounders, but it is more active as more players may be in safe positions behind the back line at any one time than could be accommodated on the normal rounders bases. Participation is thus increased as fewer players are queuing for a batting turn.

BAT-BALL

The object of the game is for a runner or a wheelchair player to score a run by going around a cone and back after another batter has hit the ball.

Figure 7.24   Bat-ball

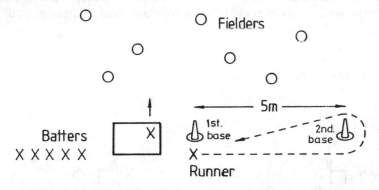

Players are equally divided into a batting team and a fielding team. The batter stands or sits on a mat, tosses the ball and strikes it out amongst the fielding team. After the strike, the runner for that player attempts to run around a cone and back without being out to score a run.

The runner is out when:

1. tagged by a fielder possessing the ball;
2. hit below the waist by a thrown ball while he is between the bases;
3. the ball is caught by a fielder direct from the strike;
4. a fielder in possession of the ball tags first base before the runner has reached home ground;
5. he fails to circle second base on his run.

The next batter in rotation then moves to the batting base and the previous batter replaces the runner. If the runner makes good the run, that player then moves to the end of the batting line to await his turn.

Both teams change over when an innings closes by a team being all out or, alternatively, after an agreed number of strikes.

The game is ideal as an introduction to a running batting game as the striker can concentrate on hitting without worrying about the immediate need to run. Many adaptations are possible by simple modifications to either the striking situation or the arrangements of the running base.

STOOLBALL (Figure 7.25)

This is a useful preliminary lead-up game for cricket and rounders, but it has been an established game in its own right in the United Kingdom for very many years. The traditional game is played on an eleven-a-side basis, but it is recommended that for maximum participation only six a side should be played.

There is a bowler, a wicketkeeper and fielders, with two batters involved at any one time. The aim of the game is for the batters to score runs by running between the wickets, as in cricket; the bowler and fielders attempt to dismiss the batters.

Figure 7.25   Stoolball

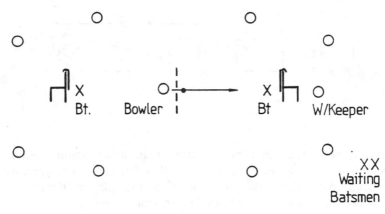

The wickets are placed roughly 10 m apart with a line marked in the centre at 5 m from each wicket, from which the bowler delivers the ball. The wickets can be made from two boards, each 45 cm square, with hooks on the back face so that they hang from the back of a chair. This allows an adequate target for the bowler and sets the wicket at a height which can comfortably be reached by players in wheelchairs.

METHOD OF PLAY

1. The batter takes up position at each wicket.
2. Two waiting batters sit behind one wicket keeping score and, if necessary, umpiring.
3. The remaining players field and spread out around the pitch.
4. The bowler delivers eight balls in an over at one wicket; delivery must be underhand and a full pitch. The type and size of ball used may vary according to the ability of the batter.
5. The batter attempts to strike the ball and, if the hit is successfully placed between fielders, the batters exchange places by running between the wickets. The batters may choose from varying shapes and sizes of bats, according to their ability to handle the implements.

RULES

1. A ball which is delivered out of reach of the batter is declared a no ball, one run is awarded to that player, and a further delivery must be bowled in the over.
2. The batter scores one run each time he completes a run between the wickets without being dismissed. Where a wall exists or a boundary line marked, four runs are awarded for striking the ball past the boundary mark.
3. A batter is dismissed out when:
    (a) the bowler hits the wicket;
    (b) the ball is caught directly off the bat;
    (c) the wicket is hit by the ball while out of home ground during an attempted run.
4. For maximum participation, each pair bats for three overs of eight balls each. The total score may be individual or summed as a pair — total runs divided by the number of times out. When the three pairs on one team have each batted for their allotted time period, the players in the opposing team take their turn to bat.

If the game is played in the above manner, allowing for all players rotating positions in the field, every player will have the opportunity, if desired, to bat, bowl, keep wicket and field according to personal level of ability.

CIRCLE CRICKET (Figure 7.26)

This game may be played indoors or out of doors as a team game or as a competition between matched pairs.

Two players are designated as batters, two players are bowlers, and the remainder of the children field in a large circle.

Two buckets are set up as wickets 8 m apart.

Figure 7.26 Circle cricket

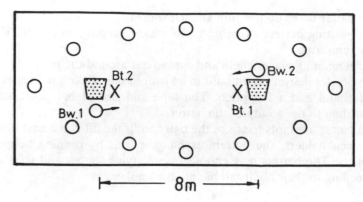

METHOD OF PLAY

The bowler pitches the ball in an appropriate way for the batter to hit it. The batters score one run if they can successfully change places before the fielders can place the ball in a bucket.

A batter is out if:

1. the ball hits the bucket direct from the bowler;
2. caught by a fielder directly from his hit;
3. a fielder puts the ball in a bucket after a hit with the batsman out of home ground.

To avoid the 'one life' situation, each pair may be awarded several lives (e.g. 4) or bat for four overs before being declared out. Their score would then be the total of runs scored divided by the number of times they were out.

Runs may also be awarded for hitting the ball through the fielders onto a wall or boundary marker.

Within a single game there may be changes in the equipment used, or in the bowlers' delivery, or in the batter's stance, according to the ability of the players involved. This game has been played successfully as a form of fist-ball with a volleyball rather than with a bat and ball.

LESSON PLANNING

Each lesson should start with some fairly vigorous fielding practices, the form of which will depend upon the disability of the children. It is essential that some time should be spent on practice of the specific striking skill inherent in the chosen game, particularly to focus on the specific type of service modification and equipment necessary for successful performance by each individual.

The lesson, therefore, becomes a simple format of:

1. Fielding warm up.
2. Striking practice. Possibly this may be linked to a serving–striking–fielding practice.
3. The main game (small sided).

Many suitable skills practices can be found in the section concerning the teaching of basic striking skills (see Chapter 4).

Chapter 8
MAJOR TEAM GAMES

Within the games programme of a normal school, particularly at secondary level, there is no doubt that the major national games predominate. Regrettably, such a programme does not always cater for the needs and interests of all pupils as there are many who do not possess the standards of physical fitness or the skills so necessary for successful and enjoyable participation. This is mainly true where the major games are presented in the sophisticated adult form without taking into account the age and ability of children. Nevertheless, when recent methods of 'teaching for understanding' are applied in small-sided versions of these games, they still play a most important role within the physical education curriculum. The major games are part of our sporting heritage and, as such, form part of our social culture.

In any kind of hierarchy of games playing the major national games are likely to be placed at the top. Many disabled children wish to take part in these games and identify with their sporting heroes. How far they will be able to play successfully depends not only on their disabilities but also on the ways in which the games can be adapted to suit their abilities. Within the mainstream situation there need to be degrees of integration in accordance with the needs and abilities of individual disabled pupils. This may vary from a relatively passive role as umpire, scorer or coach to the playing of a specific function within any given game. Certainly, mildly disabled children can play goalkeeper, act as a shooter in netball and basketball or play near the net in a range of net games. The question of integration within a games programme will be dealt with more fully in Chapter 9.

In a segregated setting it is still important that we provide children with the opportunity to take part in competitive games as part of a team. This is as vital to the development of their confidence and self-esteem as it is to the acquisition of games skill. They wish to identify with their able-bodied peers. Although team games are competitive and players try to win, this ought not to be the dominating aspect. The fostering of team spirit, the enjoyment of playing together, the development of tactical understanding and the pleasure of playing for sheer fun should be encouraged.

In this chapter several major national team games have been selected as good examples of activities that are suitable for presentation to disabled children. With appropriate adaptation, these activities may be played in both the segregated and the integrated school situation. The more usual forms of adaptation are described according to established principles and the listed activities are by no means complete. The principles of adaptation will, however, serve to illustrate methods of modifying most team games.

VOLLEYBALL

The main problems that arise when physically handicapped children attempt to perform volleyball skills occur through their inability to follow the flight of a fast-moving ball, their slowness in reacting and getting into position early enough to play a shot, and the mobility problems of covering the normal court space. The basic techniques of the game are relatively simple, but even normal children have difficulty in moving quickly enough into line with the ball in order to play the shot correctly from a sound body position. The problem of speed of reaction to fast ball flight must be solved. The degree of activity which can be developed depends very much upon the speed of flight of the type of ball used; the height of the net, which governs the flight-time of the ball; and the size of the court, which dictates how much floor space has to be defended. Raising the height of the net slows down the tempo of a game so that it is much more in keeping with the slower motor responses of the disabled. A smaller court cuts down the area to be covered by each player; in fact, courts can be zoned into various sized squares to be covered by individual players. Generally, during a volleyball game the more handicapped non-ambulant players should cover the front court under the net while the more mobile players with reasonable arm use should guard the rear court area.

The ball used in this game ought to be an overinflated brightly coloured beach ball. When inflated to a diameter of between 30 and 45 cm, the ball presents a large, relatively slow-moving target. Non-ambulant players can be provided with slim wooden bats to extend their reach.

RULES

The play area is 14 m × 7 m (or a badminton court), divided in half by a net 2 m high.

Teams consist of six to nine players a side.

The game is started by an underhand serve or an underhand throw from the centre of the court. This serving position may be modified according to the ability of players, with more able performers serving with an underhand punch from the rear right-hand corner of the court, as in normal volleyball. The service must clear the net and land within the opposite court area.

Play now consists of batting or striking the ball back over the net without allowing it to touch the ground. The ball may be struck with any part of the body, the wheelchair or the bat. Initially the ball may be played any number of times on one side of the net before being returned, but it must not be struck twice in succession by the same player. As players improve, the number of contacts by any team may be limited to three or four hits. Under certain circumstances one player on each side may be designated to catch the ball and thereby establish good control to set up the ball for team mates to follow a sequence of hits.

Points are gained by the serving team when the ball touches the ground on the opponents' side of the net or when the opponents hit the ball out of court. When the serving team loses a rally, the service passes to the other team. Only the serving team may score points.

Each player in a team should have the opportunity to serve in order of rotation, but substitute servers may be allowed when any player is unable to serve or throw the ball over the net.

A match consists of three 15 point sets. If the score reaches 14 all, then a team must win by 2 clear points (e.g. 16–14, 17–15).

Figure 8.1   Volleyball: tactical court cover (seven players)

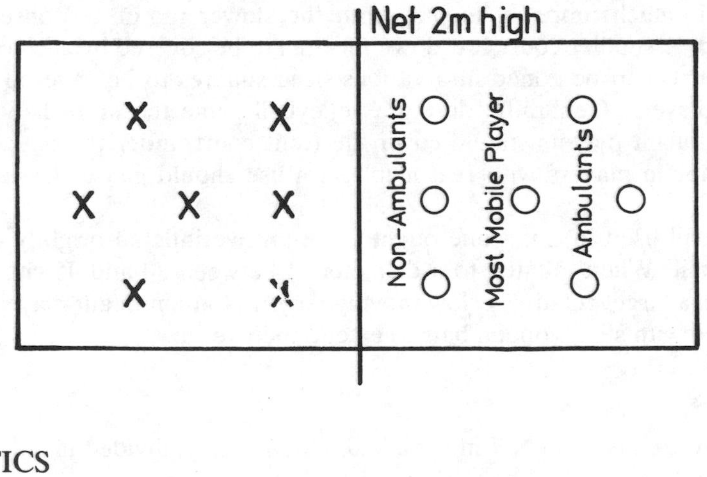

TACTICS

The most efficient system of covering the court area is for two or three non-ambulant players to play in the front court area near the net, the most skilful and mobile player to cover centre court, and the remaining ambulant players to form a defensive arc to the rear of the centre court. In this way the most mobile players cover the area in which the ball is most likely to land from service (see Figure 8.1).

On receiving the ball from the opposing service, the first shot should be played as high as possible towards the net in order to allow time for players to move underneath the ball and play a more controlled shot prior to returning the ball back over the net as deeply as possible into court.

It is highly unlikely that handicapped children could develop sufficient skill to learn the spike-and-block techniques of normal volleyball; in any case this would hinder the participation of the more handicapped players.

TEACHING VOLLEYBALL

The greatest emphasis in teaching the game should be placed on practice designed to keep the ball up in the air as long as possible. Players must be taught to pass the ball around on their side of the net with sufficient height to establish more time and control.

The *dig* is the most common shot used in defence; it is played from a ball dropping low into court. Under normal circumstances this shot is played two-handed, but for many handicapped children the one-arm shot is easier. The arms are placed straight and together underneath the ball to form a flat platform and the ball is allowed to bounce off as high as possible. The same technique is used for one-arm play or for a bat or elbow crutch using the level-platform principle.

Practice (Figure 8.2)
The feeder throws the ball onto the arc of players facing the net, and each player in turn tries to dig the ball back to the feeder. All practice situations in volleyball should be performed towards the net as this reinforces the tactical value of shots. In the first stages of practice the ball may be allowed to bounce first as this slows down the response necessary.

Figure 8.2   Volleyball: practice for dig shot

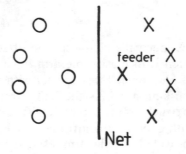

As children grow more skilful, they should attempt to keep the ball continuously in the air. Simple competitive practices can be developed by counting the highest consecutive number of hits performed in groups of four.

THE VOLLEY PASS

This shot is straightforward for ambulant players but more difficult for wheelchair users. The shot is played by bending the knees to place the head under the ball, then striking the ball with both sets of fingers and thumbs from in front of the head. Wheelchair players with good hand control can develop good technique with practice, but it is critical that the ball should be struck just above the forehead; it is difficult if players cannot get into position under the ball early enough. Ambulant players should spend a great deal of time practising the volley pass because of the high degree of control to be gained from its use.

Practice (Figure 8.3)
(a) Play the ball back and forward between two lines of players.
(b) Keep the ball in the air and try to play to the feeder.

Figure 8.3   Volleyball: practice for volley pass

Perhaps the most important teaching point to establish early is that the player must move into position as soon as possible and face the direction *in which he intends to strike the ball*.

THE SERVE

The underarm serve is much the simplest type of service and can be performed by most children with reasonable arm function, regardless of their ambulatory problems. The server faces the net with the ball held level with the shoulder of the striking arm. As the ball is released, the arm swings straight and the ball is struck off the top of the fist and punched over the net. Wheelchair players with good arm control usually have little difficulty with the underarm serve, provided that the arm rests are removed from the chair. Even with the arm rests in position it is possible for the player to lean out and strike the ball at the side of the chair.

In the early part of any volleyball lesson, great attention should be placed on acquiring the fundamental techniques of the game. Without a general ability to hit the ball fairly accurately into the air the game of volleyball is not much fun, but handicapped children are able, with practice, to acquire the skills very quickly.

ONE-BOUNCE VOLLEYBALL

This is a simplified version of the game with the normal rules, except that one bounce is allowed on either side of the net. The one bounce may be direct from service or at any stage in a sequence of shots and allows some compensation for a mishit.

CRICKET

As most special schools are unlikely to have a cricket pitch, the game as played with a hard ball on an unpredictable grass pitch has no place in the programme. However, when the game is played with a soft ball and a lightweight bat on a predictable hard surface, either indoors or on a playground, it may still retain the essential elements of the proper game and provide a very enjoyable experience for boys and girls. The eleven-a-side game reduces participation to minimum levels and should be replaced by smaller-sided games to ensure greater levels of involvement for all players. The greatest problems of the handicapped in playing cricket are obviously difficulty in judging ball flight, in handling the equipment, in coping with the space to be covered because of their limited mobility, and the invidious 'one-life' situation they experience when batting. Each of these problems may easily be solved while still retaining most of the essential features of the game.

Sufficient books have been written about the game of cricket and they do not require amplification here; therefore space will be restricted to descriptions of adapted forms of the game.

INDOOR CRICKET

Because of space problems, the game is best played on a single wicket basis with the bowler always delivering the ball from the same end. In this way the batting wickets can be set well back at one end of the hall, allowing most shots to be played into the space at the sides and in front of the batsman. This also saves time as the fielders always remain in the same relative positions and too much switching around is avoided for fielders of limited mobility.

EQUIPMENT

1 small cricket bat or lightweight bat shape;
1 rounders bat;
1 skittle to mark the bowlers' end;

1 set of indoor stumps or 1 box (approximately 45 cm high and 30 cm wide);
1 10 cm Wembley playball (vinyl).

RULES

1. Players are divided into a batting team and a fielding team in such a way as to balance the team composition by ability or handicap as far as possible. Teams toss for choice of first innings.
2. The pitch should be roughly 10–12 m long from the bowling skittle to the batting stumps.
3. All bowling must be underarm, and the speed ought to be controlled according to the ability of the batter. In the case of a very disabled player batting from a kneeling position, the ball must pitch short of a line drawn 4 m from the batting crease. (Such a player will be forced to play with a horizontal bat action; therefore the delivery must approximate to a rolled ball.)
4. Each non-ambulant batter may have the assistance of a runner.
5. Scoring system. Runs are scored by the batter hitting the ball against any of the four walls of the hall — 1 scored for the side or rear walls, and 4 or 6 runs scored for hitting the front wall behind the bowler (4 on the ground and 6 if the wall is hit direct from the shot). If the batter or runner actually runs the length of the pitch after striking the ball, then a further 1 run is added to the score (e.g. a hit to the side or rear wall counts 1 run, followed by a run taken counts 1 run = 2 runs scored). A single run may also be taken by the batter at any time after striking the ball, even if the ball does not reach the walls. One run will also be added to the batter's score if the bowler delivers a no-ball or a wide; and an additional ball will be bowled in the over.
6. A batsman is out if bowled, caught either straight off the bat or off a wall, leg-before-wicket, stumped, or run out during the course of an attempted run.

GAME PROCEDURE

Depending upon the number of players involved, all players field, including the batting team, except for the batter and runner. The game can be played with any number of players in a team, but greater involvement is achieved if the game is played with four, five or six players per team.

Each batter plays for 3 six-ball overs regardless of how many times that player is put out. At the end of a batter's innings, the score is calculated by dividing runs scored by the number of times dismissed. If the batter completes the innings of 3 overs without receiving a life, a bonus of half the run total is added to his score (half runs shall be discounted).

The scoring should be undertaken by a member of the batting side in the manner shown in Figure 8.4.

Figure 8.4 Scoring

Name	Runs	Total	Times Out	Score
A	1.2.1.W 4.2.2.W 2.2	16	2	8
B	1.1.1.1.2	6	–	9

Batsman A   16 runs for twice out
             16/2 = *8 scored*

Batsman B   6 runs scored not out
             6 + 3 bonus = *9 scored*

In this way each player participates fully as a batter, regardless of disability; even if a player is only able to defend the wicket, there is still the opportunity to benefit from the bonus system.

The winning team is obviously the team with the highest score after the scores of the individual team players have been calculated and added together.

IMPORTANT ADAPTATIONS

1. Ambulant players use a light bat or bat-shape of a size appropriate to their age.
2. Non-ambulant players move out of their chairs and kneel or lie across a support cushion. They use a light rounders bat. These batsmen play one-handed, and care should be taken in placing them in a good stable sideways position from which they have reasonable freedom of arm

Figure 8.5 Indoor cricket

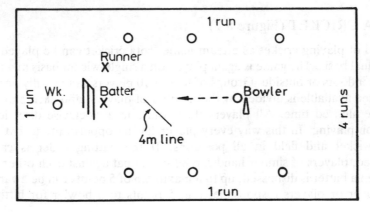

action. Many severely disabled children have been found to hit better with a backhand action.

3. Ball flight must be modified to suit the ability of each player.
4. The 10 cm diameter playball has been found ideal for hitting, yet it is small enough to be fielded and thrown.
5. Wheelchair fielders may use a lightweight plastic hockey stick to increase their reach and help them stop the ball.

This game of small-sided cricket is very easily adapted for use in a playground, provided that boundary lines can be easily marked with skittles, etc. In this case boundary lines can be marked approximately 20 m out from the pitch and 4 runs awarded for a boundary hit. In the playground, very disabled batsmen may be placed on a mat to protect their knees. The problem of handling a larger class while maintaining high involvement levels is solved by playing two games of single-wicket cricket back-to-back with the batters hitting in opposite directions for safety and convenience (see Figure 8.6).

Figure 8.6   Two games of single-wicket organized in a playground

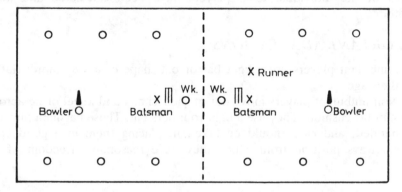

ROTA CRICKET (Figure 8.7)

Instead of playing cricket as a team game, rota cricket can be played on an individual basis. The game is again played on a single-wicket basis and may be played indoors or outside. Groups of 8, 9 or 10 players can be fully occupied. The time available is divided by the number of players, and each player bats out the allotted time. All players then rotate in a clockwise direction and carry on playing. In this way every player has an opportunity to bat, bowl, keep wicket and field in all positions. If the batting order is carefully arranged, players of similar handicap bowl and bat against each other.

When a batter is dismissed, up to a maximum of 5 points can be awarded to the player or players responsible, e.g. 5 points to a bowler for hitting the

Figure 8.7   Rota cricket

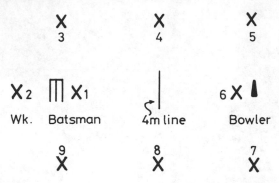

wicket, 2 points to the bowler and 3 to a fielder for a catch. These points are added to the total runs scored by any player when he bats.

The winner is the individual with the highest batting average (total of runs scored plus fielding points, divided by the number of dismissals), e.g.

A has 21 runs for twice out plus 11 points for bowling and fielding:

average $\dfrac{21 + 11}{2} = 16$.

B has 15 runs not out, plus 4 points for fielding:
average $= 19$.
B is the winner.

Much valuable time can be spent at the beginning of a cricket lesson in setting up skill practice situations in twos or threes at the basic techniques of batting, fielding and bowling. Suitable practices may be selected from Chapter 4 on the development of striking, throwing and catching techniques.

HOCKEY

Field hockey presents the difficulty of controlling and hitting an awkwardly bouncing small ball with a very narrow stick on a large pitch. These are the major factors to consider in simplifying the game for presentation to handicapped children. The game can suitably be modified for play in an indoor space or on a hard playground area where wheelchairs can be easily manipulated. Experience has shown that a form of hockey can provide a most enjoyable activity, particularly for wheelchair players where the use of a lightweight stick enhances their reach and increases their opportunity for fully active involvement much more than in many other games. The game is best presented as a form of Unihoc or shinty where both sides of the stick-head may be used.

Snarl-up in a hockey game

APPARATUS

The commercially available Unihoc plastic sticks are ideal as they are light-weight, can be simply shortened to any required length, and have a flat head on each side. They have the further advantage of being available in different colours, which simplifies the identification of the players in each team. Shinty sticks may also be used and cut down to an appropriate size for each individual. The important factors are the lightness of the stick and the length of the shaft, so wheelchair players can use one hand for play and the other for chair control.

The ideal ball for play is the airflow plastic ball of approximately 8–10 cm diameter; it does not bounce and is light enough to be hit firmly but easily. A plastic puck is supplied with the Unihoc kit, but it is too small for handi-capped children to manipulate. A simple puck can be made from a wooden block 10 cm in diameter and 4 cm deep. A large plastic ball, slightly deflated to reduce bounce, may be used by younger children to simplify hitting and stopping.

The goal may be a portable indoor goal net or merely an area marked by large skittles. The goal should be not more than 2 m wide.

The pitch may be any size. Indoors, the only markings need be a goal restriction area marked 2 m from each goal post on the goal line and a 2.5–3 m line drawn parallel to the goal line (see Figure 8.8).

Figure 8.8   Hockey pitch

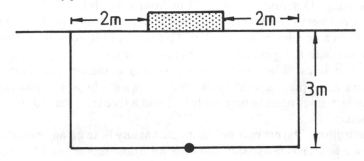

BASIC RULES

1. The team. Each team consists of a goalkeeper and three or five other players, according to the space available. If there are more players than this, conditions indoors become overcrowded.
2. The game. A game should consist of three or four periods of 6 minutes as agreed, with a 2-minute interval between periods. This allows for a rest between periods of vigorous activity and helps to maintain concentration during play. Teams toss for choice of ends or possession of the ball from the centre. The team which is behind in the scoring at the end of each period starts the game in the subsequent period. Play is started by a hit forward from the centre spot to a supporting team mate.
3. Scoring. A goal is scored whenever the puck crosses the goal line fully, between the posts, and on the ground. No goal is scored if the puck goes into the goal above floor level. After a goal, play restarts from the centre spot.
4. Restricted goal area:
    (a) No other player is allowed to go into the goalkeeper's area with wheelchair, foot or stick. This is a violation, and possession is given to the opponents as a free hit from which a goal may not be scored direct.
    (b) The goalkeeper has total freedom of movement within the restricted area but may not move out of that area. This is a violation, and a free hit

is awarded to the attacking team from the spot where the violation occurred. A goal may be scored direct from the free hit.

5. Fouls:

(a) Rough play resulting in hacking or striking with the stick, pushing a player or direct contact with a wheelchair is a foul. The penalty is a free hit. Any player guilty of two such fouls within a period of play is temporarily sent off to the 'sin bin' for 2 minutes, leaving the team one player short.

(b) Dangerous play is the raising of a stick above wheel height while within playing distance of another player. A free hit is awarded to the opposition. Defenders withdraw 1 m from a free hit.

(c) A deliberate foul committed to directly prevent a goal being scored results in a penalty being awarded. This is a free hit from the centre of the 3 m line with the goalkeeper restricted to remain on the goal line.

6. Out of bounds. Where the game is played in an uncluttered sports hall or gymnasium, play is continuous off the walls. In a playground area, boundary lines need to be established and a free hit awarded from out of bounds.

7. Substitution. Players may be substituted at any time on an unlimited basis when a team has possession and calls for 'substitution', or when the puck is dead.

8. In the event of a draw at full time, there may be extra time (2–3 minutes) as agreed, a sudden-death play-off to the first goal, or a penalty shoot out of an agreed number to each team.

METHOD OF PLAY

The game should be played on the basis of five or six a side according to the principles of play of all invasion games. Where a man-for-man marking system is used, players may be paired off according to matched ability. Teams of mixed ability may play either as walkers or crawlers, or in wheelchairs. Walking players should be restricted to no more than three successive touches on the puck while on the move. This forces the more mobile players to involve the more disabled in team play. Severely disabled players in electric chairs may play a vital role as goalkeepers. The chair should be turned sideways to the field of play and operate forwards and backwards parallel to the goal line. If the goalkeeper can handle a short stick and simultaneously operate the joy stick, it is a distinct advantage. Where a ball or puck is trapped under the wheels, a dead ball may be called and a free hit may be taken by a mobile defence player from the edge of the area. A simple game may be played with great enjoyment and activity, so long as the strict rules of safety governing stick play and body contact are upheld.

VARIATIONS
SCOOTERBOARD HOCKEY

Price (1980) suggests a game of scooterboard hockey for ambulant children and those normally confined to a wheelchair. The scooterboard is rather like a large wooden tray on castor wheels and is propelled by pushing against the floor with either hands or feet, with the player lying face down on the board. A short stick is necessary for one-handed manipulation. Even severely disabled children demonstrate great mobility at ground level after practice. Normal hockey rules can apply, except that a collision of scooterboards must count as a physical contact foul and stick work at floor level must be carefully controlled.

ISLAND HOCKEY (Figure 8.9)

This is a game suitable for all levels of disability because it requires some skill but very little movement. Children can develop certain hockey skills in a static environment without the direct interference of mobile opponents. In action it resembles a game of table soccer with live players instead of miniature teams. A normal indoor pitch is used with restricted goal areas, but all players are restricted to static positions. The team is divided into defence and attack positions, with each team placed around the pitch in alternate spaces. Wheelchair players have a small chalk circle marked around them, while standing and kneeling players are stationed within a hoop on the floor. No player may leave the circle. If the circular islands are kept 2 m apart, it is possible to cover most of the court. Each player is allowed to reach beyond his personal space with arm and stick only.

The object of the game is for each team to pass an airflow ball from island to island, without the opponents gaining an interception, until a shot at goal

Figure 8.9   Island hockey

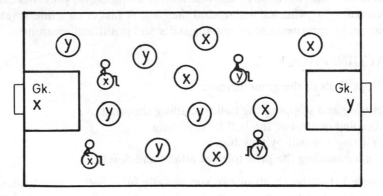

can be set up. After a goal or a save by the goalkeeper, the game is restarted by a hit out or a roll out by the goalkeeper. If the ball rolls out of reach of all players, possession is awarded to the nearest opponent of the player who last played the ball. Simple modifications may be made to increase the amount of gross motor activity, otherwise normal safety rules of hockey will apply.

ZONE HOCKEY (Figure 8.10)

In the figure, two defenders and two attackers are restricted to playing in each half of the pitch. They are not allowed to cross the halfway line. These players should be matched pairs of approximately equal ability levels, the most handicapped participants playing in attack or defence. Two mobile players (X1 and X2 and Y1 and Y2) on each team act as midfield fetchers and carriers who are allowed to play over the full court.

Figure 8.10

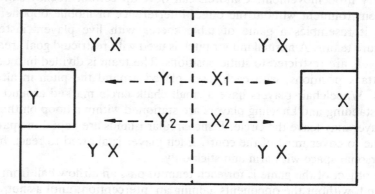

This game allocates players to suitable positions according to their functional ability and, because of the restrictions on mobility, prevents excessive overcrowding by wheelchairs around the ball. A fast open game results with considerable improvement of passing skills and positional awareness.

TEACHING HOCKEY

The basic skills of the game involve:

1. Hitting and stopping the ball, including shooting.
2. Keeping control of the ball by dribbling.
3. Winning the ball by tackling.
4. Understanding the principles of attack and defence.

Provided that the children can successfully hit a ball, a small-sided game based on simple rules may be introduced almost immediately. As the need for successful performance of techniques arises from playing the game, each lesson should include lead-up stages to the game. The safety aspects of stick play must be introduced at the outset.

INDIVIDUAL SKILLS PRACTICE

1. Dribbling anywhere around the playing area. Use both sides of the stick head to flick left and right while on the move. Kneeling players wear knee pads; wheelchair players dribble with one hand (short stick).
2. Dribbling around obstacles such as skittles. Keep the airflow ball close to the stick.
3. Free dribbling — stop and start on command.
4. Dribble and control the ball along any lines marked on the floor.
5. Shoot at the wall, stop the return and repeat.
6. Dribble freely, shoot at a wall, and pick up the return.

Teaching points
- Correct grip on the stick for right-handed players is left hand at top of the handle and right hand held low with hands well apart.
- Control with the top hand; hit with the bottom hand.

SMALL-GROUP SKILLS IN TWOS OR THREES

1. In pairs, passing and stopping the ball. Get in line with the ball early; use the bottom hand to cushion the ball when stopping. Increase the distance as skill improves.
2. In pairs, passing on the move. Pass and move to a free space. Pause and check a free path to partner before releasing the pass. Avoid other players. Encourage children to stop the ball, look up and scan the play before passing.
3. In threes, passing in a triangle. Stress angles of support play. Change direction and try to use both faces of the stick head while passing.
4. In threes, passing and stopping while on the move. Stop the ball, lift the head, look and pass.
5. In pairs. One keeps goal against a wall while the other shoots. Change places.
6. In threes. One goalkeeper against a wall. The other two pass and shoot at goal alternately. Stress the sequence — pass, stop, look up and shoot.

OPPOSED PRACTICES

1. 4 v. 1 in a grid square. Six consecutive passes, then change the defender. Stop the ball after each pass.
2. 3 v. 1 plus a goalkeeper. Play three consecutive passes, then shoot for goal.
3. 5 v. 2 in half a gymnasium. Count number of consecutive passes. Encourage good supporting positions, especially between the two defenders.

4.   4 v. 2 plus a goalkeeper. Four consecutive passes gain a permit to shoot at goal.

LESSON PLAN

The exact form of lesson plan will depend upon the age and skill level of the children. Younger disabled children require concentrated technique practice whereas older groups need to play in the game situation rather more.

Warm-up: Individual skill practice on the move.
Skills training: Partner work and practice in threes.
Opposed practice: Appropriate to the skill level.
Final game: Six-a-side hockey.

BASKETBALL

Wheelchair basketball is now a highly developed international game played to Olympic standards by fit and skilful disabled athletes. Standard rules of normal basketball operate, except for very obvious adaptations which are necessary because the teams play from wheelchairs. The complete international rules are available from the British Sports Association for the Disabled.

Although this form of basketball is an extremely fast and energetic game with highly complex rules, it can easily be adapted to suit the school situation. As it is unlikely that two complete teams of skilled wheelchair players can be found in one small school, it is necessary to produce a kind of game where ambulant and wheelchair players can perform together in a fair situation. Provided that the children have achieved a reasonable standard in passing and catching a ball, a very simple game can be played almost immediately with beginners. In its simplest form basketball is a team passing game, involving the use of the hands only, where two teams attempt to throw the ball into a basket and prevent their opponents from scoring or keeping possession of the ball. At the start only two main rules need apply: no running with the ball and no physical contact between players or wheelchairs. As the skill of the players grows, a further rule can be added allowing a player one dribble. (Ambulant players must only move their feet when dribbling with one hand at a time; the dribble ends when the player holds the ball in two hands or when the ball comes to rest. When performing a dribble from a wheelchair, the player alternately pushes the wheels of the chair and bounces the ball on the floor. When the player takes more than two consecutive pushes on the wheels without bouncing the ball, the dribble must end.) Any infringements of the above rules result in the ball being awarded to the opposing team for a throw-in from the nearest side line.

EQUIPMENT

The basket and backboard should be lowered to a height of 2 m from the ground. Portable baskets adjustable for height are now available commercially.

As a basketball is too large to handle easily, a size 5 vinyl indoor football should be substituted.

FIELD OF PLAY

This may be any size of hall with boundary lines drawn 1 m from the walls.

In a playground, boundary lines should be drawn to limit the playing area to approximately 20 m × 14 m, with a centre restraining circle of 2 m radius.

TIME

The game is divided into two equal periods of time by arrangement between the teams.

RULES

1. Two teams of five to eight players with equal numbers of wheelchair and ambulant players. If some of the ambulant players are athetoid or ataxic, they should be shared equally between the teams.
2. Play is started with a throw-up of the ball at the centre of court between two opposing players. They must tap the ball with one hand out of the centre circle to bring the ball into play. At the tip-off, other players may be in either half of the court.
3. Ambulant players with the ball in their possession must not take more than two steps. Similarly, wheelchair players must not perform more than two pushes while in possession of the ball.
4. All body contact is strictly forbidden, including contact between wheelchairs.
5. No ambulant player may encroach within 1 m of a wheelchair player. This would be classed as 'overguarding'.
6. Any severely disabled player unable to pass the ball correctly is regarded as a 'safe ball' player. Only a player from the same team may remove the ball from his grasp. (This ensures minimum participation for even the most severely handicapped within the team-game situation.) No opponent may encroach within a 2 m radius.
7. A player may not kick the ball.
8. When the no-dribble rule is in operation, a player may take up any position on the court at any time in the game.
9. For all infringements (except personal contact when shooting) the ball is awarded to the opposing team from the nearest sideline.

10. If a personal contact foul is committed on a player in the act of shooting, the shooter is awarded three free throws at the basket from which he may score two shots. Free throws will be taken from behind a line marked 2 m from the basket.
11. A player may block any shot while the ball is on its upward flight. Once the ball commences the downward flight, no player may interfere with either the ball or the basket.

SCORING

Two points are awarded when the ball drops in the basket as a result of normal play.

One point is awarded for each shot scored from a free-throw award.

If the game results in a tie at the end of normal time, a further 2 minutes will be played. If the game then remains a tie, play continues until the next deciding basket is scored.

TEACHING THE GAME

It is suggested that basketball should not be introduced initially by a series of isolated skills practices but should be developed as a simple free ball-passing game with full participation immediately. During this phase of teaching, the teacher should be most concerned with enjoyment, vigorous exercise and a thorough understanding of the principles of play. The minor games of captain-ball or skittle-ball can then be developed towards the more formal game of basketball by the gradual introduction of rules and further specific techniques as the need for them is demonstrated.

The principles of support play and possession are far more important than technical detail, and it is necessary to work for a complete understanding of basic rules from the outset. Certain rules must be emphasized again and again with beginners to avoid chaos: two step or two push, physical contact, overguarding and infringement of the 1 m encroachment. It is assumed that handicapped children have a thorough grounding in ball handling techniques and the tactics of minor team games before specific attention needs to be given to the fundamentals of basketball.

PASSING PRINCIPLES

Use two hands when possible and give the simplest pass as early as possible to keep the ball safe. Pass and move to a new position to receive a return pass. Support the ball player from all angles around the ball, particularly ahead. Spread out as wide as possible when in possession to create space and cause defenders to move quickly.

PASSING TECHNIQUES

In all types of passing there is a passer and a receiver, and the receiver must work hard to find space.

1. The two-handed chest pass is most useful when the ball carrier is not too closely guarded. The ball is drawn to the chest with both thumbs and fingers behind the ball, the elbows being bent outwards. The ball is released with a rapid extension of both arms and a sharp wrist flick. This pass is extremely efficient for most handicapped children.
2. The one-handed pass is best used when a player is closely guarded and can be played overhead, underhand or sideways.
3. The bounce pass is played off the floor past a guard. This pass can be played with one or two hands. It is useful when closely guarded and particularly useful when passing to a player who has problems in assessing ball flight. The ball should be bounced firmly enough to rise above waist level for the receiver. The receiver should attempt to catch the ball with both hands behind the ball and allow the elbows to 'give' to cushion the pace of the pass and ensure a safe catch.

PASSING PRACTICES

Initially the above techniques may be practised in unopposed situations in pairs or small groups until the fundamentals are learned. As early as possible, however, these techniques should be applied in more realistic but simplified practices involving the use of opponents to simulate game conditions.

Handicapped children need to learn when to pass as well as how to pass, and timing can be learned in simple practice situations. Small-sided practices involving 3 v. 1, 4 v. 1, and 4 v. 2 in limited space include the basics of tactical understanding in offensive basketball and are enjoyable games in their own right.

SHOOTING

The two basic shots are the two-handed set shot and the one-handed shot.

1. The two-handed set shot is held as in the chest pass but with the ball positioned just below the chin. The wrist snap is critical in gaining a high enough flight to enable the ball to drop from above the basket. Handicapped children must be taught to understand the principles of aiming:
    (a) In the early stages of learning it is most important to emphasize the visual aspects of the skill. Line up the hands, the ball, the eyes and the basket before shooting.
    (b) The 'feel' of the movement is only important when direction is

standardized. The shooter must now learn how much power to apply in the shot from varying distances.

2. The one-handed set shot is best used by ambulant players and, of course, by hemiplegics and amputees. The ball is held up in front of the forehead with the fingers and thumb under the ball. The arm is extended completely towards the basket and the ball released with a snap of the wrist. The ball flight must be in a high arc so that the ball drops down from above the basket. Ambulant players should initiate the shot with a drive from the legs, and two-armed players should steady the ball with the free hand before shooting.

SHOOTING PRACTICE

Groups of players in a circle around the basket take turns to shoot. Ambulant players return the ball.

When players become reasonably proficient they must then practise in threes shooting at the basket over a passive defender with the third player returning the ball.

TACTICS AND TEAM COACHING

The tactics of basketball can be found in any coaching text, of which there are many, but certain simple principles are basic to a better understanding and appreciation of the game.

Good, safe passing and sound support play are the basis of ball possession, which is critical in attack. Pass often and support fast. Always attempt to overload the defence by getting more players to support the ball in attack.

In defence, the basic principles are to take up a position between the opponent and the basket at all times and, within the rules of the game, prevent him from receiving the ball or shooting by an aggressive arm action. The two basic systems of defence are man-for-man marking and zone defence.

Man-for-man marking is highly energetic but should be taught at the outset to instil the principles of defensive play. As far as possible, players on both teams ought to be matched against each other in pairs according to their ability levels, in particular those related to their mobility around the court.

Zone defence can also be taught to handicapped children where the team forms a zone of defenders around the basket area and attempts to keep the ball out of shooting distance. Where teams of more than five players are competing, however, the number of players allowed to form a zone should be restricted to five, otherwise the under-basket area of court becomes rather congested.

Very handicapped youngsters can be placed in positions on court which do not require great mobility. The end-court positions of attack and defence are highly suitable as the children are then involved 'at the death'.

To achieve maximum participation with classes of 20 children or more, a sound variation of the game is half-court basketball. Five players defend one basket against five attackers in one half of the court while a further game is played in the opposite half. After a set period of time the two teams exchange roles. Most basketball tactics can be taught in this situation; then, when a full court game is played, spare players may act as substitutes, thus ensuring a regular interchange of players.

BADMINTON

Normal badminton is a fast and exciting game requiring high standards of mobility about the court, the acquired ability to monitor the decelerating flight of a high-speed shuttlecock, a wide range of wrist techniques, and an understanding of court tactics. The growth of PHAB (Physically Handicapped and Able Bodied) clubs with indoor sports facilities throughout the country makes badminton an ideal game for mixed participation between the physically handicapped and their normal peers. The basic problems in adapting the game are to slow down the decision-making and motor responses of the players and considerably reduce the size of the court to decrease the range of movement needed within the game. Wheelchair players may use the normal 1.5 m high net, but if the net is raised to 2 m for ambulant players this produces a slower and higher game pattern. The adapted form of the game is suitable for ambulant and wheelchair players of a wide variety of physical handicaps, provided they have the use of one good arm and can learn to judge the flight of a shuttle. The normal racket is extremely lightweight and, therefore, few players have difficulty in handling the equipment. In developing the game in the early stages of learning it is better to use a cooperative series of skill practices to produce longer rallies between players and thereby concentrate practice. As players acquire the various techniques to a reasonable level, competitive games can be introduced successfully. Good technique dominates the game, so it is important that handicapped players achieve competence at a few strokes before they begin to play. Constantly missing or mishitting the shuttle in a game is not much fun.

TEACHING THE GAME

The game is best taught as a singles game with the more complex tactics of doubles being introduced when children achieve competence at controlling the shuttle.

Class practice is best organized in pairs playing *across* a normal hall with the nets strung along the length of the space available. An ideal size for a singles court is approximately 3 m × 11 m. The narrowness of the court reduces sideways movement of the players to a minimum as they can reach each sideline in one or two steps to return the shuttle. With three badminton nets strung together along the hall at least six narrow singles courts can be marked.

This set-up occupies 12 players simultaneously, and by taking frequent turns a good number of children can be kept busy.

All teaching should relate tactical awareness, decision making and stroke play within the practice situation. Although technical teaching points concerned with stroking the shuttle are important, the game is much more than a series of strokes. It is a sequence of correct strokes appropriate to the tactical situation, and we must teach for understanding of these principles. Each practice must reflect the purpose of shots together with the many technical points concerned with making contact with the shuttle.

SEQUENCE OF TEACHING

THE GRIP

The normal 'unigrip' should be taught for it is important for children to play forehand and backhand shots to reduce the amount of movement necessary within the game. The chopper grip used by many handicapped children prevents control on backhand shots and causes more running.

The butt end of the handle should be placed on the heel of the hand (opposite the thumb with the handle laid diagonally across the palm and the base of the index finger). The thumb and index finger then close over and grip the sides of the handle while the little finger closes onto the base of the racket handle. With the racket head vertical to the ground, the grip appears to 'shake hands' with the racket and the 'V' between thumb and index finger lies on top of the handle.

Handicapped players with grasp problems may gain greater control by shortening their grip to further up the handle. This grip should be taught at the outset to avoid bad habits from developing and interfering with the learning of strokes.

THE SERVICE

'Can you put your opponent in the back of his court from your service, as far from the net as possible?'

Until children can bring the shuttle into play with a fairly high service it is not possible to set up practice drills.

The ambulant player stands in the centre of his court as well balanced as possible. A single crutch held under the non-striking armpit may help stabilize balance. The shuttle is held by the feathers with the thumb and index finger, while the racket is held up and back with the wrist cocked. As the shuttle is dropped or tossed slightly to the side, the arm swing commences and the shuttle is struck with a distinct snap of the wrist. The upward sweep of the racket should drive the shuttle high and drop it into the opposite court.

If the chair interferes with the more normal action, wheelchair players may be allowed to throw the shuttle high and hit with an overhead action.

Constant serving practice is needed before children can consistently bring the shuttle into play.

HIGH CLEAR

'Can you move your opponent to the back of the court with your return of service?'

The player moves under the shuttle as early as possible and attempts to make contact with an overhead shot from as high a point of overhead contact as possible. The racket ought to be taken down the back early to leave enough time to throw the racket head towards the shuttle. Teaching the overhead throwing action is critical to the development of the overhead clear shot.

Overhead rallies should now be practised with the objective of cooperating with the partner in hitting as many continuous shots as possible back and forward over the net. This can be played as a class game with the winners being the pair who achieve the highest number of hits in a given time.

LOW CLEAR

'When the shuttle falls short, can you still hit it high into the back of your opponent's court?'

This shot is played with a strong underhand wrist action, like the service from about knee height. Players with weak wrists and grip problems may still play with a long, straightish sweeping arm action.

HIGH BADMINTON

Once children can play high clear and low clear shots with reasonable success, high badminton can be played either as a singles or doubles game. A normal badminton court can be used, with the game being performed on a half-court basis, two matches per court.

The singles game is played half-court, with the area between the short service line and the net being excluded to prevent the use of drop shots, which necessitate too much movement by the defending player. Thus a player standing or sitting in centre court will always find the shuttle landing within his reach.

Normal badminton rules apply, except for overhead service from wheelchair players.

The doubles game is also played on a long narrow court with the non-ambulant player covering the front of court area from a standing, sitting or kneeling position near the short service line. In doubles play the front court area is, of course, fully used.

Depending upon the skill and locomotor ability of the players, the rules may be modified to allow two hits in succession by alternate players on one side of the net.

THE DROP SHOT

In games of singles between fairly mobile players and in all doubles games the use of the drop shot should be taught. This is used when opponents are in the back of the court and the shuttle is delicately dropped into the space near the net.

Practice can be organized in pairs with the players tipping the shuttle over the net for continuous rallies and trying to use finger control to keep the shuttle flight low and short.

BASIC TACTICS

PRINCIPLES OF ATTACK

1.   High service.
2.   Force the opponent into the back of court.
3.   Draw the opponent close to the net.
4.   Use the space created in the court to aim the next shot.
5.   Generally move the opponent away from the central 'control' position.
6.   Use disguise to mask intentions.

PRINCIPLES OF DEFENCE

1.   Avoid playing the centre-court area.
2.   When out of position gain time to recover by playing the shuttle high into the back of court.
3.   Change defence into attack by using an unexpected drop shot.
4.   Always attempt to regain the controlling position in centre court after each shot.

TEAM BADMINTON

This game is well suited to groups of handicapped children of mixed ability and as a game to integrate handicapped and normal children. The game is played on a normal badminton court with teams of four players on each side of the net, thereby considerably reducing the space to be covered by any one player. Two mobile players cover the rear-court area with the two more handicapped players in the front court. No rear-court player may return the shuttle from the front court while the shuttle is above net height. This is to allow mobile players to pick up low drop shots but prevents them from smashing down close to the net. The position of the server can be varied according to individual ability, but the shuttle may be hit anywhere into the opposing court. Under certain conditions, with players of lower ability the shuttle may be struck twice by alternate players on one side of the net.

Points may only be scored by the serving team as in normal badminton. Loss of a rally gives service to the opposing team. The sequence of service follows the pattern of normal badminton doubles, that is, when service has been lost by one pair of players, it reverts to their opponents. Each player must serve, but the servers in each team must consist of a mobile player plus a front-court player.

Exactly the same tactical principles apply in attempting to cause the opposing players to move in order that the shuttle may be hit to the floor in the spaces created.

REFERENCE

Price, R.J. (1980) *Physical Education and the Physically Handicapped Child*, Lepus Books, London

Chapter 9
GAMES TEACHING IN THE MAINSTREAM SCHOOL

Traditionally, physical education has always been taught in classes of mixed ability. Where schools have implemented a policy of streaming, the criterion for placement has been based on academic ability. As no relationship exists between intelligence and motor ability, it follows that children in a physical education class have always shown a wide range of ability in motor performance. Good teachers of physical education have, as a result of this experience, developed a sensitivity to the needs of individual children and an ability to select activities which match the performance level of the children. For the most part, however, this approach has been intuitive and often based on an assumption of particular needs. Through trial and error it has been possible to include most children in a programme of skill development. The implication of the 1981 Education Act means that many more pupils are entering mainstream education who may, to a greater or lesser extent, be impaired in their movement capacity in relation to their peer group. The new challenge facing the physical education profession is to integrate these atypical children within the programme and ensure that the children not only achieve success but feel that they are being successful. These children have a right to receive physical education appropriate to their unique needs. This means that the teaching of physical education must become even more orientated towards individualized instruction. It would be unrealistic to expect disabled children to reach the same levels of performance as their able-bodied peers, but they must have the same opportunity to learn and improve their movement skills. The problem facing teachers is how such opportunities can be presented in an integrated setting.

Integration into mainstream education may take place in three ways:

1. The development of campus sites which include the main school plus special units within a common environment. Integration may be partial, by ability in different subjects, or it may only be social by virtue of using common social and dining facilities.

2. Specially adapted schools may be designated as 'area schools' taking in all children with special needs from a given catchment area.
3. Children may be fully integrated into their local neighbourhood school.

Whichever system of placement is in operation, the teacher of physical education will ultimately be faced with atypical children sharing a lesson with their able-bodied peers. It would be a mistake to split any class into separate groups of disabled and able-bodied, for this is patently not integration. This would only highlight the differences between them and work against peer acceptance. The integration of disabled children into gymnastics, dance, athletics and swimming is a relatively straightforward process because teaching in these activities is focused on the individual. Although children may cooperate with a partner in dance and gymnastics, the essential feature is the individual nature of the activity. The teaching of games presents the biggest problem, particularly in the secondary school where the basis of play is to cooperate with team mates and compete against opponents.

There are a number of methods which may be used to improve integration of the disabled children into the games programme:

1. Disabled children may be taught games in a segregated setting within special units. Once the children have achieved a standard of competence in the basic skills, it will be possible to look for ways of integrating them into the mainstream programme. This will particularly apply in the area of individual and partner activities, as already described. Where children of the same age in the mainstream school are programmed for minor games within the PE curriculum, it should be possible to include many disabled children in group games of an adapted nature.
2. It may be possible within the flexible timetable of a primary school to programme a remedial class for children with special needs to improve their personal skills. This will obviously depend upon the availability of facilities and staff, but could be a valuable asset in supplementing the normal physical education lessons. Children within any given age range could be grouped together for teaching geared to their individual needs, making eventual integration more possible.
3. Children entering secondary school at age 11+ years may come from an integrated primary school, or may be transferred from a special school. In either case it is to be hoped that they will have developed some basic games skills, however limited. It may still be necessary, from time to time, for these children to be withdrawn on an individual or group basis to concentrate on a period of basic skills acquisition. This will boost confidence in their ability to succeed before they are returned to the mainstream class.

In physical education we are seeking to develop the full potential of each child. In the pursuit of excellence outstanding performers receive extra coaching in clubs after school. Perhaps in the pursuit of competence, similar opportunities ought to be provided for disabled children to supplement their skills.

4.   Children suffering from mild or moderate disability will benefit greatly from being taught in a fully integrated setting geared to the requirements of all the children. There will obviously be certain activities in which they cannot take part because of the nature of their disabilities.

5.   Within any games lesson there may be different degrees of integration.
(a) All children should be fully integrated into the skills-training part of the lesson.
(b) All children can be integrated within small group games practices where the games are appropriately adapted.
(c) Where team games are being played, it may be that disabled children play a particular role within the game.
Thus there is likely to be a great deal of variety in the approach and practice of the principle of integration. Teachers should, in general, produce individualized programmes applicable to either remedial or whole-class teaching according to the context in which they operate. Whichever system is in operation, there will be many barriers to overcome before any success is gained.

ATTITUDE

There has always been a high correlation between teacher expectation and pupil performance. It is important, therefore, that the teacher should take a positive attitude in attempting to discover a child's capabilities and work from that starting point. The focus of attention must be on what a child can achieve within the limits of any given disability. We must establish the principle of a games curriculum which is based upon achievement. Teachers must recognize that it is possible to integrate, given that we are concerned firstly with the children and then with the disability. There is currently a natural fear on the part of teachers that they will be unable to cope with the problems of children requiring special attention. This is based on a lack of knowledge and experience in the situation. The necessary knowledge can be gained from in-service courses which will alleviate fear of inadequacy, provide for revision of teaching methods, and advise on individualizing the programme. Disabled children, in common with the able-bodied children, need to be physically challenged. Provided that medical limitations are fully understood and appropriate safety precautions are observed, teachers should not be afraid to extend these children.

From experience we know that able-bodied children seem to accept their disabled peers without difficulty while recognizing the differences that exist. It is adults who often raise the barriers. The role of the teacher is to foster a cooperative spirit in each class so that everyone can play a full part in the programme. This may well depend on the organization of the programme and on the realistic objectives set by the teacher and the pupils.

INDIVIDUAL RECORDS

No teacher should be expected to teach any disabled child without first receiving a detailed profile report. Well before any child is transferred from teacher to teacher, or between schools, a complete pupil profile document must be sent in advance of the transfer. The teacher must be aware of the type of handicap and the effect of that handicap on performance in physical education. This highlights the necessity for pupil profiling ready for mainstreaming so that appropriate planning may be implemented. This profile must include evidence of what the child has already achieved and present guidelines for future development. The pupil profile should include:

1. Description of the disability.
2. Description of motor problems.
3. Description of associated problems — learning difficulties, concentration, distractibility, perceptual, spatial, visuo-motor, etc.
4. Special restrictions — precautions and safety measures.
5. Description of 'hidden disabilities' — Spitz–Holter valve, incontinence, minimal neurological dysfunction.
6. Criterion-referenced checklist, or at least a list of basic skills and activities where the child has achieved competence and enjoyment.
7. Special teaching methods found to be successful.
8. Doctor's approval for physical education — medical limits.

This profile provides early warning for preliminary planning in placement, selection of suitable activities, and appropriate adaptation procedures.

INDIVIDUALIZED TEACHING

In Chapters 3 and 4 I described a teaching method for individualizing instruction in games skills based on the continuous achievement of success. Where teaching is tailored directly to the pupil's needs, motivation will remain high as children succeed in their efforts. On the other hand, games skills are often introduced on a group basis where the level of expected performance is geared more general abilities and the needs of the children are assumed rather than assessed. Such a teaching method in a mixed ability situation is doomed to failure as the less able children fall further behind in their skills learning. In the special school a teacher can individualize teaching within a small group as classes are small, although the range of ability will be wide within the group. The current situation in mainstream schools, with limited numbers of children with similar disabilities in any one school, makes it unlikely that teaching can be done in homogeneous groups. Except in specially designated area schools, the teacher will be faced with one or two disabled children, several children with minimal movement problems, and a large group of able-bodied performers. In reality the problem combines a high teacher–pupil ratio yet with a need for individual attention. Administrative planning must, therefore, take account of the need to help physical education teachers provide individual or small-group teaching within a large class on occasions when the lesson material is not appropriate for the whole class. Individual teaching does not necessarily mean a one-to-one relationship all the time but implies that this will occur for at least part of the time. The problem, therefore, is to explore administrative possibilities to obtain the necessary supervisory assistance. There is no magic panacea, but, through sensitive teaching and careful planning, there may be a way ahead. Several procedures have been described which have been found to work well within large class situations in special schools with a wide range of age and ability levels, and it should be possible to transfer these procedures to the mainstream school.

SUPPORT PERSONNEL

Teachers in the special school sector tend to be well supported by auxiliary helpers, not only within the classroom teaching situation but also in the handling of disabled children around the school. As more physically disabled children are transferred into mainstream education, it is essential that adequate support services are provided by local authorities. This is standard practice in primary schools, and the classroom auxiliaries provide invaluable assistance in physical education under the guidance of a teacher. They play an important role in ensuring that children are placed in the most appropriate positions from which they can perform. They can constantly monitor the quality of practice in games skills and check that children are receiving the most appropriate kind of service in catching and striking activities. Primarily, they can be responsible, after suitable training, for the assessment of performance through the use of criterion-referenced checklists. This job needs the experience of an adult supervisor to be effective.

In the secondary school, auxiliary helpers can play the same role, particularly in the lower school. They make a valuable contribution in the skills learning section of a games lesson and can also help to support the integration of disabled children within group games. Some children will require assistance in moving from the classroom to the physical education facility and may also need help with changing and showering. It is important that such help is available on a regular basis where necessary, but it is equally important that the assistant is supervised by a teacher who can control when a 'hands off' policy should be applied. Children wish to be as independent as possible and there is a fine dividing line between necessary support and overprotection.

The role of assistant to the physical education teacher can be fulfilled successfully by non-professionals in an attempt to reduce staff–pupil ratios within a class. Students taking a year out of school prior to entry to a university course often serve as community service volunteers in special schools. They could provide a valuable service in a similar position in our comprehensive schools attached to a physical education department for a year. Sixth-form pupils could also be invited to perform such a community service in their free periods. This would provide valuable experience for those sixth formers intending eventually to train for teaching as a career. Many schools use the sixth form to give individuals help with reading and number work within the department for special needs. Assistance in physical education lessons is a logical extension of such work. Parents often provide help in special schools, particularly in giving one-to-one assistance with swimming, and there is scope for increasing this degree of involvement. A close liaison between school and home could be of inestimable value to any children requiring help in personal skill development. Under the guidance of a sympathetic teacher, parent intervention programmes can supplement work done in school and help to bridge the gap between the skill levels of disabled children and their peers. Given a programme of simple games skill practices geared to the abilities of their child, together with specific instructions relating to teaching points, most parents would be only too eager to help improve their child's skills at home. The use of simple skills checklists would enable parents to evaluate progress and enhance cooperation between teacher, child and parent. A recent innovation in the United Kingdom has seen the appointment of community teachers to primary schools. The community teacher is based in a school but provides a direct link with the home in cases of special need, by regular visits to liaise with parents. Where such a service is provided this would be of great benefit in the development of parent intervention programmes.

Regardless of the source of assistance, it is vital that opportunities are sought to increase the teacher's capacity for individualizing the teaching process. The teacher will always be the professional in control of the planning and teaching, but well-directed support personnel make the whole process a much more viable proposition. For insurance purposes, all helpers should be nominated by the local authority and work under the direct guidance of the teacher.

PEER TEACHING

Non-disabled class members can provide a valuable service in helping disabled children take a full part in the lesson. This is particularly valuable throughout the learning of basic games skills where accuracy in feeding a ball is critical to the success of the practice. Disabled children working in pairs of similar disability often fail to make progress because of their inability to pass the ball accurately to each other. The social benefits of mixed ability practice are often enormous as both children can gain shared pride as success is achieved. The role of feed player must be rotated to ensure that peer tutors do not miss out on their own development. The same principle may be established in small group practice in ensuring that the children succeed as a group.

It will often be found that older and more experienced disabled children are keen to offer their services to help in the teaching of skills to their younger colleagues, both in lessons and in after-school activities. Skilful disabled performers often make the best coaches because of their better understanding of some of the learning problems, and they are often able to come up with better solutions in ways of adapting performance.

SELECTION OF ACTIVITIES

The extent to which integration in the games programme is a practical possibility will vary with the nature of the game and the disability. A pupil in a wheelchair could play basketball, volleyball, netball or indoor hockey, but obviously would have the greatest difficulty in playing football, rugby, cricket or rounders on the field. This is surely common sense applied to the manoeuvrability of the disabled child. Each individual needs to be assessed separately in terms of ability and, not least, in terms of interest.

In the primary school where the teaching of games skills is child-centred, disabled children will be able to take part in the same individual or small group practices as the rest of the class. They will be working at a lower level of performance but nevertheless they can be accommodated within the same central theme, provided that some adaptation is arranged for them. When children are divided for group games it is quite common practice for the various groups to be involved in different games. Instead of disabled children rotating through the full range of games in a single lesson they may remain within the activities in which they can play a full part. There are such a large number of games from which to select lesson material that it will always be possible to choose enough activities to satisfy the movement needs of those with special problems. It will be necessary to assess how well disabled children relate to their peer group before planning for social game situations. Whether or not they will share apparatus or cooperate with a partner, or within a small group, are also factors which affect choice of games activities. Children who are relatively inactive may feel the cold outdoors and this may well govern the suitability of certain activities in relation to environmental conditions. At the upper end of the primary school when major national games are introduced, albeit in 'mini' form, care must be taken that these activities are appropriate and at this stage it may be necessary to find a particular role within the game for the disabled child to play. Chapters 3, 4, 5 and 6 deal specifically with the problems of selection of activities, teaching the basic skills, and are entirely relevant to formulating a games programme for the primary school.

Although the games programme in the secondary school is dominated by the major national games, there is a vast reservoir of minor games, often used as an introduction to the skills and tactics of the major games. These activities are described in Chapters 6 and 7, together with the appropriate adaptive procedures. Many secondary schools include a minor games programme, particularly in the lower school, and disabled children can be integrated fairly easily into such a programme. On entry to the secondary school it is important to assess the skill levels of each child, and this obviously affects the subsequent choice of activities for inclusion in an appropriate programme. How far disabled children can be included within the major games programme depends upon the type of game, the children's disabilities, and the organization of games in any school department. In a large school with good facilities, including a games field and sports hall or large gymnasium, it is usual for all the facilities to be programmed simultaneously. Where a disabled child can obviously not take part in outdoor activities on the field, one solution is to switch the child into the group working indoors. Most of the indoor games can be easily adapted to include disabled children; therefore they can be offered a fairly wide choice.

It is likely that some severely disabled children of normal intelligence will be integrated into mainstream schools. It is important that they should be given the opportunity to develop their basic skills and that they should be included in the skills training part of a lesson. Opportunities should be sought to include them in individual and partner activities and within small group games. Although they will not be able to play team games in an integrated setting, these intelligent children can often gain satisfaction from an active role as umpire, scorer or team coach, if that is what they choose to do. The game of cricket at club level contains many disabled people as umpires and scorers playing a full part in the life of the club. They need the chance to learn rules and tactics while at school.

In the end, selection of appropriate games comes down to the extent of each disability. There will be very many mildly disabled children requiring little or no restriction on their activities. In fact these children will be the first to complain if restrictions are placed upon them as they fervently demand to be given the chance to behave just like the rest of their schoolmates.

EDUCATION FOR LEISURE

Educating children for the fulfilment of lifelong leisure has always been a major aim in physical education. It is entirely appropriate that this applies equally to children with special needs who are likely to have more leisure time on their hands because of the current problems of employment. If at the end of their school life they have discovered at least one games activity which they can enjoy and carry on with after school, then the games programme can be deemed a success. This is normally achieved through the provision of a broadly based curriculum to develop competence in a range of activities, some of which can be carried on after school through choice. Following a basic grounding in a range of games, older pupils are offered a choice of options in games lessons. Disabled pupils must be offered the same opportunity for choice of their favourite activities, plus the opportunity for specialized coaching to increase their skill. In the earlier years of secondary schooling, individualizing the programme may be seen as working to secure a basic level of skill and helping to improve weaknesses. In the upper school the emphasis should be on the development of areas of strength where the pupil can succeed and develop further interest. This may depend on the interests and abilities of the physical education staff, the numbers of disabled pupils, and the facilities available within the school and the neighbouring community. Where a pupil has developed particular strengths there should be an opportunity for reinforcing these skills in clubs after school, and these pupils must be integrated into the usual leisure activities offered in the extracurricular programme.

It is now current practice in the United Kingdom for schools to have use of local community sports centres in an attempt to broaden the recreational experience of senior pupils. This is an important policy in helping to build an interest in lifelong leisure activities and to bridge the gap between school and adulthood. Where such a link is established between school and leisure centre a great opportunity exists for the promotion of integration beyond the scope of a normal school programme. Provision can be made to introduce disabled pupils to a range of activities appropriate to their potential. In most cases these activities will realistically be based on games played individually or in pairs and requiring only a limited range of movement, unless adapted group and team games are organized on a mixed ability basis. Through the auspices of the local leisure centre, and under the guidance of local authority recreation department coaching schemes, disabled children can be introduced to bowling, crown green bowling, ten-pin, carpet bowls, table tennis, golf and archery. The social carry-over value of these activities is obvious in providing the entry to community sport.

It is difficult to advise on methods of integration in games teaching, for every situation is different and requires its own solution. Preparation is the key to success. Provided that initial teacher-training courses include appropriate preparation for dealing with these children, and provided that more in-service courses are available, then the teaching profession will be better equipped to deal with the latest challenge. Teachers must be prepared to individualize their teaching, evaluate their methods, and experiment with adaptive procedures to enable all children to play a full part in the games programme. Success breeds success and our challenge is to help children with special needs appreciate the pleasures to be derived from playing and from watching games.

INDEX

achilles tendon, 19
adaptation,
   environmental, 48–9
   motor, 46–7, 74–5, 178–9, 211
   perceptual, 47–8, 74–5
   principles, 46, 76, 194
aiming games, 126–33
   checklist, 38
amputees, 224
anaesthesia, 24
arm control, 66, 186
asthma, 26–7
ataxia, 19, 21, 47, 65, 75, 170, 221
athetosis, 19, 21, 47, 65, 75, 170, 221
attention span, 20, 31
auditory imperception, 20

badminton, 225–9
balloon activities, 84, 146, 147, 188
basal ganglia, 19
basketball, 220–5
beanbags, 64, 66–8, 79, 96–108, 178–9,
   189, 196
behaviour modification, 33
body awareness, 32, 55
body image, 20, 21
body management, 7, 50, 54–8
bowls, 119
bronchoconstriction, 26
BSAD, 220

cardiac disorders, 27–8
cardiorespiratory problems, 30
catching,
   assessment, 81
   checklist, 39
   programmes, 76–82
   techniques, 74–6
cerebellum, 6, 19

cerebral palsy, 18–23, 28, 30, 61, 62, 100,
   148
   definition, 18
   implications for teaching, 20–3
cerebral dysfunction, 30
cerebrum, 6, 19
chasing games, 125–6
chutes, 72, 119, 121
clumsy children, 29
coaching grid,
   see invasion games
community service volunteers, 235
community teachers, 235
competition, 204–5
conditioning, 183
cricket, 209–13
criterion referencing, 37, 44, 233, 234

directionality, 32
dissociation, 32
distractibility, 20, 24, 31, 45
dodge and mark, 58
dodgeball games, 133–7
Duchennes muscular dystrophy, 25

epilepsy, 28–9
eye focussing, 65
eye-hand accuracy, 44, 50, 64, 90
eye-hand coordination, 44, 50, 74, 91

figure-ground, 20, 32, 42
free and caught, 58

grand mal, 28
grasp-release, 18, 22, 60, 61, 65, 226
gross body coordination, 58
group games, 124–160

hemiplegia, 19, 21, 224

hockey, 213–20
hydrocephalus, 24
hyperacoustic, 48, 188
hyperactivity, 31
hyperventilation, 28

incontinence, 24, 25
individual records, 233
individualized teaching, 37–41, 232–5
information processing, 3, 18
Intal, 27
integration, 23, 204
interval training, 27
invasion games,
  coaching grid, 165–7, 179–81
  definition, 162
  opposed practice, 165–6
  principles of play, 163–5, 178
  scheme of work, 167–70
  severely disabled, 178–81

kicking, 108
kinaesthesis, 6, 10, 12, 14, 18, 19, 22, 42,
  60, 63

laterality, 32
learning difficulties, 20, 30–4
  teaching strategies, 33–4
lesson plans, 90–4, 160, 181–5, 192–4,
  202–3, 220
locomotor, 65, 96, 163, 185, 194

mainstreaming, 230–8
  see also integration
man-to-man marking, 216, 224
maturation, 2
mental subnormality, 20
miscellaneous games, 144–7
mixed ability, 162–3, 230
motor function, 1
motor learning, 2
motor performance, 2
  cues, 22
  effects of handicap, 16
  problems, 16, 20
multisensory, 33, 58
muscular dystrophy, 25–6

net games, 185–94
  principles, 185–6
  tactics, 192
neuromuscular disorder, 29

paraplegia, 19, 21, 24, 25, 121, 191
parent intervention, 235
peer teaching, 235–6
perception, 3, 65
perceptual-motor,
  abilities, 6, 50, 75
  definition, 3
  feedback, 3, 5, 10, 12, 19
  model, 17, 46
  problems, 45
  process, 3, 18, 64
  training, 58
performer analysis, 20, 43–6, 63
perseveration, 20, 32, 45
PHAB, 235
prescriptive teaching, 45, 52
proprioception, 13, 48, 60, 80
  see also kinaesthesis
puck, 214

quadriplegia, 19, 21, 26, 61, 96
quoits, 68–9, 110–11

relays, 147–60
rheumatic fever, 27

selection of tasks,
  approach, 36
  evaluation, 37, 237
  guidelines, 30, 236–7
severe arm involvement, 108–10
severely disabled, 187, 198, 216, 221, 237
  see also invasion games
skill,
  closed skills, 9, 10
  definitions, 1, 166
  open skills, 9, 10
  task classification, 8, 9, 10
spastic, 18, 19
spatial disorientation. 61
spina bifida, 23–5
  implications for teaching, 24–5
Spitz–Holter valve, 24, 25, 233
stages of learning,
  associative phase, 13
  autonomous phase, 14
  cognitive phase, 12
  guidance, 11
  manual, 11, 13, 22, 52, 53, 59, 63, 76,
    87
  verbal, 11, 22, 52, 53, 59, 87
  visual, 11, 64, 223

stretch reflex, 20, 21
striking games, 194–202
striking skills,
    adaptations, 83–4
    analysis, 82–3, 87
    checklist, 39–40
    principles, 86
    programmes, 84–9
    two-handed, 87–9
swingball, 67, 78–9, 119

tactile cue, 61
target beanbag, 91
task analysis, 13, 14, 20, 30, 41–3, 63
team games, 161–203
technique, 166
throwing,
    assessment of potential, 65–6
    checklist, 38
    development, 44, 64
    programmes, 66–74
    teaching methods, 63–4
throwing techniques, 59–62
    modified sidearm, 61–2

overhand, 44, 59, 96
rear-facing, 62
sidearm, 44, 60–1
underarm, 44, 59–60, 68–9

Unicurl, 119
Unihoc, 213, 214

Vental, 27
video, 44
visuo-motor problems, 74
visuo-spatial, 83
volleyball, 205–9

wall games, 112–18
wheelchairs,
    boccia, 119–21
    kicking, 108
    position, 60
    throwing, 61–2, 65
whole-part-whole, 32, 182, 184–5

zone defence, 224

ACTIVE GAMES FOR
CHILDREN WITH MOVEMENT PROBLEMS

Alan Brown trained at Loughborough College from 1953 to 1956, and then taught physical education in secondary schools. He is currently a University Lecturer in physical education involved in teacher training, and has been Consultant and teacher of physical education at the Percy Hedley Spastics Centre since 1964, and organizer of the Northern Spastics Games since 1969. He is the author of numerous articles in educational journals and a key speaker at National and International Conferences. He has been a professional cricketer and amateur soccer player, and is staff coach to the Football Association.